U.S. – China
RELATIONS

诚邀北园
请指教

张三
8-1-205

U.S. – CHINA RELATIONS

MAINSTREAM AND ORGANIC VIEWS

—⁓—

Dr. Ifay F. Chang

ISBN: 0977159426
ISBN 13: 9780977159420
Library of Congress Control Number: 2015900946
TLC Information Services, Katonah, NY

Air Defense Identification Zone (ADIZ)
Asia Pacific Economic Conference (APEC)
Arm Race
Air Sea Battle (ASB)
Balance of Power
Brazil
Cambodia
Corruption
Currency
Cyber Security
Defense Budget
Democracy
Diaoyu Islands
East China Sea
Economy
Energy
Environment
Financial Crisis
Gas and Oil
Global Warming
Hackers
India
Inflation
Japan
Naval Blockade
Network Security

North Korea
Nuclear Threat
Pivot To Asia
Rebalance
Regional Development
Russia
Trade Deficit
South China Sea
South Korea
Space Technology
Spratly Island
Thailand
Trans-Pacific Partners (TPP)
Vietnam

TABLE OF CONTENTS

ACKNOWLEDGMENT

—ɯ—

I WOULD LIKE TO EXPRESS my appreciation to many people who have influenced and improved my writings for this book. I am also grateful to many people who have encouraged me in taking the writing endeavor. I must also acknowledge the benefits I received from many who either alerted me on certain issues and particular media reports or debated with me on some topics and views covered by the media, mainstream or organic.

In particular, I would like to thank my family, my wife Teresa and my children for tolerating my working on this manuscript in odd hours. My odd working pattern was certainly quite annoying to them who had a normal 9-5 or regular school schedule to adhere to. Despite of the inconvenience I gave to them, my family had also influenced me in selecting topics to write about.

I would also like to thank the ten US-China Forum editors, in particular, Paul Tung, Richard Chen and Nelson Mar who had always dealt my papers with timely editing and keen enthusiasm. The Forum editors collectively offered invaluable spiritual support for me to keep up with the weekly publishing schedule.

Many of my friends have encouraged me to keep writing and they have communicated with me by weekly emails. These emails have given me inspiration plus satisfaction. I apologize for not able to acknowledge them all here since the lists of my 'fan' friends are fairly long. However, I must mention one individual, Mr. Richard Haddad, who is a classic 'paper' reader and he does not own nor touch any computer. Mr. Haddad writes to me in handwriting letters commenting on my writings and always attaching newspaper clippings (from Wall Street Journal, New York Times, Washington Posts, local newspapers and magazines which he subscribes) to feeding me food for thought. I truly appreciate getting his letters but I must apologize for not diligent enough to reply them in writing. However, our verbal dialogues have always been enjoyable.

Finally, I would like to thank the 'publisher' of this book for making it easy for an inexperienced author like me to sail through the book publishing process in a breeze.

PREFACE

—∿—

THIS BOOK IS DEDICATED TO my parents, Dr. and Mrs. Paul C. L. Chang (Zhang Zong Liang in Hanyu Pinyin and Betty Chu, my mother's maiden name) who brought me to the world during the Second World War, the cruelest and deadliest war in the history of mankind and the saddest and longest war in the land of China.

While my father was engaged in the war front defending his country, China, against the Japanese invasion, my mother had to raise me under extreme difficult conditions, no milk, shortage of food, inadequate medical supply, and terrible dwelling with frequent air raids for kids to tell time. A delivery of 31 hours with a 'doctor' pronouncing me dead, I owed my life to my aunt, Rong Xian, who fought the doctor to perform mouth-to-mouth resuscitation. A soft-hearted nurse secretly agreed to do resuscitation, and here I am now living in the land of opportunities.

To the Chinese, the WW II began in 1937, when the Japanese invaded China. The recent Chinese history from 1829-1949 is sad and complicated for any student to master in comparison to the American history of the same period. The Qing Dynasty suffered unprecedented foreign invasions from eight western powers including Japan, an Asian country transformed herself (through Meiji Restorations, 1868-1912) to become an imperial, militant and ambitious nation. Japan strived to be an industrial giant to be superior to the western powers to conduct Japanese style colonialism with a secret plan to conquer China all for herself and eventually to colonize all Asia.

The Qing Dynasty was corrupt and slow to react to the foreign invasions, but there were multiple short-lived internal revolutions until Dr. Sun Yat San, the

Father of Modern China, who led a treacherous struggle of the Chinese people to establish a Republic nation under the Three Principles of People (it is Sun's book and his beliefs reminiscing "for the people, by the people and of the people). Dr. Sun was educated in the U.S.; he attended Panuhou High School (1883) in Hawaii where President Barak Obama graduated in 1979. Dr. Sun was benefitted from private assistance from his American friends in his revolution. The partial success of Sun's revolution toppling Qing did not stop the foreign powers, only accelerated the Japanese invasion plan. After Japan had won the Sino-Japan war (1894-95) by which she captured Taiwan for 50 years and forced Qing to give up control over Korea and to recognize her independence, Japan continued her encroachment in China until she eventually declared an open war against the Republic of China in 1937 which lasted till 1945

Born during WW II made my early childhood as a part of that complicated and sad Chinese history, but I had very little memory of my early life. I had rarely seen my father as my mother and I lived behind the war zone which moved with the retreating front lines. The Allied victory of WW II brought joy to the world, but the Chinese fared poorly, partially because of China was led by two strong-willed leaders, Chiang Kai Shek and Mao Ze Dong who happened to be backed by the United States and Russia respectively and partially because of China was poorly represented in the post-war settlements and treaty negotiations. As a result, the defeated Japan fared better than the victor, China, in protecting her sovereignty. Hence, the dispute of Diaoyu Islands persists today.

My family moved to Taiwan with the Kuo Ming Tang (KMT led by Chiang Kai Shek) in 1949 as the Chinese Communist Party (CCP led by Mao Ze Dong) succeeded in four years taking over the Chinese Mainland after the WW II was ended. Despite of the miseries prolonged in the next two decades under the communist rule, a United China without the presence of foreign powers was still a significant accomplishment for China. As a war child, my fate could be anything but certain. I could be easily killed or starved to death between battles or I could be left in a province where the hidden communist organization suddenly emerged and declared me a communist child or I could be brought along with the retreating KMT army to Taiwan as they ultimately decided to retreat to with the consent and support of the U.S.

My youth years in Taiwan were relatively peaceful owing to a stable truce although maintained with a hostile relation between the CCP controlled mainland and KMT governed Taiwan. The United States, emerged as a super power after WW II, played a significant role in maintaining the hostile truce across the Taiwan Strait by having a military alliance with the Republic of China (KMT) government in Taiwan and denying recognition of the People's Republic of China (CCP) with a purpose of stopping the expansion of communism. The influence of the U.S. in Taiwan was very significant, for my generation and beyond. Most young people in Taiwan had their dreams of 'go America young men' very much like America's 'go West young men' fever in the early 19th century in America, except that the Taiwanese students had little other choices as Taiwan is just too small a province to accommodate a sudden surge of population.

The opportunities of education (university and beyond) and employment (professional careers) were extremely limited then.

The Taiwan students in the U.S., though restricted by the U.S. immigration quota, steadily increased from 1950 to 1994 when it peaked at about 37,500, but today, the attitudes of Taiwan students changed as Taiwan's population stabilized and economy improved, the number of Taiwan students in the U.S. is reduced to about 20,000, less than 3% of the total number of international students. However, since the normalization of the U.S. and China relation in 1972, the number of mainland Chinese students coming to the U.S. has been steadily increased to over 200,000 today, more than 25% of the US international students. There is no question that the U.S., as a country of immigrants, has benefitted from the continuous incoming youthful, intelligent and motivated students. Many of these students become naturalized as American citizens obviously motivated by the land of opportunities.

After seven decade post WW II, the world has evolved into a fast paced globe interwoven by networks of communication (through ocean cables and satellites) and transportation (through air, sea and land travel) enabling vast amount of commerce and culture exchange. As a result, the complicated and sad part of history mentioned above is fortunately getting its light of the day. The two governments, in the continental mainland and Taiwan island, are finally opening up and offering a fact-studded presentation of the Chinese history from 1897 to 1947, especially giving a mutually accepted "Politically correct" description of the Sun Yat-San's revolution (1897-1912) and the eight years of brutal war against the Imperial Japan (1937-1945). This is seen at the scholarly conferences and museum exhibits held on both sides of the Taiwan Strait. Recognizing the same factual history, the two Chinese governments were able to jointly refute Japan's effort in distorting the war history and Japan's war crimes such as Nanking Massacre, comfort women, and biological experiments on human. Finally, the historians and governments on the two sides of Taiwan Strait are united together to condemn the Japanese government's methodic and Ill-intentioned false description of WW II history in the Japanese school textbooks and the Japanese government's scheme to claim the sovereignty of the Diaoyu Islands.

My father was a political scientist. I was always fascinated when listening to his analysis of world affairs when his friends came making house calls. He was a young scholar sponsored by the Republic of China to study political science at the London University in England; his Ph.D. thesis was on "Government and Police Administration". Naturally he served his government after he completed his study and had a bright career as a young man, but his fast rising government career was essentially truncated when CCP took over the mainland. In Taiwan, he felt frustrated as many bright young men did as the national government by default had to shrink its size and functions to govern just one province. My father chose a semi-dormant political career reserved to lecturing in government training and strategy institutions on world affairs and served as university presidents. He was the first president of the Chinese Culture University and later the president of the Taiwan Normal University.

Although his background and passion was in political science, he steered away all his sons and daughter away from politics and constantly encouraged us to pursue science or engineering discipline which eventually became my profession. Yes, I came to America in 1964 and successfully completed my graduate studies in 1968 at a time that the U.S. economy was prosperous and I was luckily offered with seven prestigious jobs to choose from when I received my Ph.D. from the University of Rhode Island. I selected to work for IBM with a goal to pursue a R&D career. Eventually I have served as an IBMer for 31 years, a rare mutual commitment in today's career market.

In 1972, a political event rattled my peaceful life – Nixon visited China. For many Chinese who emigrated to the U.S. from Taiwan, this is a political wake-up call. From 1972 to 1979 when the U.S. finally recognized People's Republic China as the official representative of all China, many Chinese went through an agony of reconciliation: How could the U.S., the protector and supporter of Republic of China of six decades, betray Taiwan and the People there? There were protests and there were opinions, but eventually, the mainstream media prevailed in declaring a new China era with a new China policy. Many Chinese students residing in the U.S. elected to be naturalized as American citizens before the U.S. recognized China, So did I. I would have to admit that my decision was obviously not strongly motivated by political or ideological reasoning but more by personal career consideration. Given that I could not possibly find a satisfactory career path in Taiwan or Mainland in the early seventies, I decided to become an American citizen and pursue my technology career in the United States.

To my surprise, when I brought up the citizenship issue with my father, he was clearly supportive and he said "there is no better place to pursue a science and technology career than do it in the United States, just make sure you bring up your children with the good part of Chinese culture. Eventually, China will rise but no one can predict Taiwan's future since its future is not in its own hands but in the hands of the U.S. and China. The U.S. foreign policies are self-interest driven and short-sighted. So long you do not pursue a political career; you would not be burdened by the Taiwan issue. However, as a Chinese American, you should be aware of the development of the U.S.-China relationship, not that you should or could do anything about it, but knowledge would lead a peaceful mind." Honestly, I did not give too much thinking to his words until I have sort of retired from my professional career.

Today, the U.S.-China relationship is one of the important issues in the world since China indeed has risen to be the no. 2 economy second to that of the U.S. Almost daily in the media, there are news, analyses, comments about China and her relationship with the U.S. The mainstream media seem to adhere to an anti-China and anti-Communist legacy touting a 'China Threat' theory and preparing an inevitable confrontation between the U.S. and China. As an American citizen, I am not sure, the mainstream media is always right. Now, in my semi-retired life, I recalled my father's advice, "to stay away from politics" and indeed I had followed his advice. I also recalled his words, "you should be aware of the development of the U.S.-China relationship and knowledge would lead a peaceful mind". Since my retirement, I began to pay attention, study and write about the U.S.-China relations with a purpose to reaching a peaceful mind.

This book is the accumulation of my effort. I dedicate it to my parents. I, as a Chinese American citizen, wrote honestly on the relations and issues of the U.S. and China, based on my readings and research in the mainstream and organic media. I am grateful that I have followed my father's advice to pursue a science and technology career which has offered me a peaceful and fulfilling life. I am also grateful to my father's words regarding paying attention to the U.S. – China relations as an American citizen. As I collected and reviewed my writings, which included historical facts, thoughts of many scholars and political analysts and my opinions, into this book in an objective way, I felt peaceful in my mind. I spoke the truth and felt relieved. I hope my readers will feel the same way when reading this book, if not, please feel free to vend your opinion to my column, Mainstream and Organic at http://www.us-chinaforum.org, you will feel peaceful in your mind.

INTRODUCTION

—⚬—

THIS BOOK IS A COLLECTION of individual essays about the issues concerning the United States, China and both, altogether they portray a picture of current relationship between two countries and its outlook. The comments and opinions in these papers sometimes go beyond describing the picture of the relationship between the two nations; they delve into history, discuss media's analysis, right or wrong, and offer advice from a U.S. Citizen's point of view. This book is entitled with a short name, "The U.S.-China Relations", because it is the most faithful way to represent the 60 papers collected here each having a distinct title of its own. This book and its title also reflect the author's main concern in his retirement life. Aside from personal health issues, which are not avoidable as one reaches retirement, the U.S.-China relations do occupy my mind.

Since the United States and China are now the two greatest economies in the world, what happens in these two countries do have impacts on other nations by intention or not. Therefore, this book is really about world affairs and issues occurred in the recent two years that have connections with the U.S., China and the rest of the world. The individual chapters in this book are mostly taken from a weekly column, Mainstream and Organic, which the author committed to write for a syndicate of six small newspapers and a website, named US-China Forum (www.us-chinaforum.org and www.us-china.com) in the past two years.

As an introduction for the book, I would like to explain first why I wrote for the small newspapers, then why I named my column, The Mainstream and Organic and finally my motivation for compiling my column papers into a book.

In the Acknowledgment page, I have told you my father's words that have urged me to pay attention to the U.S.-China relations as a naturalized Chinese American citizen. I should, however, elaborate more on the background of reasons that has elevated my attention to the U.S.-China relations to be a daily focus.

I am a Chinese American citizen, born in China, grew up in Taiwan and immigrated to the United States 50 years ago. Taiwan, a beautiful island where I lived sixteen years often appears in my dreams as homeland with familiar images. China, a vastly populated country where I was born always attracted me with its rich culture and long history but remained as a mystic land, even though she is my ancestry land. The general people in Taiwan and China can be characterized with similar words, simple, peaceful, frugal, diligent, competitive with strong motivation to strive for success. These traits and virtue and their family orientation and traditional believes from Confucius and many other philosophers nurtured their characters to be Chinese. Unfortunately and sadly, Taiwan was under Japanese occupation for fifty years (1895-1945) after Japan won the first Sino-Japanese war (1894 – 1895); Taiwan suffered from a systemic discrimination and a savage colonial rule but that part of history was very faint in the memory of the younger generation(s). History dealt Taiwan an unfair hand in her path of uniting with China; Potsdam Declaration was dishonored and the internal squabble between the Chinese Communist Party (CCP) and Kuo Ming Tang (KMT) caused many decisions regarding war reparations made by world powers without the participation and approval of the governments of China. The U.S. supported the KMT based on the anti-communism policy even after KMT lost the entire mainland and retreated to Taiwan. Taiwan became part of the U.S. military alliance in Asia and was protected under the U.S. – Taiwan Mutual Defense Treaty, but in 1979, the U.S. officially recognized China as the only China representing all China explicitly included Taiwan with an expectation of a peaceful reunification.

The failure of the CCP to improve the mainland economy and the success of Taiwan's development with the U.S. aids have accentuated the ideological difference and retarded the effort of uniting Taiwan with Mainland even after President Carter formally recognized the people's Republic of China in 1979. A small fraction of people advocated independence for Taiwan but the majority were more concerned with the economic future of Taiwan if reunited with China.

Mainland China is the ancestral land and cultural roots for many overseas Chinese including the Chinese Americans living in the U.S. The Vietnam War left a deep scar on the U.S. as a war against communism, but ironically, it was Russia more than China backing the North Vietnam to a bitter war with the U.S. The Vietnam War in fact caused China to depart from the Soviet Union's style of communism and she eventually decided to 'reform and open up'. The economical development initially was gradual until recent decades that China had advanced significantly to be the envy of the world.

China had shredded her paper tiger image by her fast impressive development; however, along with her economic success we also witnessed many of the ills and evils of a non-transparent governing body that exhibited amazing official corruption, judicial injustice, and widening gaps of wealth in societies. The recent leadership of CCP seems to be aware of these ills and have initiated party cleansing actions, to destroy the "flies" as well as "tigers" in corruption, and policies, to improve the social programs aimed at reducing the wealth gap. China is now driving a slogan of China Dream to bring more of her population to middle class.

The United States became the true country of immigrants after the Chinese exclusion act (1924) was repealed in 1943, even though there was only a small quota of 105 for ethnic Chinese regardless of nationality. Later, in 1946 the immigration quota was extended to Filipino and Asian Indian and in 1952 to all Asians. Finally, in 1965 the quota system based on National Origins was abandoned altogether. All immigrants appreciate the United States as the land of opportunities, where they live, work, get married and have a family and career. Like many other Americans, the immigrants have independent views on political issues and do not necessarily agree with all US government policies, for example, the invasion of Iraq, the support of the military government in Egypt, and especially the US-Japan alliance which is very sensitive to Asian Americans. By encouraging Japan to re-arm and revise her peace constitution to permit first strike can potentially lead to uncontrollable situations possibly to wars. The 'China Threat' depicted by the right-wing Japanese politicians to justify Japan's military expansion is so obviously far-fetched and yet it seems to have received many favorable reporting from the U.S. mass media as well as some echoing voices from the anti-communism 'think tank' experts based on a legacy theory.

As a US citizen, I felt compelled to voice my opinions regarding the 'China Threat' and the many inconsistent China policies our government is conducting such as the Pivot to Asia strategy and Air Sea Base deployment targeted at China essentially inviting military confrontation. Especially alarming is that the mainstream media seems to have adopted a 'target China' position in beating the war drums for an inevitable military conflict between the U.S. and China. Rarely, we see any objective analysis about the U.S.-China relations published in the mass media except occasional discussions circulating in the Internet or appearing in blogs and small publications. I call these unbiased media organic in contrast to the mainstream which regrettably seems to share a bias. When the editors of US-China Forum approached me about writing a column, I was delighted to have the opportunity and proposed that 'Mainstream and Organic' to be the name of the column. Mainstream media is defined as the established large media reaching to the mass including television, major newspapers and prominent magazines whereas organic media represent publications or individual writings in limited distributions. It was my goal to write about issues concerning the U.S. and China with reference to the views expressed in the Mainstream and Organic media so that the issues get a fair discussion.

My purpose of compiling the Mainstream and Organic column papers in a book is to share them with more American citizens in an easy to read format. Hopefully, this book will be in print form and eBook format about the same time so the readers will have a choice. We know that not all American citizens agree on every issue and we also know that not all citizens are aware of all issues, even just in the domain of US foreign policy, or particularly in the narrower subject domain of the U.S.-China relations. However, in a democratic society, we must raise the awareness of our citizens to current events. We cannot afford to be just led by the mainstream media, especially on the important topic of US-China relations. We need to be aware of the opinions of the organic media in contrast to the mainstream media. We need to make fairer and deeper analysis on issues. We need to resonate in agreement or in opposition to bring out our citizens' views. It is for this purpose, I present this book, The US-China Relations - in Mainstream and Organic Views to you.

President Nixon's ice-breaking trip to China in 1972 enhanced the US-China relations. Recognition of China and a soft policy towards China had contributed to the final collapse of the Communist Soviet Union. The United States had won the final victory of the Cold War! China had also benefitted from the shaded help from the United States to open up and reform leading to China's miraculous economical development. For Americans' past role, the Chinese people appreciate and give credit to the Americans openly, and it is manifested in the record number of Chinese students studying in the United States. Now China has risen economically as the second largest economy in the world. Does she pose a threat to The United States as often reported in the media? Should the U.S. transform the Cold War strategy to target China? Is the U.S. China policy heading in the right direction? Is China being reactive to the U.S. Pivot to Asia strategy or is she preparing an unavoidable war between the two nations? Should the U.S. embrace the rise of China instead of target China as the enemy? Is it possible for China and the U.S. to collaborate to create win-win opportunities for the benefits of both nations and world peace? These and many more are questions this book intended to answer by tracing the history of the past century and half to find causality roots for what happened and what might happen and by analyzing the current events without a legacy view to project the trends of the U.S.-China relation development. I hope you will resonate with me and many American citizens after reading this book, in agreement or in opposition to any opinions expressed, so that a fair view is elevated to the mass level.

Author, Ifay Chang. Ph.D.
Producer/Host, Community Education - Scrammble Game Show, Weekly TV
Columnist, www.us-chinaforum.org - Dr.Wordman
Trustee, Somers Central School District
President, Somers Republican Club
Facebook.com/ifaychang
Twitter: ifaychang@drwordman.com, DrWordman@scrammble.com
Email: DrWordman@gmail.com

Publisher
TLC Information Services
3 Louis Drive, Katonah, N. Y. 10532-3122
Tel. 914-248-6770
Email: info@tlcis.us

CHAPTER 1

WHY AN UNINHABITED ISLAND MAY

DRAW THE U.S. INTO A WAR

—ɯ—

OUR MAIN STREAM MEDIA SOMETIMES showing a bias in their selective reporting of global events, the case in point is the Diaoyu Island dispute which has the potential of erupting into an Asia War drawing US into it. Yet, you hardly find enough fact reporting and analysis in our TV and major news media. Why? Is it none of American's business? Or is the presidential election and the money it raised is saturating our news media? No, I hope not, we Americans need to know any possibility of war because it matters to everyone of us. In fact, in a presidential election year, we don't want to hear just blaming and bashing; we want to elect a president who can fix our economy as well as understand current events and foreign policies to protect our homeland and maintain world peace. Therefore, the explosive situation of this tiny Diaoyu (also named Senkaku) Island deserves our attention.

Many Asian news media have vividly reported the current events related to Diaoyu Island. Protests occurring in China, Hong Kong, Taiwan and around the world including San Francisco, Houston, New York... (yes, US cities) denouncing Japan's aggression and her maneuvering to capture the Diaoyu Islands were like an emotional volcano, suppressed more than 100 years, exploded. This sentiment not only was brewed by Japan's war crimes against the Chinese people and her occupation of Chinese territories but more so by the cruelty, humiliation and shame the Japanese applied to the occupied Chinese. Moreover, the Japanese government and its emperor never showed remorse nor apologized after their defeat in WW II. Adding salt to the injury, the Japanese school textbooks consistently white wash Japan's criminal acts before and during WW II. The recent militant aggression, flamed by Japan's right-wing extremists party, which tries very hard to restore

Japan's pre-war glory and military might, included not only ambitions towards East and South China Sea but also territorial disputes with Korea. In many ways, the Asian victims just like the Jewish victims during WW II suffered irreparable atrocious harm. Germany at least officially apologized for her war crimes and compensated the war victims. The Japanese on the contrary continues to deny her war crimes: Nanking Massacre, comfort women, biochemical human experiments, killing millions of unarmed people, etc.

Some protests unfortunately led to violence such as destroying Japanese made cars. Violence should not be encouraged by any means but the harsh verbal dialog and militant actions (arrests) against Chinese fishermen from Taiwan and mainland provinces made by the Japanese forces in the disputed region are more responsible for this kind of world-wide break-out. Examining the past 70 years, the two Chinese governments due to their internal conflicts have exercised extreme constraint in dealing with the Japanese aggression to the point they angered many Chinese on two sides of the strait and around the world. No wonder this suppressed shame is now boiling over especially on September 18th, the Memorial Day for Japanese invasion of China in 1931. That invasion had cost China tremendous lives, money, land, sea and pride. All Chinese people buried that humiliation deeply in their memory while their leaders showed mercy to Japan by accepting Japan's surrender with no penalty except the condition for Japan to return all captured Chinese territories including these tiny islands back to China.

The global factions broke out immediately after the WW II; China was divided internally and influenced externally by superpowers, respectively, the U.S. and the Soviet Union; it is this situation that has given Japan the opportunity and ambition to brew expansionism leading to the current forceful plot to capture the Diaoyu Islands. Unfortunately, the U.S. has contributed to the mess by giving back Japan the administrative authority of Okinawa in 1971 with access (so called administrative rights) to the uninhabited islands for strategic military consideration. This became the basis for Japan, especially the right-wing party to foster its expansionism. The recent blocking off Chinese fishing boats from the island region to scheming to "purchase" these islands by the Japanese government are part of the expansion plot.

Why is this dispute a potential of igniting a war in Asia and a possibility of drawing the U.S. into it? The two fundamental reasons are the 'century shame' still felt in the hearts of the Chinese and the 'aggressive behavior' continuously exhibited by the Japanese as alluded to above. However, the real sparking issue is unfortunately attributed to the actions of the United States. From the legal stand point, this type of dispute could be settled by international courts. Japan knowing her weak legal claim is not motivated to take that path, hence resorting to a phony scheme to buy the islands taking advantage of two factors: 1. The two Chinese governments hamstrung by their internal squabbles unable to cooperate in defending their islands and 2. The US strategy - Returning to Asia by strengthening mutual defense treaties with Asian countries. The United States although took a neutral position on sovereignty rights of these disputed islands but declared that these islands would be covered under the US-Japan mutual defense treaty. This emboldened Japan to take a hard line approach threatening to deploy defense military forces to 'manage' these disputed islands. The famous and successful former Japan's Prime Minister, Nakasone Yasuhiro, remarked about Japan's foreign policy: Japan should endeavor to procure U.S. power to serve Japan's interests and objectives. Apparently, the US-Japan mutual defense treaty is regarded by Japan as such power. Will Chinese swallow this aggression? I am afraid not. The Chinese people have felt and experienced foreign threats from the North and the West for centuries especially the past one hundred years; there is a strong sentiment that they must find vindication for victimization.

Why are these tiny islands so important? From the point of view of the U.S., these islands are strategic in terms of having a strong US presence in the Pacific-China sea, but from the Japanese point of view, these islands give them expansion of her sovereignty not just in terms of the islands but more the ocean for fishing rights (The giant Japanese fishing industry, dominating world-wide, can block off fishing boats from China and Taiwan) and the energy resources lie in the East China Sea. (A 1969 UN study and later estimates claim 100 billion barrels of oil reserve in the region)

For the sake of world peace and justice, it seems that US ought to take a sincere neutral position not to encourage Japan's aggression in territorial claim. The U.S. with her oil drilling technology can help the region to develop energy resources. The U.S. and the world stand to gain by working with the Chinese to jointly develop energy resources in that region to share with the world.

CHAPTER 2

TRUE AMERICAN EXCEPTIONALISM

—⚍—

US-CHINA FORUM FIRST LAUNCHED ON August 17, 2013, is a new medium devoted to views and opinions on US-China Relations. Its coverage, from history to current events, matters not only to people living in both countries but also to the entire world in a 'G-2' sense. **Mainstream and Organic** is a new column within the US-China Forum primarily written in English with the hope to better connect the US and China mainstream media and the organic thinking circulated in the brains, clouds and dotcoms of the internet world. Through this column we attempt to highlight mainstream media news and essays, offer analyses and rebuttals and most importantly provide organic thinking and thoughts for the readers. Just as people would prefer healthy organic produce to mass processed food, we know readers would prefer reading original organized opinions offered in a compact column. We welcome your feedback and will publish your response if deemed organic to keep this column always organic.

When you correspond with me, I will sign my name, Ifay Chang, but Dr. Wordman is my media name used in this column and my TV show, nicknamed Dr. Wordman Show, a weekly public-access TV for community education aired in the Westchester and Putnam counties in the state of New York.

To kick off the first column, I choose to talk about "American Exceptionalism" which is a hot media term Russian President Vladimir Vladimirovich Putin used in his 'exceptional' letter to the New York Times to criticize Obama and his Syria policy. Exceptionalism in a positive sense means a country (applies to an individual as well) is exceptional in her behavior thus exempted from normal rules or principles in general expectation. Putin disagreed with Obama's statement, "the US policy is what makes Americans different. It is what makes us exceptional"; and referenced these words to fault the US attempt to attack Syria without the UN Security Council's authorization. He further remarked, "It is extremely dangerous to encourage people to see themselves exceptional" which actually triggered a response from a Washington Post Columnist, Robert J. Samuelson. Putin's letter reads like one from an American presidential candidate. It is no surprise that Putin and his letter, with NY Times' help, grabbed the limelight in the Syria chemical weapon saga.

Samuelson responded to Putin's above remarks by interpreting American Exceptionalism as just Americans' core beliefs, 'value freedom more over government's protection', 'all men are created equal', and 'government of the people, by the people and for the people'. He also quoted historian Charles Murray, "(The United States was) the first nation in the world to translate an ideology of individual liberty into governing creed". Citing some survey results he showed that more Americans than Europeans believe the above principles and consider them superior hence making Americans exceptional. As an American, I do believe in these principles and can resonate with the American Exceptionalism. However, I also believe that every nation could have Exceptionalism if her people felt exceptional.

Americans had their revolution and independence early with many exceptional leaders honoring the above said principles advocating a democracy with limited government. She had more than a century (1776-1900) to develop a strong United States. In the 20th century, the United States benefitted from two world wars emerged as a victor and world leader stronger militarily. Americans felt exceptional and American Exceptionalism grew as a result, but as pointed out by Murray, the American Exceptionalism is eroding as the total spending of US governments bloated from 4% to 40% of GDP over the past 100 years or so. The recent US leaders are far less exceptional yet insisting on military intervention as means of settling issues. The US government's behavior (large government, financial debt, weapon sales, spying on citizens, etc) is the primary reason for the erosion of American Exceptionalism – people feeling exceptional.

Stalin believed in Soviet Exceptionalism based on communism so did Mao in Chinese Exceptionalism for his time. Soviet Union had her role as a world great power but eventually communism failed. Mao had little success despite of his stubborn belief and tight control of his party; it is Deng who altered the policy and took a low-key approach to grow China's economy under political stability. Deng and his followers were exceptional leaders in China not only brought China to the second largest economy in the world but for the first time over nearly two centuries made Chinese people felt exceptional. Communism failed, Soviet Union collapsed, but China is holding onto her rise and trying hardest to keep improving her people's living standard. The US foreign policy of flirting with Japan and bashing a reforming China makes no sense and it doesn't make Americans feel exceptional.

A nation's Exceptionalism can only be expressed by people not by political leaders making military threats. China making more friends in the UN makes her people feeling exceptional. The American people dislike war, do not trust big government and are losing freedom to achieve life's goals. It is time for American leaders to wake up to stop aimless foreign interventions and to fix the domestic issues. They must try to be exceptional leaders to make Americans feel really exceptional again. This is the true American Exceptionalism.

CHAPTER 3

US-China Relationship and a Dangerous Xiaosan

—ⵯ—

Mark Leonard (ML), the author of best seller, 'Why Europe Will Run the 21ˢᵗ Century' and 'What Does China Think '(Public Affairs '05 and '08), wrote a long essay in Foreign Affairs on 9/6/2013, entitled, 'Why Convergence Breeds Conflict – Growing More Similar Will Push China and The United States Apart'. ML's essay contains good observations, an enjoyable piece; however, its conclusion seems illogical. One may describe world affairs in a simplistic manner but may not produce simple conclusion. The US-China relationship is one of those situations. I don't agree with ML's conclusion – 'growing more similar pushes them apart'. Rather, I suppose, the two countries haven't examined their similarities diligently enough, on both historical and current developments, to discover and nurture a warm relationship. Further, I suppose, the two countries are marching on a dangerous path guided by faulty foreign policies, deriving from a worst-case scenario with no historical perspective. I shall use a simple metaphor and ML's observations to prove my points. Marriage can be used as a metaphor for the US-China relationship. The workings of marriage had gone through many changes in many ways and so did the US-China relationship. From two unrelated parties in a world arena to a possible 'G2' relationship may be simply viewed as two partners getting married dealing with growing and adjustment pains. In time, similarities develop but some intrinsic differences still persist; they need to be recognized by the two partners.

Historically, the United States never engaged any meaningful relationship with Chinese people when China was weak and victimized by the Western powers and an imperialistic Japan. The relationship started when China woke up to reality seeking to form a republic nation. The United States was sympathetic and her history and governance served as a model but US-China relationship was neither close nor warm until WW II. China and the U.S. were true allies in WW II in every sense, saving each other's lives on many battle grounds fighting a common enemy, Japan. This relationship was deeply memorized by all Chinese then and now, not erasable by any effort of the Soviet Union and the early Chinese communist regime. The US made a strategic mistake by not accepting China as a whole to force a coalition government to evolve into a Chinese republic more or less democratic. The two Chinese factions unfortunately also made strategic errors in not treating the dispute as an internal affair but clinging to two opposing external partners, the Soviet and the US. Then the external partners made a settlement so arbitrary and selfish treating China almost as a defeated country, dividing her in two; a treatment both Chinese factions opposed and a settlement was far worse than the real defeated aggressor. (Japan kept her sovereignty intact) The settlement not only broke China in two but worst of all caused hundreds of millions of Chinese people to undergo many decades of miserable life under communism. The generous US aid helped Japan and Taiwan to recover fast from WW II but her relationship with the Chinese people went through decades of dark ages. This part of history should be recognized and reconciled by both partners going forward in a G-2 relationship.

ML described a "Chimerica" relationship when China had divorced from Soviet style communism pursuing economic growth under political stability. He described the two countries as different as a lock and key, but symbiotic and complementary during the 'Chimerica' period. In my opinion, the relationship worked when the United States had a secure 'lock' on the world and China was practicing Deng's low 'key' philosophy. As time progresses, the US lock is not so secure any more, the 9/11 attack and Middle East wars changed the image of the United States. As a superpower advocating democracy, yet, the U.S. lost the support of the United Nation (ML: the U.S. finds many world organizations not workable) and relied on military power to settle issues. In contrast, China made more friends in the world and gained the support of the UN. So the 'Key' has become bigger than the 'Lock'. In the marriage metaphor for G2, two bread winners in the family must make adjustments when their earning power and external circles change. To keep a warm relationship, they must make adjustments for mutual benefit. ML talked about "trading places" and "double bypasses" but what they needed is to examine their similarities and intrinsic differences to find more symbiotic and complementary opportunities. This is not a chess game nor a go game as referred by ML but a bridge game; they need to develop a communication convention to improve their mutual understanding. G2 partners are bridge partners; when the world hears a G2 language, a convention all players understood, there will be neither fear nor dispute in the game. The U.S. and China should begin practicing a two-party bridge (like a honey-moon bridge in real card games) to establish a convention: language, rules and each other's playing style. With a convention, the two countries will find many historical, geographical and political reasons they can work together sharing technologies, know-how and resources.

ML rightly pointed out that the US and China are not fighting for ideology rather than status. Then what should they do to create a new 'Chimerica' respecting each other's status? Recognizing the history and the present facts is the first step. Each country must examine the past history honestly, tracing back to WW II at least, to revive the warm relationship between the Americans and Chinese. Recognizing and respecting history is the basis for building a warm future relationship, never slogans nor worst-case assumptions. Like a good marriage, a 'G2' relationship with good intention and proper behavior will work for mutual benefits and the world.

Just as in a marriage, flirting with a third party, a xiaosan, to provoke the partner is unwise and extremely damaging to a relationship. The current US behavior flirting with the Japanese right wing leader Abe Shinzo is exactly a taboo in the Sino-US relationship. Japan, refusing to recognize history and showing no remorse on her war crimes against China, Korea, Philippine, USA, etc - cannot be trusted. Japan, historically eyeing China as her supplier, market and subject and savagely applied bacteria and chemical agents to the Chinese civilians and prisoners of war including Americans cannot be a fair player. Today Chinese people socially are disgusted with the term "Xiaosan", a third person wrecking a marriage and causing betrayal and dangerous behavior. The Chinese media and Internet blogs portray Japan as a xiaosan, when Abe is wooing the United States. Encouraged by Clinton's gestures and McCain's untrue statements regarding Diaoyu Islands, Abe wants to revise Japan's peace constitution to build attack military power. While the U.S. and Japan held joint military exercises, should anyone be surprised that Obama's G2 idea received a lukewarm response from the Chinese?

A workable G2 like a marriage must be built on mutual trust and sincerity with patience never an eye for an eye. ML quoted Sigmund Freud in describing, "the more similar China and the United States become, the less they like each other", I would say, Freud would probably diagnose the flirting as insane, an act leading to wreckage and war. Now I can understand why 'xiaosan' as a frightful word is used by media in describing the problem of the US-China relationship. The more wooing and flirting are going on, the more dangerous the xiaosan becomes and the less likely a warm G2 can work – a clear and simple fact.

Hopefully both Americans and Chinese will realize the simple fact that flirting with a xiaosan will lead a marriage or G2 to a dangerous path. Both Chinese and Americans should ponder and realize that similarities and differences can coexist in a nurtured relationship built with trust. The US-China relationship would be fine and the world would stand to gain if they both could resist the intrusion of a xiaosan. A xiaosan is a danger to the US-China relationship, period!

CHAPTER 4

TRUE CONFLICT IN US-CHINA RELATIONSHIP

—✦—

THE TOPIC OF MY FIRST column in Mainstream and Organic was 'True American 'Exceptionalism'. Before getting to the main topic, I briefly explained why the column was called Mainstream and Organic. As the column was sent to the press, immediately I received a comment: Why didn't you write a piece as a clear example to show how Mainstream and Organic Opinion may differ. The comment hit me like a rock, sure, the readers deserve and want to know precisely how differently mainstream and organic media are dealing with an issue. That is the goal of this column. So today's topic, the true conflict in US-China relationship will be discussed in terms of Mainstream versus Organic views.

The US-China relationship and their conflict haven't been crystal clear due to the fact that the relationship can be looked at through multiple lenses: political (world arena), economic (trade deficit and debt financing), military (security threat), cultural (communication and exchange) and many other different aspects (cyber warfare, immigration, tourism, etc. etc.). If one is diligent enough to study the mainstream opinions on this issue, one comes away with the following view: China is evil and a threat and the U.S. must target China as a potential enemy not just an economic competitor. The US foreign policy of Pivot to Asia is portrayed by mainstream media in the U.S. as a necessary measure to curtail China who is growing too strong for the benefit of the rest of the world. On the other hand, this US foreign policy is being viewed, by China's mainstream media as purely a hostile action targeted at China, despite of multiple US official denials to the media stories. The mutual defense alliances, joint military exercises and trade agreements such as Trans-Pacific Partners (TPP) led by the US with Asian countries are characterized as for the benefit of Asia-Pacific countries and the world. Furthermore, the US mainstream media have for a long time blaming China's cheap manufacturing for taking away US jobs (blaming China for US domestic problems). Trade disputes and cyber warfare are other topics of contention, even though clearly, the U.S. had conducted cyber espionage on China while accusing China doing the same thing.

In US, under the freedom of speech law and a capitalistic system, nominally all sorts of voices and opinions are permitted, but money and size of media enterprises influence and form the mainstream media. If you had to buy an ad in NY Times to express an opinion than you knew you were not part of the mainstream. With the advancement of Internet, there are websites, blogs and social media tools available for individuals and small groups to express opinions but these media, I called them organic, live in the shadow of the mainstream media - syndicated news agencies, newspapers and televisions. In today's world, in order to get a true representation of any controversial issue, we must constantly seek out the organic media to avoid being force-fed or overwhelmed by the mainstream. In China, mass media are controlled more by the government than by enterprises; hence the official newspapers and televisions are the mainstream media. The domination of mainstream media in China, however, also faces the challenge from the Internet-supported organic media. The more advanced the internet becomes the more difficult it is for any government to control the proliferation of the organic views. Therefore, it is very healthy and revealing to have a column where both mainstream and organic views can be presented together.

Now what may be the view of the organic media on the conflict of US-China relationship then? Among many opinions circulated, one particular view, seemingly logical and persuasive, deserves to be summarized here. This view interprets the true conflict of US-China Relationship as an insecurity issue rooted in people's life style and unwillingness to make adjustments to the life style.

Americans are used to live in an easy credit world with all their material needs handily satisfied. People accumulate debts and governments accumulate debts. The US national debt has been growing and sustained by the government borrowing money guaranteed with her printing machine printing US dollars or treasury bills. Other people in the world also desire to have a better life with their material needs satisfied. They work harder and they earned through trade and acquired wealth in US dollars; naturally they want to cash out their wealth to improve their standards of living. However, they can't cash out their dollars but have to keep them as loans to the US Treasury. Since the US has the control of the dollars as the predominant instrument for global trade exchange, Cashing out dollars by those other countries will depreciate the dollar hence reducing their acquired wealth. When China and Japan, both holding enormous amount of the US Dollars, started to agree on not using US dollars for trade exchange, essentially denying the U.S. the privilege of printing as much US dollars as needed to fund her deficit and sustain her life-style. To avoid this to happen, the US employs the strategy to revive Japan's territorial ambition to go head to head against China so to derail their trade currency agreement. With China and Japan at odds, the US dollar is secured; hence Americans' life style living in ever increasing debt can be continued. You don't hear this opinion from the mainstream media but you can from the organic media. As the US government is being shut down lately due to financial and budgetary concerns in the US Congress, this organic view seems to make a lot of sense. The US and China are not fighting over ideology but over life-style.

Let's recount the history of the US-China relationship over the past 150 years. China was a victim of the Western powers and Japan. As China struggled with her revolution to build a republic modeling after the United States, the US stood essentially a sympathetic bystander. Not until the Pearl Harbor and WW II, the U.S. and China were brought together as real allies defending against a common atrocious enemy – Japan. That relationship was genuinely warm and imprinted on the Chinese people's mind even till today. The Soviet communism tried to conquer the world and caused China (and many other countries) to be divided in two, but communism has failed. The communist China had abandoned the Soviet style communism for decades searching for a system suitable for her, and achieved an obvious economic success today. Shouldn't we question the long-standing mainstream view on the conflict of the US-China Relationship? Is China really an imperialistic nation like Japan was? Is it possible that China's military effort is a response to the US pressure and the US-Japan military alliance and Japan's desire to re-arm with liberty to attack? Should we blame our domestic problems and financial woes on China? Is bashing China and cultivating the revival of a militaristic Japan really a good solution or in the long term interest of the United States? Shouldn't we think about this issue more open-mindedly not getting stuck with an old strategy based on obsolete, perhaps even false, assumptions? Do ask ourselves what is the true conflict in US-China relations! Take your pick, life-style and economic competition or ideology and military confrontation?!

CHAPTER 5

A NEW MODEL FOR US-CHINA RELATIONSHIP

—ɯ—

EVER SINCE INDEPENDENCE, THE UNITED States has embraced liberalism, supporting ideas such as free and fair elections, civil rights, freedom of the press, freedom of religion, free trade, fair taxation and private properties. The American Revolution overthrew the British imperial rule and established a democratic nation. Through WW I and II, the United States emerged as a superpower and took upon herself a duty to maintain world order and peace. The United States consistently promotes liberalism and liberal democracy worldwide (albeit selectively when economical self-interest dictates in the example of Saudi Arabia), helps establishing and safe-guarding democratic regimes and upholds a capitalist economy. Many countries adopting the democratic system and capitalism have reaped their benefits in high-er standard of living and industrial development. Since the New Deal created by President Franklin D. Roosevelt, the United States has absorbed the welfare-state concept. The liberalism has evolved into a social liberalism and the liberal democracy has accepted the element of social democracy.

The evolvement of the American democracy and capitalist economy in the United States seems to hit a wall in the recent decade. The congress is unable to get things done. The US government was forced to be shut down again, this time by a Tea Party movement. Instead of reviving her economy we see persistent high unemployment rate and continuous rise of national debt going beyond 17 trillion. The ever-increasing taxation, federal budget and government size not only make this generation of Americans in heavy debt but may lead the next generation to bankruptcy.

A recent article by Ms Rosa Brooks in Foreign Policy (foreignpolicy.com 10-16-2013), It was Nice While It Lasted – Reflection of the End of America, expressed the frustration of the American people and her feelings of despair. However, cynicism dos not solve problems, wisdom does. The American democracy and social liberalism with many virtues have been adopted as a model by many countries in the world, but, the recent EU crisis and troubles facing Greece, Spain etc raise the concern whether or not these governments can maintain an effective political system and a sustainable economy. This concern is amply exhibited in the debates among political scientists and economists in the US and China.

When our country is led by her 'political correctness' which is principally evolved from social liberalism, our society seems to become fractured rather than bonded, our citizens seem to become less tolerant individuals and the minority activists 'do what they please and demand what they want' with a standby silent majority caring little about the long-term consequences inflicted on our nation and society. This diabolic phenomenon is exhibited in many domestic issues, campaign finance, taxation, welfare benefits, healthcare reform, poverty and wealth, affirmative action, birth control, civil rights, church state separation, gay marriage, immigration, school violence, sex education, etc.. This diabolic phenomenon is also exhibited in our foreign policies such as foreign aids, military spending and wars, United Nations, economic and military alliances, cyber warfare and spying, etc. Hence it is understandable that traditional conservative philosophy is rising to challenge all the 'political correctness' evolved from social liberalism. Ms Brooks blamed the conservative Tea Party for the government shut-down and imagined the end of America but offered no clue to cure our domestic problems and social ills. We should ask ourselves: Did the decades of social liberalism bring us to our current plight? Should we pivot back to America to balance our political philosophies (liberalism versus conservatism) to solve our fundamental problems?

The United States is still the superpower in the world militarily but China has risen to the world's no. 2 economy. Capitalism certainly has its hand in the Chinese economical development, even democracy has its influence in the Chinese one party government system but the principal success factor for China is attributed to the country's conservative philosophy – shared sacrifice and focused economical development under stability. In their conservative philosophy, Chinese people traditionally do not trust their government rather they believe in hard work, shrift, and self-reliance. The early communism in China not only did not destroy that belief, it reinforced it, people realized not to count on the government to give them benefits, welfare, never mind prosperity. The communist party and the Chinese government also realized the same, hence, came with Deng's open reform. China gradually applied capitalism in economical development but all the while leery of a total free democracy and liberalism. Today, the American society and all its current problems are fairly transparent, clearly visible through Hollywood movies and the mass media. It seems, through this observation, China is struggling to find a workable model of governance instead of following the US model with lock, stock and barrel.

No doubt going forward, the U.S. and China will be the kingpins of the world's stability, peace and prosperity. However, the current US-China relation and foreign policies are on the wrong track leading to possible military conflict even war. The US-China relationship needs a new model rather than a replica of the old cold war. The concept of G2 has been introduced but it lacks substance as a workable model. Ironically, the two great nations despite of their economical and military powers and somewhat different political philosophies, they both have serious domestic issues and social problems. Some problems are common but having different root causes. The number one common issue is 'the chasm or gap between the rich and the poor'. It is an old problem in the United States only more acute recently. It is a new problem in the transforming China only more intense caused by the rampant corruption and extravagant behavior. The root cause and cure for this problem is in 'how the wealth is generated, controlled and distributed' under a right moral and legal framework, a not entirely similar or different problem in the two countries.

Can we envision a workable new model for the US-China relationship? The G2 concept is actually a plausible one, but it needs to be built on a correct assumption. The two countries must treat each other as partners with respect then the G2 can lead to and guarantee the world peace with mutual prosperity. The two countries must adopt a correct foreign policy based on their strong domestic programs solving their social problems by learning from and helping each other. There are plenty of collaborative opportunities, in agriculture, energy, finance, resource sharing, industrial production, medicine and healthcare. Since a military cooperation rather than confrontation between The US and China can certainly become insurance for world peace, the two countries must collaborate militarily.

Under this model, the two countries should develop a language convention – like a language between bridge game partners - openly exchange and discuss political philosophies and governing systems and their applicability in a G2 scenario. Under this model, the two countries must accept the concept there is no absolute right or wrong in any particular evolving political system, rather they must adopt policies accommodating the differences of each system for mutual prosperity.

CHAPTER 6

ABC TV'S MISTAKE REFLECTS AMERICANS'

INSENSITIVITY TO US-CHINA RELATIONSHIP

—⟋ⱲⱾ—

JIMMY KIMMEL OF ABC IN his 'Jimmy Kimmel Live' or 'Kid's Table' show aired the following episode with no effort of editing the insulting dialogue out:

Jimmy: OK, next question. America owes China a lot of money, 1.3 Trillion dollars. How should we pay them back?

Kid 1: You came the other way around and kill everyone in China.

Jimmy: Kill everyone in China, ok, [chuckles], that's an interesting idea.

-

Jimmy: Should this country be forced to pay our own debts?

All Kids: Yeah!

Jimmy: Well you just said kill everyone in China a while ago. What happen to that?

-

Jimmy: Should we allow the Chinese to live?

All Kids: Yeah, No!

The scene showed a group of kids including an Asian looking face in a playful mood exhibiting obvious innocence. Kimmel was the only well poised adult raising a serious question. Allowing the above scene and dialogue to be aired in a (not-live) program is a huge mistake on the part of ABC. The kid's innocent remark: "Kill everyone in China" was an incorrect blurb but it came out of kid's innocence. However, Kimmel's remark: "Kill everyone in China, ok, that is an interesting idea." was grossly insensitive coming from an adult, a TV program host and one who led the dialogue. Furthermore, Kimmel's dwelling on the "kill everyone in China" phrase and his follow-up question after kids showed silence: "Should we allow the Chinese to live?" was even more disturbing. Thank goodness, the majority of kids answered yeah! Anyone with any sensitivity to racial, violence and moral subjects watching this TV program would wonder what went through Kimmel's mind. What was he trying to promote? Doesn't ABC understand what is politically correct and incorrect in a public TV program? What is a racially insulting statement?

This episode raised an uproar of anger among Chinese Americans. Request for apology, petition to the White House and public protests have yet to obtain an open sincere public apology from ABC. The Asian civil rights PAC 80-20 may be proud that they were the only one who had received a verbal and private written apology from ABC Executive Vice President, Alternative Series, Specials and Late Night, Lisa Berger, and Vice President, Talent Development and Diversity, Tim McNeal, but the entire Chinese American community deserves an open apology from ABC and Jimmy Kimmel himself. The reluctance of making such a public apology compounds the mistake of airing such an insulting episode and allowing it to be linked to YouTube. ABC may select any mainstream media to deliver such an apology. In this organic column, we will reserve a space for publishing such an open apology from ABC and Mr. Kimmel to the Chinese American community.

Why is such an episode of any significance today when many insulting TV shows are produced? Many would cite the **discrimination issue** by saying, if you replace the word Chinese by Jews, Africans, Indians, Japanese or Mexicans in the sentence of "should we allow the Chinese to live", you would have more than uproar; Jimmy Kimmel would lose his job. I certainly agree with that, but more importantly, I would state: ABC's mistake is more than insulting the Chinese Americans. It reflects **Americans' insensitivity to the US-China relationship**. This is the most important international relationship today regarding world peace and prosperity.

There are enough essays and political opinions expressed in the main stream media about China's rise in economical power, US debt to China, China's nervousness towards the 'pivot to Asia Pacific' policy of the United States and the delicate relationship of a 'G2' scenario. The predominant view seems to be lingering on from the cold war era, now casting China as the communist enemy replacing the collapsed Soviet Union. Others have pointed out that China has divorced from the Soviet style of communism since the 70's. China's current policy is essentially adopting the capitalism in her somewhat insecure one party political system to maintain her economical growth hinged on political stability. Her rise in economical power carries a baggage of history in the past 150 years being a victim to aggressors from Western Powers and Japan. The United States by and large was the model of governance in Chinese people's mind ever since her founding father Dr. Sun Yat-Sen started the revolution in the late 19th century and wrote his political philosophy, "Three Principles of the People", essentially agreeing with Lincoln's concept of "for the people, by the people and of the people".

The Japanese invasion in the early 20th century, intended to conquer China, ushered into China communism which on the surface advocated for the welfare of the people. As an ally of the United States and a victor of WW II, China struggled to develop herself into a modern country only to see her falling further behind Japan, the defeated aggressor. Deng in the late 70's recognized that reform was China's only option after Mao's death. The recent miraculous rise of China is not only owing to the economical reform process for the past three decades, but also owing to her low-key foreign policy putting all her energy into economical development.

Today's US-China relationship is symbiotic in nature. China exports low-cost manufactured goods to the U.S. and takes the US debt. The U.S. has vast advantages in agriculture, energy and technology to export to China. Through collaboration each can prosper with ample energy to focus on domestic issues such as raising the standard of living, improving healthcare, education, enhancing national infrastructure and energy development. The opportunities for cooperation are plenty. On the other hand, it is extremely dangerous to posture a hostile policy towards each other making military threats while each possesses nuclear weapons and missile technologies. The world cannot afford to have a large scale war between these two giants. It could lead to the annihilation of the entire population of many countries. This is the very reason, "kill everyone in China" and "should we allow Chinese to live" are not joking matters. If American kids blurted out and adults found them amusing and reinforced their impression, we must recognize them as serious mistakes and stop them.

The above ABC's episode is a demonstration of the failure of our education and a failure of our mass media. This kind of violent thought is far more damaging than bullying in schools or killing at a mall. It is worst than genocide. Hence, I demand ABC to make an open apology to all American Chinese and every Chinese descendant in the world.

ABC, you have made a grave mistake!

CHAPTER 7

CAROLINE KENNEDY'S HISTORICAL MISSION

—ɷ—

CAROLINE, THE ONLY DAUGHTER OF the well-respected and world-famous US President, John F. Kennedy, (youngest elected US President, 1961-1963, assassinated on 11/22/1963) is the new US Ambassador to Japan. Her job, as an ambassador, is to maintain a good relationship between the United States and Japan. However, her responsibility will be a historical one since her role will relate to a much bigger picture in the eyes of many political analysts. Some western media have cast her assignment as an appeasement to the Japanese vanity of worshipping the rich and famous Americans, but that is a shallow opinion. Both the US and Japanese media have also voiced concern on her lack of diplomatic credential and political experience, but again that is a misunderstanding of the Kennedy legacy. In her role as ambassador to Japan, Caroline Kennedy's smarts and beliefs are far more important than her skills at this juncture when the stability in Asia Pacific means much more to world peace.

John F. Kennedy made a historical decision in carrying out a naval quarantine around Cuba preventing the Soviet Union to build an intermediate ballistic missile site in Cuba. The United States was fully aware of the threat to the US security by the Soviet's nuclear military presence in Cuba. It was risky in confronting Nikita Khrushchev of the Soviet in the Cuban missile crisis since the confrontation brought the world closer to a nuclear war than ever before. However, Kennedy's decision eventually prevailed. The Soviet backed down because the Justice was not on their side. There was no justification for the Soviet to bring nuclear threat to the Atlantic near the tip of Florida. Kennedy's resolve improved the image of American will power and established his credibility as a young President. President Kennedy's approval rating soared to 77% in 1962.

Now half century later, the Soviet Union has collapsed. Communist countries are half embracing capitalism. The United States rightly recognizes the importance of Asia Pacific in a global view of peace and prosperity. The 'Pivot to Asia Pacific' would be a logical foreign policy if it did not carry a military focus with increased naval force and military exercises in the Pacific. This policy would be beneficial to the world and welcomed by all AP nations if the United States did not reignite the ambition of the right-wing Japanese forces to restore the pre-WW II glory of the imperial Japan. Since the pivot or rebalance policy, Japan has reelected Abe Shinzo, Japan's right-wing leader, as her prime minister. Abe is taking advantage of the US 'pivot' policy as the opportunity for declaring "Japan is back" to re-dominate the Asia Pacific region. The Japanese government, despite of the protests of her neighboring countries, China, Koreas, and others as well as Japan's internal opposition, is energetically trying to revise Japan's peace constitution to allow Japan to rearm with attack right and to attempt territorial expansion. Japan's disputes with China and Korea have become a hidden fuse in the AP region.

Hillary Clinton, the former US Secretary of State, whether intentionally or not, did inflame Abe's ambition. The current pivot to or rebalance in Asia Pacific does contain a military component which draws close similarity to the Cuban Missile Crisis – the Soviet's intention in building a military presence in the Atlantic. If arming Cuba with ballistic missiles by the Soviet was perceived as a threat to the United States and other American States, then allowing Japan to rearm with attack capability would definitely be viewed by China and other AP nations as a threat to the security of the AP region. Caroline Kennedy as a new ambassador working under the new Secretary of State, John Kerry, should easily comprehend such a similarity. Recognizing the legacy of President Kennedy in insisting the Soviet to back off from Cuba and remembering the history of the imperial Japanese army invading nearly every nation in the AP region during WW II (including a Kennedy family history - a Japanese destroyer sank John F. Kennedy's boat, PT-109, on the night of August 1, 1943 in the South Pacific which made Kennedy a hero of WW II), it is obvious to draw a conclusion that there is no justification for the United States, especially with Japan, to hype a military focus in the 'Pivot' policy if gaining world prosperity and peace were the real objective. Ambassador Caroline Kennedy in her confirmation process said: "I am conscious of my responsibility to uphold the ideals he (her father, John Kennedy) represented – a deep commitment to public service, a more just America and a more peaceful world."

Caroline Kennedy's mission along with that of Gary Locke, the US Ambassador to China are of historical importance at this juncture judging on the acute tension build-up between China and Japan. Gary Locke, a first Chinese American serving as the US Ambassador to China, has gained enormous respect and popularity among Chinese people for his low-key style (Confucius teachings) in conducting his public appearance and interaction with people. His accomplishment in improving US embassy efficiency in cutting visa approval time from 100 to 3-5 days has been widely praised. Unfortunately, Ambassador Locke has announced his resignation to return to his family in Seattle in early 2014. Hence, the mission of Caroline Kennedy is extremely critical, not only as the ambassador to Japan but the key US representative in Asia Pacific while a new US Ambassador to China is being selected by the Obama-Kerry administration.

Managing an adversary US-China relationship with a competitive partner, Japan, a former world's second largest economy, in a triangular mingle, is not as easy and productive as cultivating and managing a straight-forward partnership between China and the United States. Japan has been persistently denying history of her aggression towards other nations and exhibiting resentment to the rise of China replacing her as the second largest economy in the world. The United States as the supreme power has the responsibility to keep the globe in peace and has the obligation to stand behind justice never forgetting and encouraging imperialism. Caroline Kennedy has a historical mission in her role as the ambassador to Japan upholding the ideals of President Kennedy and committing to a more just America and a more peaceful world

CHAPTER 8

RIGHT CYBERSPACE STRATEGY AND POLICY

FOR THE U.S. WITH RESPECT TO CHINA

———ᘛᗝᘚ———

EVER SINCE NSA CONTRACTOR EDWARD Snowden disclosed the US cyber spy activities to the world, the media worldwide drew attention to privacy protection, cyberspace conducts by multi-national companies and possible cyber war between nations. We shall first review a few recent publications then come to the title subject.

First article by Abraham Newman, Privacy Pretense – How Silicon Valley Helped NSA (Foreign Affairs 11/6/2013), described how cyber data companies such as Google, Yahoo, Facebook the like pursued weak privacy policy and self-regulation in Internet security. They lobbied in the U.S. and in foreign countries. The firms had adhered to an old 1997 government framework, "Privacy and Self-Regulation in the Information Age," which maintained that the best way to protect consumers was to let the technology market handle sensitive issues on its own. However, these lax rules created fertile ground for NSA snooping. What was good for Google et al was also good for the NSA (and foreign hackers) in taking advantage of the lax rules and accessible data. After the surveillance scandal, the public is aware of that now. People are less trusting of IT giants, telecommunication companies and governments. Therefore, Congress legislators are working to enact laws to strengthen privacy protection and limit State surveillance of citizens albeit facing resistances from Internet industries and government security agencies for different reasons.

The second article, The End of Hypocrisy – American Foreign Policy in the Age of Leaks, appeared in November/December issue of the above cited publication, Henry Farrell and Martha Finnemore presented an excellent analysis of the hypocrisy the National Security Agency of the United States in conducting its cyber spy and surveillance programs. The Snowden disclosure did not really compromise much the intelligence sources or methods; rather it embarrassed the United States by revealing her double-faced approach on her cyber spy activities. Prior to the Snowden leaks, the U.S. only talked about defending against foreign cyber attacks, often accusing China and others hacking US companies for commercial gains. After the leak revealing that the US cyber spying activities were world-wide and the fact the U.S. and the United Kingdom compromised key communication software and encryption systems designed to protect online privacy and security, the U.S. began to alter her story by justifying her cyber spying for national security in contrast to other nations hacking for commercial gains. The US Defense Department and National Security Agency started to highlight the danger of cyberwar and the necessity of acquiring resources for defending our cyberspace and responding to foreign cyber attacks. These arguments seem to fall on deaf ears in other States, even in the U.S., since every one now clearly see through this hypocrisy and begin to justify their own cyber activities. What strategy should the U.S. formulate to direct her cyberspace conduct is obviously an important issue?

The third essay, Cyberwar and Peace - Hacking Can Reduce Real - World Violence, in Foreign Affairs (November/December, 2013), written by Thomas Rid, argued that cyber attack did not qualify as an act of war. Based on historical evidence, he illustrated the ineffectiveness of cyber attack code to cause violence. Mr. Rid's conclusion is only based on limited facts but his concerns that the escalating use of cyber spying and espionage by NSA and Defense Department actually diminishes people's trust in the US government are indeed valid. His essay intends to make an impression on readers that cyber war will not happen and cyber attack will not cause serious violence, therefore, we may forget about it. This conclusion is questionable. Therefore, we will return to the title subject, Right Cyberspace Strategy and Policy to China and present an analysis referencing to the above three papers.

By lightly brushing aside the creative cyber wars in novels and movies and citing only a few past incidences Rid concluded his analysis - the effect of cyber attack is inconsequential. We all know that modern weaponry has become more and more dependent on computer and software control. The rapid technological advances in both computer hardware and software can change the possibilities of cyber wars and their outcome, both in scope and in effect, far beyond our current knowledge.

For example, nuclear weapons are the most dangerous threat to all mankind. The deployment of a nuclear weapon (even modern conventional weapon) normally depends on human intelligence to operate and launch, but if a cyber code were imbedded into a nuclear weapon system then it could replace or bypass human intelligence to launch such a nuclear weapon. If cyber attack could be used to sabotage the construction of a nuclear bomb in Iran, most likely a cyber attack could ignite a nuclear bomb elsewhere. Therefore, a nuclear (and conventional) threat can be heightened by cyber code. Another conceivable example is a cyber code infected GPS system dictating or even replacing human intelligence in exercising actions to cause violence and massive disaster. A nuclear test can go haywire, an army of drones can be directed to inflict major damage and well planned accidents can happen at a specific time and a specific city. So NSA and Defense Department are correct in calling cyber war a serious danger.

However, the US Defense Department and NSA are wrong to instigate a cyber arm race by building a huge organization of cyber personnel. The argument of building only a cyber defense skill is flawed since defense skill has little difference from offensive skill in cyber warfare. The simple argument for not having a cyber arm race can be drawn from our experience or mistake in nuclear arm race. It is a wrong strategy to instigate a nuclear arm race since it leads to proliferation of nuclear weapons, raising the chance of having a nuclear war. So by the same logic, we should develop a clear strategy to thwart a global arm race in cyber space. To prevent a cyber arm race with China, for instance, it is essential to define a 'Hackless' agreement between two nations, a H2 agreement including IT industry and multinational companies involved with strong privacy and data security. Cyber arm race contrary to weapon race depends more on people skills (logic and language) less on hardware technologies even less on materials, hence, a prolonged race favors a country with more people skills such as China or India. To prevent a hacker-proliferated world making everyone living under stress, the U.S. should contemplate H2 or H3... or H7 agreement immediately before it she loses advantage and time.

CHAPTER 9

IMPERFECT DIPLOMACY EVIDENCED BY

CHINA'S NEW ADIZ IN EAST CHINA SEA

—◊◊—

IT IS PERFECTLY REASONABLE FOR China to declare an air defense identification zone (known as ADIZ) in East China Sea to require flights to notify China ahead of the scheduled flights; the United States, Canada, Russia even Japan had their ADIZ and guidelines for decades. In view of the tension in the East China Sea provoked by Japan by nationalizing the disputed Diaoyu Islands (Senkaku Islands called by Japan) through a government orchestrated purchase from a civilian, the Chinese ADIZ map, which included the airspace of Diaoyu Islands, would be logically interpreted as an attempt to identify and prevent hostile and unnecessary flights over the disputed region. These islands historically belonged to China for centuries as a part of Taiwan. Japan captured Taiwan in a war against China but had to return to China by the instrument of surrender based on the Potsdam and Cairo Declarations which were signed by the defeated Japan and nine allied victors. When the U.S. (as the trustee of Okinawa) offered the civil administration right of Okinawa islands to Japan in 1972 unilaterally without the consent of China, she accidentally made the status of the uninhabited Diaoyu Islands ambiguous, owing to their close proximity to Okinawa. Despite of their internal political squabbles, both the Mainland China and Taiwan claim that the governance of the Diaoyu Islands belongs to Yi-Nan Xian (like a township) in the province of Taiwan.

When China announced the ADIZ map and flight guidance, she declared that it is not aimed at any country or any aviation entity but merely followed the international practice. Why did such a legal and logical announcement arouse a strong protest from the Japanese government, even more surprisingly it received disapproval from the United States, calling it a unilateral decision raising the tension in the East China Sea? The U.S. even sent B52s flying into the newly declared East China Sea ADIZ as a protest as if flexing muscle by flying bombers in the region (although wasn't armed as reported) would reduce tension but China's declaration of an ADIZ guidance would increase tension. Whether the US reaction were agitated by Japan behind the scene or considered as a 'face' issue (like a commonly alleged oriental problem - face saving is more important than rational decision), the US behavior and this kind of development can hardly be considered a rational and logical diplomatic measure if the purpose is to reduce military tension.

Mainstream media in the West and East have ample reports and analyses on this episode, mostly arguing from legal and logical viewpoints. ADIZ is not a sovereignty issue, declaring fly path is a good public safety measure all public aviation entities would be glad to oblige; as indicated by the fact that three Japanese airlines immediately agreed to oblige to the Chinese new fly zone requirement. It is the Japanese government that pressured the civilian airlines to disrespect this requirement. What is the logic here? Are the civilian lives and safety not important? The root of the dispute (Diaoyu Islands) went back to 1895 when Japan took Taiwan by war. The seized Taiwan and other islands were supposed to be returned to China according to the Japanese surrender agreement, an undisputable fact. Post WW II, China was divided and the world was polarized by the Cold War, prompting the U.S. to develop Japan as an ally at the expense of China, a US ally in WW II. Post cold war, the US must revise her Asia-Pacific strategy especially on the fundamental assumption which country should be treated as an ally to maintain world order and prosperity. It is true Japan under the US wings had grown strong and adopted more of a democratic government system, but it is also true that the Japanese right-wing party is gaining power and influence in steering Japan back to her imperialist past. Although the U.S. maintains neutrality in the sovereignty dispute of the Diaoyu Islands, it is clear that Japan is taking advantage of her ally position under the US-Japan mutual defense treaty to gain more control of these islands and to expand her military power for territorial ambition, despite of the fact that the visiting Japanese Prime Minister Kakuei Tanaka and Chinese premier Zhou Enlai in 1972 and the Japanese Prime Minister Takeo Fukuda and the Chinese leader Deng Xiaolong Ping, later in 1978, had agreed to table the Diaoyu dispute for the sake of restoring China-Japan relationship.

What is wrong with the current development regarding ADIZ, in my opinion, is not a logic or legal issue; rather it is a diplomacy issue. For too long, the U.S.

and China were in an unnecessary adversary relationship with no open and frank diplomatic dialogue. China being historically weak in diplomacy out of a weak government perhaps has not learned the diplomacy that the U.S. as a superpower is used to. Although China might think her declaration of ADIZ guidance in the East China Sea was perfectly legal and was not directed to a particular party, but she did not take the best diplomatic approach to reach the aim. If China would first present such a plan to the U.S. along with a diplomatic statement such as: "China wishes to reduce tension in the East China Sea, hence proposing an ADIZ map and guidance. All civilian aviation shall follow the same guidance as other international ADIZ requires. The US military aviation is exempted from the civilian procedure but diplomatic channels shall be established between military organizations in two countries to ensure all legitimate military exercises can proceed without incidence. China naturally will reciprocate in regard to US ADIZs." Similarly, this kind of diplomatic exchanges should be held with Korea and Russia. Following these diplomatic dialogues, then China can make the declaration to the world publicly. Whether Japan will protest or not is utterly irrelevant.

If the above took place, what would the U.S. do? As a democratic nation, it is hardly right for the U.S. to refuse (not appearing to be a bully) the Chinese proposal aimed to reduce tension and seeking the US cooperation, particularly having no impact to civilian aviation in the region. In this column, we have talked about the need for a new model and a direct diplomatic language between the U.S. and China. This episode of ADIZ announced for East China Sea is the very example that calls for China and the U.S. to learn and develop a direct diplomatic language and process which will be not only good for mutual benefit but also soothing for the world to appreciate.

CHAPTER 10

US Secretary John Kerry's Legacy To Be

—ɷ—

On John Kerry's watch, he has managed to work with Russia in reaching an agreement to remove the chemical weapons and achieved an interim success on Iran nuclear issue. However, as pointed out by Aaron David Miller (a Middle East Analyst, author of the book - The Much Too Promised Land: America's Elusive Search for Arab and Israeli Peace and advisor to Six Secretaries of States) in his recent article, Now Isn't the Time to Negotiate over Syria's Civil War (in Newsday, Op-ed, 10/29/2013), Kerry may be overreaching in trying to convene a UN-sponsored meeting to end the Syrian civil war. Further, in another article, Confidence Man (published in Foreign Policy on 11/18/2013), Mr. Miller characterized Mr. Kerry as "a man with the skills, toughness and ego to be a great Secretary of State" but questioned "would the world let him?" Mr. Miller claims that it requires the **opportunities**, right trusted **world partners** and prudence in diplomacy in order to achieve great accomplishments. He concludes, in the article, "the era of heroic US Secretary of State tackling huge (world) problem solo is over" and Dramatic "Hollywood style (happy and good) ending is through". Presently, in the absence of strong trusted partners in the world arena, though Mr. Kerry is energetically playing the leading hero, Mr. Miller could not help but offer a tentative non-committal prediction, "time will tell his success or failure."

On the Middle East situation, Mr. Miller's expertise and experience are very well respected. He is absolutely right that the current situation is very different from 1973-75 when Kissinger could produce three Arab-Israel agreements after Iraq joined the Yom Kippur War in 1973 (The war has provided him the **opportunity**). So is different from 1991 when James Baker got the Arabs and Israelis to the Madrid conference following Saddam Hussein's invasion to Kuwait (which gave him the **opportunity**). Those opportunities presented themselves for the two

Secretaries of State to accomplish some significant peace effort at that time in that part of the world. Today, the Middle East situation has not been improved; the wars do not present opportunities for the parties to come to the conference table. Any peace solution would still require long patience and miraculous opportunities to occur. So despite of an energizer bunny image Mr. Kerry presented himself over his predecessor, a cautious Ms Clinton, in engaging with the parties in the Middle East, the Arab-Israel peace process and achievement would probably not be his signature legacy as hinted by Mr. Miller.

In the other part of the world, ever since the United States launched a 'Pivot to Asia' policy, the turn of events have not developed the way to the best interest of the U.S. and the world at large. Contrary to making a positive presence in the Asia Pacific waving a banner of maintaining stability and peace and stimulating trade and economy in that region, the U.S. essentially elevated the tension in the Asia Pacific to a potentially dangerous level. If that was by design, then the Middle East history would be a great lesson to study, since the conflicts among Asia Pacific nations could be accentuated eventually to a situation similar to the Middle East thanks to the US agitation and intervention. Even though there was no fundamental religious and racial intolerance like that between Arabs and Israelis in Asia Pacific, but the Japanese aggression during WW II against all her neighboring countries did create very deep wounds within the entire region. Those wounds were barely covered with a thin scab over the past 70 years due to Japan's continuous denial of her war crimes. Under the pivot strategy, the US seems to encourage Japan to poke open those scabs to inflict pains and bring back nightmares. Implicitly giving Japan a lead role to play in restoring a 'Pan Asia Pacific Prosperity Circle' through military alliances and trade agreements forgetting that was the sole banner the imperial Japan had used to justify her aggression to China, Korea, Philippine and the rest of Asian countries. Fortunately or unfortunately, Japan, through her right-wing party leadership, has alerted both China, Korea and possibly the rest of Asia with her desire to revise Japan's peace constitution to permit her to expand military power with attack capability, and more vividly with her aggressive behavior in dealing with territorial dispute with China and Korea. Therefore, it is no surprise, the tension in the China Sea in the Asia Pacific is heightened to a dangerous level.

The Asia-Pacific situation may turn out to be **the "opportunity"** Mr. Miller referred to in his articles for Mr. Kerry and of course Mr. Obama to build their legacy in their tenure to 2016. This situation is by far more controllable than the Middle East. China is not like Israel, she has a large population and a vast economy and a significant military power. China's new leader, Xi JingPing, has visited Muscatine, Iowa, U.S. for studying American agriculture in 1985 as a young man. He has visited Iowa again in 2012 as the Vice President and President to be of China. Obama and Xi met twice in 2013, with the second time over two days in a 400 acres resort, Sunnylands, Ranch Mirage, California. Xi, the elected Chinese leader by the People's National Congress, will serve most likely two terms (limited by law) to 2023. He would be **the world partner**, Mr. Miller referred to as necessary to partner with, to solve huge problems in the world such as the Asia Pacific crisis, over Mr. Vladimir Putin of Russia, anyone in Europe, or Benjamin Netanyahu. Facing the recent development in Asia Pacific (as partially caused by the U.S.), continuing unrest in the Middle East (with no quick solution) and lingering problems of world economy (and US domestic issues), It would be unthinkable for Obama and Kerry to consider Abe Shinzo as a strong world partner to deal with these world challenges even though Abe is very much inspired and eager to play that role to realize his "Japan is back" dream.

US Secretary of State John Kerry's legacy and perhaps his re-bid for the US Presidency in 2016 depends on his recognition of **the opportunity** and his ability to be friend and work with a **strong partner** in the world so that tough world issues can be solved with assurance of positive outcomes. That clear opportunity is in Asia Pacific not in the Middle East and the strong partner is Mr. Xi in China. Mr. Kerry must act prudently to work with the opportunity and the right partner to produce a win-win outcome as his legacy.

CHAPTER 11

SHOULD OBAMA'S ADMINISTRATION

RE-EXAMINE THE U.S. ASIA-PACIFIC STRATEGY?

—⁓—

THE UNITED STATES AS A superpower carries the responsibility of maintaining peace and freedom in the world. Entering the current century, the U.S. faced a series of challenges, the terrorists attack, the Middle East wars, the Iran nuclear threat, the North Korea's nuclear weapon experiments and the recent Syria's chemical weapon issue all squarely challenging us. The United States must have a sensible foreign policy while domestically trying to revitalize her economy after multiple recessions and financial crises.

As an American citizen, observing the events happening around the world, I am very concerned about the US "Pivot to Asia" or later rephrased "Rebalancing in Asia" foreign policy. This policy seems to be created with a principal assumption that China is our arch-enemy and a new cold war should be directed at her as we did to Soviet Union. All China's neighboring countries are encouraged to join force with the U.S. to curtail China's rise and her assertive presence in Asia-Pacific. As reported by NY Times and elsewhere, this policy had raised serious concerns in China and produced enough hyped anxiety in the right wing party in Japan resulting in the election of Shinzo Abe, a known rightwing extremist advocating stronger Japanese military, as her new Prime Minister. Furthermore, the recent missile and nuclear bomb test carried out by North Korea, annoyed China, could well have been the first offspring of the US "Pivot" strategy. These developments have made all Asian countries nervous, even Australia whose media has published warnings on the projected outcomes from this "pivot" policy.

Shinzo Abe visited Obama early this year bringing his apparent intent to win America's endorsement for his desire to expand the Japanese military perhaps even his desire to revise Japan's constitution. His visit triggered a demonstration warning the resurgence of Japanese Militarism in New York City by Chinese Americans of some 60 civil organizations. Abe's speech of 'Japan is Back' at Center for Strategy and International Studies (CSIS) is plainly boastful. As a Chinese American fully aware of the Asian sentiment towards the atrocity committed by the Japanese military and how Japan's denial of her war crimes angered the Asian countries, I question the wisdom of the U.S. picking Japan, enemy of the U.S. and China during WW II, over China, an American ally in WW II, as a partner to maintain order and peace in Asia. Although the reception of Abe by President Obama was low key by press coverage which may have suggested perhaps the U.S. has realized that her current Asia-Pacific strategy may be backfiring, however, Abe's continuing effort in visiting China's neighboring countries seeking strategic alliances definitely is raising more Chinese eyebrows. We may ask: What would the United States gain by encouraging Japan to resurge as an offensive military power in Asia? What would benefit the U.S. by stimulating an acute arms race between China and Japan and with the U.S.? Is America that cynical to wish China and Japan to destroy each other? Or do we wish to solve our national debt problem by selling weapons to the warring parties in Asia? As an American citizen, I can't believe our government would engage in such a faulty policy.

The time has changed and the world, especially China, has changed since 1972 when Nixon visited China. Today, the United States has to put her own house in order and shape her up to compete with rising global economic entities. The more sensible win-win approach seems to be working with Asian countries, particularly China and India, as partners to raise their citizens' standard of living. We all know that they are decades behind western developed countries and their governments certainly place economic growth as the highest priority unless they felt a military threat. Obama has fairly won his second term with a mandate to fix the country's economy. His focus on domestic challenges, however, requires a stable and uneventful world so the Obama administration can put our house in order. Therefore, It seems to be necessary for his administration to re-examine the US Asia-Pacific strategy - whether or not the 'pivot' strategy is creating a stable world so we can focus on our domestic woes. We need to examine whether or not is it right and beneficial to target China as an enemy or as a partner? Is it wise to cultivate Japan back to militarism or to guide Japan to face history and reality? Does arm race lead to a solution or a problem? Can we negotiate with China to contain conflicts? Studying history often can shed some light on these big issues. In 5000 years of Chinese history, most of the time China was in defense of invasions, most severely in the last century against western powers and Japan. The Chinese definitely does not want to repeat that part of history. Nor do Americans!

CHAPTER 12

WHAT ARE THE INTENTIONS BEHIND THE FOREIGN

POLICIES OF THE UNITED STATES AND CHINA?

—◊—

NICHOLAS DONABET KRISTOF, AN AMERICAN journalist, a columnist and twice winner of Pulitzer Price, is a very well respected political analyst. In his recent NY times Op-Ed (12-4-2013), he cites an American folklore story Hatfields and McCoys Feud originated in the 19th century as a metaphor alerting the danger of the Diaoyu Island (Senkaku) dispute between China and Japan. The Hatfields and McCoys were English and Irish immigrants to America, settled in West Virginia and Kentucky respectively bordered by Tug Fork, a feeder flowing into the Big Sandy River. The feud involved the ex-Confederates (Hatfields) murdered an ex-Union soldier (McCoy), the disputed ownership of a hog, a romance between a McCoy girl and a Hatfield young man and politics and justice in the trials of the Hatfield-McCoy violence. The Hatfields and McCoys have become synonymous with blood-shed involving family honor, justice and vengeance.

In three words, Kristof smartly used the Hatfields and McCoys feud to symbol-ize and highlight the Diaoyu dispute which can be traced back to 1845 when Japan invaded China and captured Taiwan to which the uninhabitable Diaoyu Islands belong historically. Indeed the Diaoyu dispute has the potential to evolve into a bloody conflict not only between the Chinese and the Japanese but possibly involve the Americans. Mr. Kristof, an expert in foreign affairs, certainly is fully aware of this possibility. However, the ordinary Americans, who most likely have not even heard about the Diaoyu Islands, really need to understand the true significance of the Diaoyu issue and comprehend why the rocky islands may impact all of us thousands of miles away. It is especially important for young Chinese Americans, Japanese Americans and all Americans to understand the historical background and the recent developments about Diaoyu Island and the possibility of war which is more serious than equating it to a bloody long feud like Hatfields and McCoys.

In a way, the Diaoyu Island dispute is a simpler story than Hatfields and McCoys; it does not involve family honor nor romance not even any people since there is no residents on the rocks as we all know. The dispute viewed by China and the vast majority of her people is simply an exhibit of Japan's territorial ambition and continued aggression against China, first in the 19th century, later throughout WW II in the 20th century using military force and then to 21st century using trickery schemes such as 'purchasing' and 'nationalizing' the uninhabited islands. The recent aggressive conduct by Japan is also likely stimulated by the existence of an UN study reporting rich energy resources in that region. Hence the Diaoyu story may also be characterized as aggression motivated by greed. The recent tension, however, is created by international politics. Politically Japan sees the heightened dispute as a perfect excuse to allow her to revise her peace constitution to give Japan "first attack" right, instead of limiting her strong military power to defense only. The current right-wing Japanese government, led by Prime Minister Abe Shinzo, advocating "Japan is back" and "returning to Japan's pre-war glory", is the very force behind in aggravating the Diaoyu Island dispute despite of some Japanese scholars and historians honestly refuting the Japanese government's claim on the Diaoyu Islands.

The United States has maintained a neutral position in this dispute, which was tabled by China and Japan in 1972 by their leaders, namely Premier Zhou Enlai and Prime Minister Kakuei Tanaka, when they both wished to have a better diplomatic relationship. Today the United States seems to go along with Abe's scheme to drag the US-Japan Mutual Defense Treaty to cover these uninhabited rocks. This may make some logical sense if the U.S. valued these rocks for their military strategy - forming an ocean chain to surround and curtail China in the Asia Pacific. However, recalling the Cuban Missile Crisis in the Kennedy era, the United States reacted forcefully to the Soviet's attempt of establishing a missile base in Cuba; Americans should understand how China would feel and react when we side with Japan in pivoting to AP with a military intent to contain her.

If the Diaoyu Island dispute involved hatred between the Chinese and Japanese as Mr. Kristof cited some remarks made by Chinese, it would not be difficult for

Americans to understand its causality. There is no doubt China was a victim to aggression by Japan and other Western powers during the19th century. After a prolonged war (1937-45) defending against Japan's invasion, ultimately at the Japan's defeat, China along side of the United States accepted Japan's surrender without demanding any retribution or penalty other than requiring Japan to return all captured Chinese lands back to China including the Diaoyu Islands. After WW II, Germany apologized and compensated to her neighbors, but Japan showed no remorse and insisted on worshipping her war criminals annually at her national shrine. By denying her war crimes and atrocities, Japan alienated not only the Chinese but also the Koreans, Filipinos and many Asians rekindling their bitter memories into hatred.

The current American foreign policy of pivoting to AP and dealing with China's rising is puzzling many Chinese Americans, Japanese Americans as well as some Caucasian China and Japan experts. There are a number of reasons for believing so. Firstly, our government and most mainstream media seem to take for granted accepting a new Cold War hypothesis targeting China as the archenemy and siding with Japan as an ally without questioning its weakness and false assumptions. Secondly, our policy makers seem to be ignoring the historical facts behind the ownership of these rocky islands and forgetting the WW II history regarding allies, hence, putting the United States on the wrong side of Justice. Thirdly, our policy seems to be confusing the world and China regarding whether or not the U.S. really wishes to steer US-China to a 'Great Nation' (G2) relationship for the benefit of world peace and prosperity. Lastly and most frightening is that the United States seems to be designing a major war to let Japan and China to destroy each other. The fact that Japan is desperately trying to get the U.S. to be locked in her defense through the US-Japan mutual defense treaty and China is fearfully trying to upgrade her naval forces to defend against the superior joint naval power of Japan and the U.S. certainly do not comfort the world at all.

Witnessing the sharp reactions over the East China Sea ADIZ announced by China, we cannot help but join Mr. Kristof to open more frank discussions on the 'intensions' of the foreign policies of the United States and China.

CHAPTER 13

NEW YEAR NEW HOPE AND NEW

US-CHINA RELATIONSHIP

—ɯ—

IT IS A UNIVERSAL TRADITION that our calendar brings us to a festival mood when a year ends and a new year begins. No matter what the past year was like, the New Year brings us a new hope and gives everyone a new start. It is this spirit that moves civilization forward and makes progress for mankind. Every human being is entitled a new hope and collectively every nation is bestowed a new opportunity in the year of 2014 to start anew, a new plan, a new goal and a new relationship.

In this journal space, US-China Forum, although launched in August 2013, it reviewed, witnessed and discussed many current events happened throughout the year concerning the United States and China, their domestic issues as well as their international affairs. In this specific column, Mainstream and Organic, we tried to bridge the gaps, analyze the differences and raise the voices from common folks to seasoned analysts, from the mass mainstream to the organic blogs and most importantly from the American viewpoints to the Chinese understandings. At this juncture of New Year celebration, we see very fitting to talk about a new hope and a new US-China Relationship.

For the United States, the past year was an eventful year, domestically we had to continue struggling with the bailout of the historically one of the most critical financial crisis happened in 2008. We continually fought the persistent unemployment rate in the high digit above 7 or 8 percent. Our housing market was still suffocated crawling out of the bottom since the bubble burst and created the credit crisis. Socially, we saw more States recognizing sam sex marriage up to 16 States now and the Affordable Care Act passed though its implementation remaining to be very challenging. Internationally, our Middle East involvement was still like stuck in a mud hole unable to make a clean break. The Iran nuclear threat, the Syria chemical weapon and the Egyptian uprising all kept President Obama and Secretary of State Clinton sleepless many nights. The pivot to Asia Pacific seemed to be creating another hot spot instead of cooling off the World which is always longing for peace. North Korea was making her nuclear threats and Japan was busy weaving her alliances with Asian countries dreaming Japan is back to her pre-WW II glory. In a way, it was good to see Obama got re-elected to a second term to avoid a frequent change at the helm. John Kerry has replaced Clinton as the secretary of the State and Chuck Hagel replaced Leon Panetta as the Secretary of Defense; we hope the new cabinet is able to contemplate a new foreign policy for the New Year, especially towards Asia Pacific.

For China, 2013 is equally eventful. Domestically, the transition of power and authority was the greatest event in China which was watched all over the world. Amid the trial of Bo Xilai, the biggest corruption and betrayal case in recent Chinese history triggered by Wang Li Jun incident, revealing the murder of British business man Neil Heywood at the US Consulate in Chengdu. Xi JinPing and Li Keqiang were elected as the President and Premier Of China. The fact that Xi was able to consummate all authorities of government, party and military in one person smoothly was indeed a feat projecting a possible decade of stable development and reform. China is revising her economic development plan, adjusting the GDP growth rate to a lower level near 8% and moving carefully to a more consumption propelled economy. The third plenum session of the 18th CPC party's congress had concluded with ten significant directives, loosening up one-child policy, equal education opportunity, and eight significant reforms including financial reform as witnessed by the opening of a special free (financial) trade zone (FTZ) in Shanghai. The Diaoyu dispute occupied much of the world media in 2013 has strengthened China's resolve in defending her sovereignty against the Japanese aggression seemingly never died since 19th century. Finally in December, China succeeded in a soft landing of a robot on the moon to perform scientific experiments powered by solar energy which signifies that China is ready to join the U.S. and Russia in collaborative space exploration to benefit all mankind.

Reviewing what happened in 2013 and going forward into 2014, it seems to be appropriate and opportune time for US and China to develop a new strategy and launch a new relationship based on the candid meetings between Obama, Kerry and Biden with Xi and Li respectively taken place in 2013. The new knowledge that the U.S. leaders gained about China and the mutual accessibility to US and China leaders, especially in the military sector, paved the way to reexamine the old assumptions inherited from the Cold War and to reset the foreign policies towards each country. At this juncture of New Year, while citizens of both countries are celebrating, we wish we will usher in a new hope and a new US-China relationship moving the world closer to peace, harmony and prosperity in 2014 and beyond.

CHAPTER 14

FROM MANDELA TO DIAOYU

ISLANDS – A LESSON FOR WORLD LEADERS

—*m*—

NELSON MANDELA WAS RECOGNIZED AS a world statesman in fighting inequality and racial discrimination in his country, South Africa. His influence reached the entire world drawing leaders worldwide to pay final tribute at his funeral. Mandela was a young man believed in using violence to fix problems in the world but he failed and ended in jail for 27 years. In his prison years he studied Marx and Maos, on communism, but what really changed his life was his realization that changing the world is a monumental task and changing one's country is extremely difficult but changing oneself is achievable. Through changing himself, he succeeded in changing the people surrounding him, then his nation and then the world. Can this invaluable golden philosophy and Mandela's experience be applied to deal with the world's hot spot – Diaoyu Islands? Is there a lesson for the world leaders?

The dispute of Diaoyu Islands is fairly well known by now, i. Historically they belonged to China since the 19th century, ii. The infamous 1972 transfer of administrative right of Okinawa to Japan by the United States unilaterally caused ambiguous interpretation by Japan to include these islands under her administration, iii. Japan's recent scheme of nationalizing these islands raised China's firm resolve to claim back the sovereignty of these islands. The recent increasing display of military forces involving the U.S., Japan and China and the declaration of an ADIZ (air defense identification zone) in East China Sea including these islands are making Diaoyu Islands the hotspot of the world. The Japanese Prime Minister Shinzo Abe is in the center of this dispute. Abe seems to be hunger for the world's limelight with a desire to restore Japan's pre-war glory but what he needs is a lesson from Mandela's experience.

Shinzo Abe was born with a lineage of Japanese powerful politicians, father Shintaro (1924-91), Japanese foreign minister (1982-1986), twice lost the chance to become the PM, once to rival Noburo Takeshita and once to an insider trading stock scandal, grandfather, Kan (1894-1946), also a politician born in a wealthy business family, and grandfather-in-law, Nobusuki Kishi (1896-1987), a far more important figure in his life. In 1935, Kishi was working for the campaign of industrial development of Manchukuo, known to have exploited Chinese forced labor, then in 1941, was promoted to minister of commerce and industry till 1945. When Japan surrendered, Kishi was put in prison as a suspect of class A war criminal but was released in 1948 without indictment. When the U.S. ended the allied occupation in 1952, Kishi resurfaced in politics helping organizing a federation of two pre-war conservative parties with 'revision of constitution' as one of the party's goals. Kishi later joined the liberal party and was elected to the diet from 1953-1979 and served as PM from 1957-60. Kishi resigned as PM due to a socialist party's demonstration against his government causing an embarrassing cancellation of President Eisenhower's visit to Japan. Kishi dedicated a tombstone for the war time PM Tojo and six other war criminals executed after the Tokyo trial which infuriated the Chinese and Koreans. When Shinzo was elected as the PM in 2006, he also worshiped at the Yasukuni shrine where war criminals are memorialized. As Japan's present PM, he is strongly advocating revision of the Japanese constitution to permit her to use attack force.

Knowing the above background, it is understandable why the current PM Shinzo Abe may want to follow his grandfathers' footsteps to restore Japan's pre-war glory and make himself the PM to claim "Japan is back". However, the time has changed. Japan was right to modernize herself through the Meiji Restoration (1868-1912), absorbing the western scientific technologies but was wrong in believing in the imperialism. When the people of the world were far apart, information flow limited and nations' knowledge of the globe incomplete, exploration was the main drive propelling imperialism and colonialism. In today's world, people gain knowledge about the globe, people's dreams and desires are similar and there is no super race only educated race. No nation can whitewash history, distort education and manipulate the media completely. In today's world, true great leaders of every nation should take Mandela as an example, accepting the history and current facts then making changes to themselves then to their countries and then to the world for fulfilling the dreams and desires of the people in the world.

For Japan, and its leader Abe, the dispute of Diaoyu Islands is a warning for Japan to recognize a dangerous path she is taking her citizens to. Japan's methodic whitewash of the WWII history and brainwashing the Japanese citizens to deny their ancestors' war crimes were grave mistakes made by the post war leaders of Japan. Continuing to deny history, to ignore the global citizens' knowledge of the world and to believe in settling problems with military force are current mistakes of the Abe administration. In 1937 Japan believed that she could conquer the entire China in six months but she was wrong; even a brutal massacre in Nanking could not scare the Chinese to surrender. Chinese people's peace loving nature and submissive to authority, was interpreted by the Japanese imperial army as cowardice but after the Chinese learned the truth of Japanese imperialism, they fought back hard and won. China is a developed military power now with nuclear, laser, satellite and space technologies at her disposal to defend any attack from Japan. Her retaliation to any challenge will not be a long stretched war like WWII but an instant destruction of Japan. If Japan ever thinking again to conquer China in a first strike it would be a suicidal thought. Abe must seriously reflect on the facts, change his attitude and think of the welfare of the Japanese people instead of dreaming of returning to the imperial past his ancestors lived in.

For China to deal with the issue of Diaoyu Islands, the Mandela experience is also a lesson. China is justified to be assertive in defending her rights but the Chinese leaders must be skillful in conducting their foreign policies in reaching an acceptable solution. Even though Japan has used a ridiculous argument to tie Diaoyu Islands to Okinawa (in its administrative rights offered to Japan by the United States illegally) and schemed to nationalize the islands, China should not use force to reclaim the islands unless she is forced to do so otherwise. China must also place her people's dreams and desires as the first priority and exercise maximum effort in diplomacy to win back the islands. The diplomatic relationship with the United States is an important key to the solution of the Diaoyu Islands. Justice is on China's side and time is also on China's side. Eventually justice will prevail especially when China can now stand up in international arena and speak loudly on her behalf. Japan must listen and other nations will have to listen as well (even when the points were made in Mandarin). It is wiser to place emphasis on energy development and scientific research which can benefit Chinese people's standard of living than waging a war, but never forgetting the need of military strength for nation defense.

Though Diaoyu Islands are remote from the United States but the hot spot status of the islands was largely created by her. Now the hotspot is a warning to the U.S. and she can learn from the Mandela experience as well. The United States has experienced many times that the hotspots in the world likely lead to war which eventually get the US involved, especially when the U.S. helped creating the hotspot in the first place. Inevitably, wars seldom settle troubles in the modern era. The United States must realize that today is different from when she had a war with the British, French, Spanish or the Mexican to settle territorial or other issues. Time and time again she failed to settle conflicts by war even when justice seems to be on her side. In the Diaoyu case, justice was never on her side, she played games with ambiguity which inflamed Japan's faulty ambition. It is time for the U.S. to take correct measures to defuse the Diaoyu hotspot.

WHY IS ABE SHINZO FOLLOWING JUNICHIRO KOIZUMI'S FOOTSTEPS ON THE YASUKUNI ISSUE?

—ᴍ—

COMMEMORATING JAPANESE WAR CRIMINALS AT Yasukuni shrine by Japanese government officials has been a critical political issue in Japan and all her Asian neighbors. Since Prime Minister (PM) Junichiro Koizumi's first visit of the shrine on 8/13/2001 this issue had become a sore foreign relation problem especially between Japan and China, and Japan and Korea. High official contacts between China and Japan were severed from October 2001 to October 2006 and similarly with Korea from June 2005. The rigid relation ended when Abe Shinzo as the succeeding Japanese PM visited China in October 2006. Later he did not visit the shrine as the PM mainly because of his awareness of the massive anti-Japanese riots in China caused by Koizumi's visits to the Yasukuni shrine and his own insecure position as a new PM compared to the charismatic Koizumi.

Why is it now, a year after re-elected second time in 2012 as the Japanese PM, Abe Shinzo chose to visit the Yasukuni shrine? This news as reported by the NY Times, Wall Street Journal and Bloomberg News all voiced puzzlement. This question cannot be answered simply even by many Japanese political analysts in view of the Japanese politics and the two principal parties' history. Abe Shinzo now leads the strong but factional 'conservative' Liberal Democratic Party (LDP), which has consistently been in power since 1955 except two brief periods of 1993-2004 and 2009-2012. The 'left and central' Democratic Party of Japan (DPJ), the main but weak opposition, took over the government during those two brief periods.

The Yasukuni issue doesn't seem to have a strong tie with the ideology of the Japanese political parties. The DPJ although loosely being labeled left and central had very little opportunity to demonstrate its ideology. During its brief administration, it supported free public schooling (through high school) and provided child-rearing subsidies. In contrast to LDP, The DPJ has always advocated against bureaucracy and large government which cannot be verified without being in power for long enough time, however. The LDP on the other hand, though long time being in power has a fuzzy ideological picture principally because its individual strong men held power as PM with long tenures acted on their own rather than adhered to a well defined set of ideological principles and goals. True, the LDP advocates preserving tradition and culture, including the Japanese monarch system and free trade and markets in the manner very much depending on the strong men's relations to businesses. The Yasukuni issue was accentuated by Junichiro Koizumi (PM 2001-2006) and by Abe Shinzo (PM since 2012) more as their individual quests rather than following a party ideology. Since this view might not have been raised in the mainstream media, a detailed discussion should follow.

Junichiro Koizumi was born during WW II on 1/8/1942, a war child born to a political family. His father Junya Koizumi served as Director General of the Japanese Defense Agency during the 60's before his death in 1969 (Junichiro in his term as PM later elevated the agency to Ministry of Defense through legislation). His grandfather, Matajiro Koizumi was the minister of Posts and Telecommunications (later Junichiro attempted to privatize Japan Post, the operator of the Japanese postal savings system and succeeded through dissolving the Diet). Junichiro took the position to build a stronger relation with the United States and had a very good personal relationship with the US President, George W. Bush. He not only elevated the defense agency but also deployed forces to Iraq in supporting the war against terrorism which, to many Japanese believing in their Fascist Constitution, is considered a violation of their constitution. Junichiro claimed that his visits to the Yasukuni shrine were his private action not representing the Japanese government. However, signing on the Yasukuni guest book as the Prime Minister reflected his desire to be representing the Japanese government on this action.

Abe Shinzo was born on 9/24/1954 also with a lineage of Japanese powerful politicians. His father, Shintaro (1924-91), served as Japanese foreign minister (1982 to 1986), twice lost the chance to become the PM, once to rival Noburo Takeshita and once to an insider trading stock scandal. His grandfather, Kan (1894-1946) was also a politician born in a wealthy business family. His grandfather-in-law,

Nobusuki Kishi (1896-1987) was a far more important political figure. In 1935, Kishi worked for the campaign of industrial development of Manchukuo (seized from China), exploiting Chinese forced labor, then in 1941, was promoted to be minister of commerce and industry till 1945. When Japan surrendered, Kishi was put in prison as a suspect of Class A war criminal. (14 class A war criminals were enshrined in Yasukuni) When the U.S. ended the allied occupation in 1952, Kishi resurfaced in politics helping organizing a federation of two pre-war conservative parties with 'revision of constitution' as a goal. Kishi later joined the liberal party and won the diet seat from 1953-1979 and served as PM from 1957-60. Kishi resigned as PM due to a socialist party's demonstration against his government causing an embarrassing cancellation of President Eisenhower's visit to Japan. Notably, Kishi dedicated a tombstone for the war time PM Tojo and six other war criminals executed after the Tokyo trial which infuriated the Chinese and Koreans.

Abe's visits at the Yasukuni shrine, like Junichiro's, seemed to have the same reason - a strong desire to restore honor to their ancestors and their war-crime associates.

Junichiro was a popular PM enjoyed a support rating as high as 85% even with his pro-military expansion and deployment of Japanese troops to foreign country such as Iraq. Abe seems to emulate the process and follow Junichiro's footsteps to gain popularity but with bolder ambition by pushing for revision of the Japanese constitution in order to expand Japan's 'attack' military power. Like Junichiro, Abe is claiming his Yasukuni visit as his private action with no intention to hurt the feelings of the Chinese and Korean people but the fact he leads other Japanese officials to the shrine gives a different message to the Japanese people and the world. It seems obvious that Abe Shinzo is continuing on Junichiro Koizumi's footsteps except with bolder actions such as enacting the new Japanese Secrecy Law and revising the Japanese constitution as his personal quest to bring Japan back to imperialism through nationalism.

The official US response to the Yasukuni event is "disappointed" which may go beyond Abe's Yasukuni visit to his sales pitch made in his US visit in 2013 - "Japan Is Back".

CHAPTER 16

THE DIFFERENCE OF GERMANS AND JAPANESE IN

HANDLING THE TRUTH OF WW II HISTORY

—֍—

A NEWS, 'GERMAN, 88, CHARGED for WW II French Massacre', published in the Japan Times on Jan 9, 2014, makes one wonder why is it published? Who is the author? What is the author's intention? Who would be reading and what would be the readers' reaction? Would this type of news remind the Japanese to reflect on its WW II history? Being an Axis partner with Germany, what and how did the Japanese Imperial Army do to its victims? Why won't the Japanese leadership make an effort to cleanse the guilt of Japanese war crimes? Why do they continuously whitewash the WW II history even to the point of fabricating lies in the Japanese school textbooks to mislead the Japanese children? These questions have been on the minds of many historians including Americans, Asians, Europeans and some Japanese historians.

There is an obvious contrast of how Germans and Japanese dealt with their WW II history. The Germans through their government have sincerely shown their remorse by apologizing, compensating the war victims and openly establishing war memorials for the victimized countries and their citizens. The German government had passed laws condemning WW II Nazi crimes and installed procedures for prosecuting the war criminals. Hence, this news about the 88 year old war criminal is another testimony of how the Germans wanted to cleanse their souls to live with the historical facts and to restore their true national pride that Germans are honest and brave people capable of handling the truth.

On the contrary, the Japanese through their government has never shown their remorse in any sincere manner. Their apologies were guarded, often denied by other officials in the same breath. The Japanese establishes WW II memorials to honor their war dead but include the war criminals sentenced by the International Military Tribunal. The Japanese war crimes are no less cruel and atrocious than what the Germans did, yet, the Japanese government denies them, the Nanking Massacre, the chemical and bacteria weapon experiments on human, the comfort women, a sex slavery denounced by UN, etc. To this day, the Japanese even try to petition the U.S. White House to remove the memorial site that was established by Asian Americans in remembering the Asian comfort women forced into sex slavery by the Japanese imperial Army during WW II.

Let's put aside how the victims felt about the very different behaviors of Germany and Japan regarding their war crimes. Let's focus on the questions above and why the Japanese did so differently from the Germans. Why isn't the Japanese people honest and brave like the Germans to handle the war truth? Many scholars wrote about this issue including some Japanese authors who could not live with what the Japanese government's white washing the WW II history. Some Western scholars often analyzed this from the Japanese culture point of view but no clear answer was offered. The Japanese people often were shocked to tears when they witnessed the war records in museums outside of Japan.

Recently, the new Japanese Prime Minister Shinzo Abe, following the footsteps of the former PM Junichio Koizumi (2001-2006), went to the Yasukuni shrine to worship the Japanese war criminals including the general of the Japanese Imperial Army, Hideki Tojo, sentenced to death by the International Military Tribunal. Abe's action naturally triggered the anger of many Asian countries and people around the world again. As one Asian American, I couldn't help but anxiously seek an answer, hoping to awaken the Japanese people to bravely and honestly accept the truth of WW II, like Germans did.

I found an answer for explaining the behavior of the post-war Japanese government in defining the Japanese war history, war crimes and war criminals. The answer lies in the fact that, after WW II, the Japanese war machine from the Emperor Hirohito down to the military officials were given a lenient treatment resulting in the creation of a post-war Japanese governance fully infested with the war elites who either escaped from war crime prosecution or reemerged after the cease of the US occupation in 1952. In Germany, the collapse of Hitler is complete and the division of two Germany made such collapse irrevocable. In Japan, the pardon of Hirohito not only spared his life but sowed the seeds of the Japanese government behavior such as denying defeat, honoring war criminals and attempts of revival of militarism. Though the U.S. and the Japanese peace constitution imposed a democratic government system in Japan, but the politicians running the government had deep roots in the Imperial war machine, characterized by traits such as rather die but never surrender and rather obey absolutely than question the motive or principle. This political blood ran through the veins of post-war Japanese government. Hence, over 70 years, the Japanese government led its people to believe that WW II was their holy war to liberate Asian people from Western countries colonization. The Japanese invasions and war crimes were justified under such a holy war banner. The Japanese surrender was solely due to the fact that the U.S. had first developed the atomic bomb and used on Japan, otherwise, Japan would be the victor.

The Japanese people place deep trust in their government, democratic or not. The citizens continuously elect the lineage of political elites with deep roots in the Imperial Japan. Take Shinzo Abe for instance, his father, Shintaro, was the longest serving foreign minister, a cabinet member of the Kan Abe, Shinzo's grandfather who married a daughter of a general. Shinzo's mother is the daughter of Nobosuki Kishi, Prime Minister (1957-60), a member of the Tojo (war criminal) cabinet. Kishi served in the war cabinet but not like Tojo was released from the Sugamo prison without indictment and reentered the Japanese politics. The action and behavior of Shinzo Abe is quite predictable. Currently Shinzo is steering Japan back to imperialism risking a war with China dragging The U.S. into it.

The above answer explains credibly the Japanese post-war behavior, but offers no easy solution for the Japanese people to remedy the mistake and to reconcile with WW II history so long the government is in the hands of politicians like Shinzo. The Japanese people must objectively elect leaders free from the 'Imperial background', and then they may finally see the truth of WW II history. When the Japanese people can elect a capable Prime Minister, perhaps a woman, like Germans did, then they may finally be able to walk out of the Japanese Imperial shadow.

CHAPTER 17

TOM CLANCY AND US-CHINA RELATIONSHIP

—⁓—

TOM CLANCY IS ONE OF my admired novelists, His book, 'Hunt of the Red October' (1984), through the movie and the actor Jean Connelly captured my respect for his writing especially his imaginative plots for his stories. His death in 2013 saddened millions of readers who were not privy to classified 'national security' information but could immerse in national security situations through his novels. His close friendly relations with US retired generals and his diligent studies of advanced technologies of military weaponry make his novels realistic and informative regarding international conflicts and national security affairs. Clancy's plots may have been influenced by the scenarios toyed by the Pentagon and CIA strategists just as likely those scenarios were influenced by Clancy's story plots.

Many of his books accidentally predicted real world events. In his 'Debt of Honor' (1984), the plot was that Japan, led by hard-line right-wing nationalists and having acquired nuclear weapons, went to war with the United States with the purpose of restoring Japan's previous glory and re-establishing the Greater East Asia Co-Prosperity Sphere, a banner used by the Japanese Imperial Army to justify their aggressions to their neighboring countries during WW II. Japan was defeated by the United States through the actions of the heroic Jack Ryan created by Clancy; but the scary plot was a Japan Air Lines pilot decided to plunge his Boeing 747 into the Capitol building in Washington DC to kill the entire American government while a joint congress was in session. Later the real 9/11 commission in its report implied that the US national security would be better served by recognizing such a suicidal plane crash as a national threat. Clancy sort of imagined the 9/11 event in his book, but would he be right also on Japan going to war with the United States again? What if Japan would win this time? Judging the behavior of today's Japanese government led by a hard-line right-wing Abe Shinzo as the Prime

Minister, one could not help but worry about Abe's intention to revise the Japanese Peace Constitution to grant her the right to first 'attack'.

Clancy's readers may find another scenario also shocking in his book, 'Dead or Alive' (2010), a plot of tracking down a terrorist mastermind, "the Emir", who instead of hiding in a mountain cave in the Middle East but actually lived comfortably in a foreign country - near a US military base in the fun city Las Vegas in the story. Why shocking? The book story bear the similarity to the case of Osama bin Laden who was tracked and eventually killed by the US special forces near a military base at Abbottabad, Pakistan, a foreign country, in 2011. Was Osama learning from Clancy's book and was the US intelligence and Special Forces learning from Clancy's books as well? Certainly Clancy followed the terrorists events for writing his book..

Threat Vector (2012), written by Clancy with Mark Greaney is about China. With internal political and economical strife, the Chinese leadership was pushed to disaster and decided to strike Taiwan hence the U.S. was trying to thwart the war. Again this scenario seems to follow some current events falling out of the US strategy, 'Pivot to Asia'. In the real world and in Clancy's book, the U.S. assumes China as the enemy threatening her neighbors and the interests of the U.S. The U.S. is currently constructing and strengthening alliances with neighboring territories surrounding China in the Pacific from South Korea, Japan, Taiwan, ... to Indonesia and India for the purpose of containing China and stopping her continued economical growth. Isn't this strategy the very reason for causing the "internal political and economical strife in China"? Judging from the role Japan is anxiously playing under the pivot strategy, Clancy's assumption of China attacking Taiwan could be a mistake, since in the real world, the U.S. is dangerously reviving nationalism in Japan and in China which may lead to another Sino-Japanese war.

Different from the book, the President of the United States of course does not have a Jack Ryan, Jr. and 'the campus' to use to mitigate the potential war but to rely on his advisors to reexamine the assumptions of the pivot strategy and its possible consequences. Assuming China as an expansionist aiming to bully her neighbors, but allowing the U.S. to act as a bully herself to stop China's rise seems to be self-serving. The assumption, that Japan will not become a real expansionist as a threat to Asia and to the interests of the U.S., may be false. Isn't Japan's eagerness to return to her past of militarism obvious or of concern? Clancy's Threat Vector may produce another correct prediction about a war in Asia except not a war between China and Taiwan but Japan and China, started by Japan dragging the U.S. into it. Does the United States profit from this scenario, China and Japan destroying each other? If so, the U.S. will not appear to be on the right side of justice contradicting Clancy's story plots.

Japan may have a motive to return to her dream of conquering China but why would China want a war if not pushed or tricked into one? China is peacefully rising raising the standard of living for her people. China's economy is doing fine, surpassing Japan and soon over the U.S. Why would China risk her prosperous future to start a war? However, if she had realized that she was pushed into a war and had understood who the real culprit was, she would have no choice but fight for survival. Most likely she would go nuclear since that is the only route to avoid a defeat setting China back another hundred years as did the West invasion and the Sino-Japanese wars. Abe Shinzo is dancing with the drums of the Pivot, buying war gears, increasing military budget, attempting to revise constitution to allow attack force, flaming nationalism and worshipping Japanese war criminals of WW II... which are all actions inviting a war and her own destruction. This time the ending would be far worse for Japan compared to WW II sine China is no longer a sitting duck. The U.S. would have to be truly impartial and sincerely trying to prevent the war in order to avoid engulfing herself into the war or being viewed as the real culprit.

Bullying does not work between great nations with nuclear power. Eye for eye only leads to more violence and military race. In today's digital world, secret diplomacy cannot remain secret for long. Hence the great nations must be clear and precise to express intentions to each other and to the rest of the world. The US-china relationship must be based on historical facts and current events and not fictional assumptions or wishful thinking. The current events created by the Pivot, Diaoyu dispute, Snowden affair, ADIZ, etc have already provided ample excitements like a Clancy's book. The ending, of course, is still to be written. The world, like Clancy's readers desire, wants to have a good ending. The U.S. and China must now take a serious effort to engage in dialogues to digest these current events and to make their intentions transparent and understandable by each other and by the rest of the world. Then, a good ending with both countries standing on the right side of justice is possible.

CHAPTER 18

DEBATE ON THE LOGIC IN GREAT POWER DIPLOMACY

DIAOYU ISLAND (SENKLAKU) CASE IN POINT

—⚍—

THE ARTICLE IN FOREIGN POLICY, China, The United States, and Great Power Diplomacy (FP 12-26-2013), written by Dr. Paul Miller, a political scientist and a national security researcher at the Rand Corporation with university academic background and work experience as an analyst in CIA's Office of South Asian Analysis, presented a rich food for thought on the U.S. foreign policy related to Asia Pacific. Dr. Miller used a logical thinking process to look at the US Asia Pacific policy through a focus on the Diaoyu (Senkaku) Island dispute between China and Japan knowing that the involvement of the United States on the issue is ambiguous. Dr. Miller took the Diaoyu case to illustrate how to think about the US national security interests, following a logical analysis to conclude a policy recommendation, urging the U.S. to take firm engagement. This thinking process is commendable, however, the arguments that Miller put into the process were debatable, some even contradictory and illogical. Hence the conclusion is not convincing. The following may be considered as a rebuttal on Miller's logic with the hope a real logical conclusion can be drawn.

Miller suggests that the U.S. as a super power should only care about her intrinsic interest and cites "learning how to stay uninvolved is an important virtue of international diplomacy" contradicting to his conclusion. He rebuts the argument, "shouldn't the United States get involved to 'demonstrate resolve' or 'reassure allies' or 'protect credibility' or 'show leadership'", by first saying that those concerns "are not ends in themselves", "they are tools to employ when some concrete things are at stake"; "organizing foreign policy around US leadership puts the cart before the horse"… "If the islands are irrelevant to US interests, it doesn't show very wise leadership to spend time and resources worrying about them". "The only reputation this (US involvement) would cultivate is that of a meddlesome bully." Secondly, Miller argues that those concerns "turn international politics into an elaborate game of psychology" and make policies subject to the scrutiny of world opinions. He further states that "making world opinion the centerpiece of US grand strategy strains credibility". "Perceptions are important, but not more important than alliances, trade relationships, and deployments of the U.S. forces abroad that give the United States the power to objectively change reality." Thus, Miller lays the foundation for analyzing the specific case of the island dispute: If the islands were irrelevant to US interests then it would appear bullying if we chose to engage; if the islands were critical to the US interests then it would be justified if we chose to get involved.

Unfortunately, Miller's logical thought process led to a wrong conclusion: "The disputed islands thus provide an excellent opportunity for the United States to force the issue with China now.... Such a confrontation need not be belligerent or mean-spirited, but it should be firm. The goal is ... to counter China's coercive diplomacy and forcibly socialize China into responsible great power behavior." In my opinion, his conclusion was false because of the false assumptions and facts he drew leading to an illogical conclusion.

Miller deduction used a set of arguments which can be summarized as follows:

i.   the balance of power in East Asia is a critical concern to the United States.
ii. China's rise is the largest shift in the distribution of world power since the fall of the Soviet Union.
iii. China is a competitor, rival and potential threat.
iv. Japan and Europe are not threats because they coexist happily with the United States within the zone of the democratic peace.
v.   China's efforts to expand its power anywhere in the world is of interest to the United States.

These statements are logical but not sufficient to elevate the otherwise unimportant disputes over a few minor islands on the other side of the world into a matter of great power confrontation. He stressed that the United States doesn't care about the islands, but it should care about how China throws her weight around, how she relates to her neighbors and what she thinks how she can get away with. To my surprise, Miller uses the following arguments to elevate the issue as a threat,

i.   China's declaration of an ADIZ over the East China Sea is unilateral rewriting the rules of international diplomacy in her favor hence a threat to the United States and the global order.

ii. Though the U. S. is so powerful, she cannot afford to ignore China's small efforts to challenge the status quo. Different from small states, China grows relative to the United States; if there is ever a confrontation between the two countries, it is to the advantage of the U.S. for it to happen earlier than later.

After reviewing the above, any learned political scientists would have enough arguments reputing Miller's essay. First, in the great power diplomacy, it is illogical to assume a great power like the U.S. will act like a superpower yet develop her policies based on insecurity. The whole assumption of China is scary is false simply because China's military power is not only in no way a threat to the United States but her 'expansion' (more like her insecurity feeling choked in the ocean passages vital to her international trade) is largely triggered by the U.S. policy targeting China as the enemy, vigorously arming her neighbors and forming an island-chain blockade. The military race during the cold war produced several nuclear powers in the world including China, whether the Soviet Union was collapsed or not, they (including the U.S.) remain to be threats to global peace. Hence creating hot spot by engaging in the island dispute does not reduce any threat to the world nor to the U.S. China like Japan are thousands of miles away from the United States, why is Japan not a threat to peace when her prime minister is inflaming a nationalist and imperialist dream fanned by the U.S. whereas China trying to gain her great power status through diplomatic means does? A proper recommendation to the great power perhaps should be 'Learning how to get involved is an important virtue of international diplomacy', especially for China and the U.S. The statues of the two countries do depend on the world opinion. The U.S. foreign policy does indeed impact perception. Ample examples have shown that military might or bullying actions do not solve world problems. In formulating foreign policies, the U.S. not only must consider her self-interest but also must stand on the side of justice. In the Diaoyu Island dispute, the world opinion, historical facts and justice are on the side of China. Global order will evolve in time with justice eventually prevailing. Therefore, the U.S. must take the position in recognizing the injustice created in WW II by Japan and engage a fair great power diplomacy with China accordingly.

CHAPTER 19

FROM 'COMFORT WOMAN' ISSUE TO US-CHINA-JAPAN RELATIONS

—m—

THE TENSE SITUATION FOCUSED ON a few rocky islands (Diaoyu/Senkaku) in the Asia Pacific between China and Japan with the United States caught in between could turn them to be a dangerous hotspot leading to world turmoil. The three biggest world's economies tangled in an escalating conflict would destroy the world economy and might even ignite a war of a magnitude unimaginable. The solution for this conflict may seem to be complicated, but it may simply lie in an honest study of the WW II history. Let the historical facts be presented to citizens of the three countries. The Japanese need to know the real facts of WW II specially the war crimes committed and why Japan should not go back to her past and repeat the history. The Chinese need to know how diplomacy was important to settle international problems and why China must stand up and carry more world responsibility, no longer weak at the mercy of strong powers. The Americans need to know the real facts of WW II about allies and enemies and why the U. S. must stand on the side of justice not being a careless bystander nor risking being blamed as the culprit of another war. The 'Comfort Women' issue, a part of the WW II history, may very well serve as such a study case for all. If all could face this issue honestly and correctly, extrapolating to other issues, a healthy foreign relationship among the three might prevail.

The recent memorial activities related to 'comfort women' in the United States (Memorial Plaque or Monuments for WW II Comfort Women in Palisades Park, Bergen County, NJ, Loretta Weinberg and Kevin J. O'Toole, Gordon M. Johnson and Connie Wagner, Eisenhower Park, Nassau County, NY, Tony Avella, Charles Lavine, and Michelle Schimel and Cupertino Memorial Park, California, Mike

60

Honda et al) came about not by accident but traceable to Asian Americans' concerns about the U.S. foreign policies. The Japanese empire had won wars against the Russians, Koreans and the Chinese since the 19th century. They captured land, islands and oceans, including the Korean Peninsula, Manchuria, Okinawa and Formosa (Taiwan, where Diaoyu Islands belong). The ambition of the Imperial Japan was further heightened in early 20th century when China was going through an internal revolution to become a republic nation. Japan's goal was to conquer and subdue China in six months with her mighty Japanese Imperial Army. The invasion of China, however, turned into eight years of Sino-Japanese war, a major part of WW II. It was during this war that the Japanese Imperial Army had implemented the 'Comfort Women' program, forcefully capturing and deceptively recruiting Korean, Chinese, Philippine, Indonesian, Dutch and other Asian women into sex slavery serving the Imperial Army during the war.

The 'Comfort Women' issue is just as horrible as the other Japanese atrocities during the war such as the Nanking Massacre, Bacteria and chemical weapon experiments, etc, but it is now a better recognized Japanese atrocity by the international community owing to the UN investigations. The 'Comfort Women' has been determined by the UN as a military administered sex slavery program, coordinated throughout the Pacific during the war by the Japanese Imperial Army. Many Japanese scholars, authors and women's websites have admitted and condemned this shameful program. The UN human rights sub-commission had adopted a resolution (1998) citing the report by Gay J. McDougall, an independent expert on human rights, on the systematic rape, sexual slavery and slavery-like practices during armed conflicts. "The McDougall report, followed by the significant resolution, made a milepost.... .has made it difficult for the Japanese government to refuse to take legal responsibility for the crime and make state compensation to surviving victims," said lawyer Totsuka Etsuro, a leader in appealing the sexual slavery issue to the international society.

In 2012, the Universal Periodic Review (UPR) of the UN Human Rights Council, had sent a report to Japan with 174 recommendations and a compensation request for comfort women suffered in the Japanese military. For years, UN human rights bodies have criticized Japan for failing to address the Comfort Women issue, but the Japanese Government has always ignored them as not binding. The governor of Metropolitan Tokyo and the mayor of Osaka even openly claimed (8/2012): "no evidence supporting the forcible recruitment of the women". Abe Shinzo, in his first term of PM in 2006-7, ignored Congressman Mike Honda (D-CA15) resolution (2007) calling for Japan's acceptance and apology of 'comfort women' and created a controversy by his 'double talk' diluting the 1993 'Kono Statement'- acknowledging and apologizing for the 'Comfort Women' war crime. Today, Abe continues to deny this historical fact, calling it an academic issue for historians to study and siding with the Japanese Diet Committee's claim of no coercion in the comfort women program, contradictory to the UN findings.

Abe Shinzo, a leader of Liberal Democratic Party (LDP), is the master mind in steering Japan back to her Imperial and militaristic past. His strategy seems to be exploiting the several generations of post-war youth who were deprived of the historical facts on Japanese war crimes, whitewashed out from the school textbooks. Abe and his right-wing supporters have been raising Japan's nationalism to restore Japan's past military glory, elevating the territorial disputes with China and Korea and honoring the war criminals. Currently, Abe, gaining approval rating among the young, is beating the war drums by increasing military budget, buying weapons and attempting to revise the Japanese peace constitution to allow Japan to have first strike 'right' as a 'normal country'.

The denial of the Japanese war atrocities by Japan is the fundamental cause of the Asian conflicts. The United States is aware of that. The US 'pivot' to Asia-Pacific, had run into a trap - Abe Shinzo's nationalistic agenda, in his own words placing Japan at the eve of WW I. What did he mean? On the one hand, he is building military power and on the other hand, he is elevating territorial disputes, busy making military alliances and visiting the Yasukuni Shrine to worship Japanese war criminals disrespectful of the US advice. What next will he do?

The attention on the 'comfort women' is a wake-up call. The American citizens and government must now face the facts, uphold the justice and never let the history repeat again. Looking at this issue and Abe administration's irrational behavior in general, the US congress' resolution on 'comfort women' attached to the 2014 appropriation bill is a right move but not enough. Abe had made the 'double talk' in 2007 in his first term. Now Abe is back as PM and yelling "Japan is back". We Americans must think hard: What did he mean and what will he do? We must use 'comfort women' to open the eyes of the Japanese citizens, especially women and youth, to understand the Japanese war crimes. A nation denying her war crimes and going back to the glory of a military state is a dangerous state. A nation building military power in the name of peace under a peace constitution is not really peace loving. Americans, Chinese and Japanese must be frank and sincere to face the historical facts together to avoid any nation to be hijacked again by Military Fascism.

CHAPTER 20

NATION DEVELOPMENT OF THE U.S. AND

CHINA IN PAST 250 YEARS AND FORWARD

—ꝏ—

THE PAST 250 YEARS, 1764-2014, is the most interesting period of human history in terms of nation building. The history witnessed two dramatically different processes of nation development. The United States achieved the world superpower status through an early and successful revolution forming a unique American style democracy, whereas China achieved the world's second largest economy through a treacherous path fending off foreign invasions, devastating wars and a late revolution till this day still incomplete. As the world is embracing globalization, an understanding of the past 250 years of history about China and the U.S. can shed a bright light on our future.

The United States, a new nation born out of a British colony, declared her independence in 1776. Luckily, her first and only American Revolution (Rebellion against the British rule) was successful and brief, concluded within twenty years (1763-1783). The open rebellion started in 1773, with the first shot fired only in April 1775. The revolution started from the North (1775-1777) then spread to the South (1778-1781) with the turning point occurred in 1776-1777 when France signed a treaty of alliance and commerce. The British had the upper hand initially, but the guerrilla style hit and run tactics of the revolutionary army had done the British in. With the help of the French, the revolutionaries defeated British General Lord Charles Cornwallis in Virginia in 1781, set the fate of the British to fail. A preliminary peace treaty was signed on 11/20/1782 then a final treaty, Peace of Paris, on 9/10/1783. A mere two decades marked the successful American Revolution creating the foundation of the United States.

China was a rich and prosperous country (Qing, 1644-1911) with a great economy peaked about 1766 but deteriorated because of ill policies rooted in the insecurity of the ruling Manchurian. Long braided hair in men and bound feet in women were to hamper People's agility. Possession of weapons was banned to prevent rebellion but it made Chinese vulnerable and defenseless to foreign invasion with guns and ships. The British lost in America but won big in the two opium wars (1839-1842 and 1856-1860) against China resulting in the infamous looting and burning of the Old Summer Palace and signing the most humiliating and unequal Treaty. The treaty of Nanking forced Qing to pay huge sum of war reparations, to open five ports for British trade, to cede Hong Kong Island to the Great Britain; the treaty was extended to grant the British and French more concessions, to open all of China to British merchants, to legalize Opium trade, and to exempt imports from internal and transit duties. In the same time frame, the United States annexed Texas (1845) and obtained the West, California, Utah, Nevada, Arizona, and New Mexico through the Mexican-American War (1846-1848), eventually growing from 13 to 50 states.

The Chinese people did rebel (Taiping Rebellion, 1849-1864) but the uprising failed as the bloodiest civil war with 20-30 million died. China was essentially besieged by foreign powers then. Japan, one of the foreign powers and a great learner of western imperialism and militarism, had an evil ambition to conquer the entire China. Japan first invaded China in 1894 over the control of Korea, challenging Chinese suzerainty over Korea. With success, the Japanese Imperial Army and Navy escalated the war and forced China to sign the Treaty of Maguan Tiaoyue. By the terms of the treaty, China was obliged to recognize the independence of Korea, to cede Taiwan, and the Liaodong Peninsula (south Manchurian, this was later reprieved by the intervention of Russia, Germany and France) to Japan; to open the ports of Shashi, Chongqing, Suzhou, and Hangzhou to Japanese trade and pay reparation equivalent to (then) 510,000,000 Japanese yen, 6.4 times the Japanese government revenue. While China was humiliated by Japan, The United States won the Spanish-American War and signed the Treaty of Paris (1898) ceding control of Porto Rico, Guam and Philippines to the U.S. Hawaii was also annexed in 1898 promoted by the American sugar planters with three Presidencies involved, encouraged by Benjamin Harrison (1889-1893), opposed by Grover Cleveland (1893-1897) and finally supported by William McKinley (1897-1901) with the argument to Congress (6/11/1898), "we must have Hawaii to get our share of China", not a honorable argument. Hawaii was made 'Territory' in 1900 and became an official state in 1959 along with Alaska. The State of Hawaii extends the U.S. way into the Pacific but that's hardly the justification for "pivot to Asia-Pacific".

The Boxer Rebellion (revolution, 1889-1901) was another failed uprising in China to protest against the eight foreign powers and the miserable Chinese government, but it failed, causing the government to pay 67 million pounds of silver (more than China's annual tax revenue), as indemnity to be paid over 39 years to the eight nations involved. (The U.S. kindly turned the miscalculated payment to her into scholarships for Chinese students to study in the U.S.) The next uprising, Xinhai revolution, was launched by Dr. Sun Yat Sen in 1911, modeling the American revolution with the aim to establish a Republic nation based on his Three Principles. The Qing government was toppled, but not like the American revolution fighting only the Great Britain, the Chinese revolution was facing complicated foreign intervention as they were all present in China. Multiple factions were dividing China having different foreign power involved, while Japan was busy executing her plan of conquering the entire China. The Japanese provoked another Sino-Japanese war (1937) lasting eight years and making China as a major battle ground of WW II (1941-1945). The Chinese revolution was first interfered by the foreign powers including Japan (1911-1936), interrupted by WW II in China (1937-1945) and further delayed post-WW II (1946-today) by the Cold War staged by the Soviet and the U.S. China was split into the Mainland and Taiwan in two camps. Hence the Chinese revolution, unlike the Ameriucan Revolution, is not complete even over 100 years. As the Cold War has ended, the unification of China should complete the revolution forming one Republic nation without any foreign power intervention.

Taking the side of justice to fight aggressor and fascism and being remote from the war zone, the U.S. benefitted from WW I (1914-1918) and WW II as a victor without severe damage to her homeland. It was not so lucky for China; the nation and her people suffered a great deal under the eight years of Japanese invasion. It took nearly 150 years since her independence (1776) for the U.S. to develop an unique democratic system (granting voting rights to the white males in the 1820's, to black males in 1870 and to women in 1920), one would not be surprised that

China, given her steady development and progress, will develop her unique governing system in the coming decades.

Recently, my respected friend and an anti-war writer, Dr. John V. Walsh, published an article in Unz Review (1/21/2014) questioning the validity of US foreign policy of targeting China as the enemy in a 'cold war' manner. I wholeheartedly support his view: A prosperous China posts no threat to the U.S. From the above review of history, it is evident that China had never had any overseas expansion nor any overseas military base. China had no desire to impose her political system to anyone since she is still searching for reform to tune it into a unique system suitable for China. Therefore, it would be a serious mistake for the U.S. to target China as the enemy; rather, the U.S. , as a model, should help China complete her revolution and unification. It would be also a grave mistake for the U.S. to partner with Japan and encourage her to rearm, in view of the two facts: 1. The war crimes and atrocities Japan has committed in the past 150 years and 2. The aggressive behavior and ambition the current Japanese Prime Minister Abe Shinzo has exhibited. In today's nuclear age, no one can profit from a major war without being injured. On the other hand, as said correctly by Dr. Walsh, global prosperity is not a zero sum game; in partnership, the U.S. and China as two great nations both will be prosperous and will be able to maintain world peace collaboratively.

CHAPTER 21

INTERPLAY OF US-CHINA-JAPAN NATIONAL STRATEGIES
AS REVEALED BY THE DIAOYU ISLAND DISPUTE

—⚏—

CAN WE SEE WHAT IS going on with the U.S., China and Japan from the world's hotspot, the Diaoyu Islands? Yes, we can.

The Diaoyu Islands are physically small, but the recent flare-up of their sovereignty issue is not a small matter. Historically Diaoyu Islands were under China's sovereignty but they were lost to Japan along with Taiwan when Japan won the war against China in 1895 right after Japan invaded and took Okinawa in 1879. When Japan was defeated in WW II, Taiwan and these islands (part of Yinan Township of Taiwan) were supposed to be returned to China. However, China was split by two Chinese regimes, People's Republic of China and Republic of China, both claiming representation of full China, the mainland, Taiwan and these islands. Since these islands are close to Okinawa, the United States, as the trustee of the islands surrendered by Japan, included the Diaoyu islands in an administrative zone together with Okinawa islands. Post WW II, the United States has helped Japan to rebuild into a democratic nation and an US ally. In 1972, the United States turned over the administration rights of the Okinawa and the Diaoyu islands to Japan despite of the protests from the two Chinese governments. China has always claimed sovereignty over these islands but China and Japan agreed to table this dispute for the sake of normalizing their relation then. Recently, with the right-wing leader, Abe Shinzo, being re-elected as the Prime Minister, Japan has been trying to nationalize these islands, rejecting the notion of them being ever a disputed territory. Abe is promoting a nationalistic agenda of restoring Japan's pre WW II glory and aggressively pursuing military and territorial expansion.

Under the administration of the United States Occupation Government, Japan had been recovered quickly from the WW II damage and had rebuilt herself up economically. In 1951, a US-Japan Security Treaty was signed, stated in which, Japan would rely on the U.S. for her security and defense and the U.S. was permitted not only to act for the sake of maintaining peace in East Asia, but also to exert its power on Japanese domestic quarrels (the latter part was deleted in1960). Focusing on economic development with no defense burden, Japan rose rapidly as a strong manufacturing country supplying goods to the U.S. and to the entire world. Japan trailed the U.S. as the world's second largest economy until China overtook her.

Apparently, Japan was happy to be an economic partner of the U.S. but was never content to be the no. 2 economy as shown by her growth strategy. The rise of China produced a great concern among Japanese political leaders. Japan's current behavior, particularly on the Diaoyu Islands dispute, reveal a methodic national strategy to bring Japan back to her Imperial glory with a desire to dominate Asia again, with or without the United States as a partner. This methodic strategy includes three prongs. The first prong is fabricating and dramatizing 'The China Threat Theory' to gain world's attention and possibly sympathy to Japan's hostile activities targeted at China. The second prong is playing into the new foreign policy of the United States, 'Pivot to Asia Pacific', to strengthen the US-Japan Security Agreement, obligating the U.S. to get involved in Japan's dispute with her neighbors. Japan is very eager to play an aggressive role to build alliances with Asian countries. The third prong is drumming up nationalism in Japan to bring Japan back to her pre-WW II glory, specifically by revising Japan's peace constitution to expand militarily with 'attack right', by whitewashing WW II history and denying the war atrocities (Nanking Massacre, Comfort Women etc) committed by the Japanese Imperial Army, and even reinterpreting Pearl Harbor and Atomic Bombing of Japan. Abe may try to explain these away by saying that Japan needs to be rejuvenated from an aging society and mindset, but in reality, the aggressive behavior of his government not only worries her close neighbors, China and Korea but even Australia. No wonder, some political analysts are urging the United States to take a pause to reassess the 'Pivot' effect with a possible uncontrollable Japan.

The United States has earned her super power status through the world conflicts. Although the United States champions democracy and human rights but her foreign policies seem to be more in tune with the 'Hegemony Theory'. According to John J Mearsheimer, a political science professor at the University of Chicago, the hegemony theory means that a great nation will always pursue hegemony to dominate over other states, and in the process will always want to prevent another country to be a hegemon or a competitor. The United States, by defeating Germany (1900-1918), Japan (1931-1945), Germany again (1933-1945) and Russia in the Cold War (1946-1992), has essentially achieved her hegemon status over the West hemisphere. As pointed out by many analysts, despite of her diplomatic language, the 'Pivot to AP', is the US strategy to exert US presence in AP, to align her AP partners, Korea, Japan, Philippine, Taiwan, ... to prevent China to become a competitor or a regional hegemon. However, maintaining a hegemon status is very costly as seen from the collapsed Soviet Union. The current economic woos in the United States certainly makes her ill affordable to pursue a global hegemon alone. Hence, flirting with Japan in the 'Pivot' policy to let Japan bear some costs in containing China is not out of love for Japan but more as an economical consideration. However, Japan's willingness to play with the US strategy and more comes with a huge risk. Japan has her own agenda (above) which may lead to an uncontrollable situation, damaging the US interest including the possibility of a global economic chaos or an unimaginable nuclear war destroying the world.

China claims that her rise in economical power is peaceful and beneficial to the world, never intended to be a hegemon. The history of China and the fact that China having no military base outside of her sovereignty lend a good credit to her claim. However, in Mearsheimer's hegemony theory – well followed by the US military and national strategists, China will inevitably pursue the path of hegemony. It is this assumption that drives the U.S. to take measure to prevent the rise of China to become a hegemon. What is illogical, of course, is that why does preventing a hegemon justify another's hegemony behavior? China is concerned with the US intention and hegemony behavior in AP as well as the possible revival of the Japanese hegemony ambition. Therefore, out of fear and self-defense, China engages in military research and development. China's recent achievements in rocket, laser, satellite and space technologies are impressive, but then that success fed right into the US national strategy (hegemony theory) justifying her to deploy the 'Pivot to AP' policy to stop China to become a hegemon. History tells us, arm race only leads to war not peace. World Politics tells us, no one can precisely predict what a country may or may not do in any given condition. Therefore, the current foreign policies between the U.S. and China, assuming each other is pursuing hegemony, or must pursue hegemony do not make logical sense.

The U.S. and China both have achieved great nation status, owning the world's two largest economies with intertwined mutual dependency. The military might of the two may not be equal but both possess enough nuclear weapons to boot. The two nations are separated apart on two hemispheres with no direct territorial conflict. Why should the two countries engage in a hostile foreign relationship simply based on the 'hegemony theory'? We know, a great nation must pay a big price to be a regional hegemon and the costs for being a global hegemony is prohibitive for any nation to bear. One may then ask what will be the gain for the U.S. and China to play a hegemony game? If the U.S. and China can establish a friendly relationship with open communication, other countries in the world would adjust accordingly. Take Japan for instance, her government will soon realize it makes more sense to focus on her aging population than drumming a belligerent tone towards her neighbors. Under a harmonious G2 relationship, the issue like Diaoyu Islands can quickly evolve into an international collaborative development project beneficial to the world.

CHAPTER 22

CAN JADE RABBIT (YUTU) HELP WIN THE

SPACE EXPLORATION FOR MANKIND?

—ᗡᗡ—

PEOPLE HAVE HEARD THE STORY of a race between the fast rabbit and the slow turtle. The turtle won the race because of its persistence and steady progress while the rabbit took a nap thinking the slow turtle would never catch up. This legendary tale is simply a motivation story: If one would work hard and never give up, eventually one could reach the goal as a winner even with a slow start. In real life, this story is more significant about achieving a long-term goal, over a life-time or an eternal goal.

Space exploration is just such a long-term eternal goal of human kind to find the unknown in the Universe, to find whether or not a brethren of another civilization existed, and to determine whether humans could live in another planet outside of the Earth. Space exploration is an eternal goal simply because the Earth is so small compared to the Universe and human civilization is so minute and short compared to the infinite space and time. Unfortunately, the space exploration had started like a race simply because humans on Earth had always had internal squabbles, making space exploration as a space race rather than a collaborative project. This is laughable; If there were other more advanced civilizations in the Universe beside humans, they would be laughing for sure.

Sadly, Space exploration has often been used as a proxy competition for geo-political rivalries and show-off of national strength. The early era of 'Space Race' started between the Soviet Union and the United States during the cold war, the launch of the first man-made object to orbit the Earth, the USSR's Sputnik 1, on 4 October 1957, and the first Moon landing by the American Apollo 11 on 20

July 1969 are the major milestones of the initial race. The Soviet space program achieved many of the first milestones, including the first living being in orbit in 1957, the first human spaceflight (Yuri Gagarin aboard Vostok 1) in 1961, the first spacewalk (by Aleksei Leonov) on 18 March 1965, the first automatic landing on another celestial body in 1966, and the launch of the first space station (Salyut 1) in 1971. However, the first man stepped on the moon on July 20, 1969, was an American, Neil Armstrong, who had made Apollo 11 the most sensational achievement in space exploration by his statement, "That's one small step for (a) man and a giant step for mankind."

After 20 years of experience, humans wised up shifting from one-off flights to renewable Space Shuttles, and from competition to cooperation in the example of International Space Station (ISS), although China was excluded from ISS. Reusable hardware and collaboration hopefully will make human space exploration long lasting and eventually successful, apart from reducing the generation of garbage in the space.

In the 2000s, the People's Republic of China initiated a successful manned spaceflight program, while the European Union, Japan, and India have also planned future manned space missions. In this century, China, Russia, Japan, and India have advocated manned missions to the Moon while the European Union has advocated manned missions to both the Moon and Mars. Interestingly, from the 1990s onwards, private interests began promoting space tourism and private space exploration of the Moon. This hopefully will make further sharing and collaboration feasible on a commercial basis.

The moon has been a fascinating space object in many literal writings and romantic stories. The Chinese ancient story about a fairy, **Chang'E**, living on the moon with a **Yutu (Jade Rabbit)** was so in-grained in the folklore; the recent Chinese lunar landing robot named Jade Rabbit and the Moon exploration program named Chang'E were very exciting to the 1.3 billion Chinese people. The Jade Rabbit is commissioned to live through the lunar day and night cycles (14.77 earth days and 14.77 earth nights cycle) and to carry out a host of experiments. The soft landing of Jade Rabbit and the vast amount of observation and the experimental data Jade Rabbit collected would be useful information to share with the world. Although, Jade Rabbit is not as sensational as Neil Armstrong, it is still a very significant milestone in mankind's space exploration. The American mainstream media has very little coverage of the event. It is very puzzling to news watchers. We hope this is not a sign of turning space exploration back to a space race like what happened in the Cold War era.

Space exploration is a long-term eternal goal for mankind. As humans, we should place our energy and wisdom together to continue this endeavor. Just like the legendary story of the race between a rabbit and a turtle implied, persistence will eventually win. We hope the Jade Rabbit currently on the moon will beam back lots of useful data and give human's space exploration another giant stride. A recent article by Phil McKenna, 'Red Star Rising: China's Ascent to Space Superpower' (New Scientist, 2-12-2014), stated, "Jade Rabbit's successful launch, landing and exploration is evidence of China's meteoric rise in the space stakes, and one that will only accelerate." Indeed, the advances China had made in her Space program including space rocket, satellites and the Beidou (GPS) communication technologies have made significant impact to the world. The weather reporting and even the US military now depend on the Chinese Satellite and communication system. McKenna urged international collaboration to include China by saying: "perhaps the most utopian consequence of China's space ambitions would be a renewed realization that space is not divided according to national boundaries." I fully agree with this notion. At a space science conference, the US deputy secretary of state William J. Burns announced, "an international space road map aiming to unite the separate paths of the national space agencies", apparently not excluding China. The new road map by including China would create a realistic prospect for expensive long-shot projects such as human missions to the Mars or any asteroid shield or space garbage collection system or mining Helium 3 and other minerals on the moon. Hence, I believe, Jade Rabbit, even though with a late start, may just help win the Space Exploration for mankind in the long run.

CHAPTER 23

FROM RUSSIA'S ANNEXATION OF CRIMEA TO

INTERNATIONAL DIPLOMATIC PLAY

—ɯ—

HISTORICALLY, CRIMEA WAS PART OF Russia. Its population is mainly Russian speaking people. When Ukraine's government developed problems, the unrest was understandable. Russia's interference in the name of protecting innocent Russian speaking citizens in Crimea is predictable from a behavior pattern of a powerful aggressive nation exerting her influence. What is surprising is that the annexation was done by a referendum voted by overwhelming majority of voters in just a few weeks. Russian President signed a bill of annexation on March 18, 2014 and the United States and EU voiced protest and denied recognition of this referendum.

From peace loving people's perspective, if this annexation was supported by Crimea's majority of citizens without a bloody or prolonged battle, it is not a bad thing. Why is main stream media overwhelmingly condemning Russia, even though the de facto feat is already done. There is no lack of comments and opinions in the press criticizing Russia's obvious bullying behavior. However, as to why Russia did what she had done, we find the analysts' commentary fuzzy but largely leaning towards the thought process of Cold War, when the Soviet Union was considered the chief target of the Cold War.

Some arguments say Russia is concerned that Ukraine may join the NATO (the chief Cold War Instrument). Russia will lose her naval base in Sevestopol of Crimea if that happens. Sevestopol is a strategic base for Russia's Black Sea Fleet (BSF). Hence, Russia's annexation of Crimea was motivated by military strategy. Be it that may, the fact this annexation was done swiftly by a democratic process without bloodshed, does speak for the ideology, 'people has the ultimate right for self determination', a UN endorsed principle. Apparently, the overwhelming majority vote was not a product of coercion, the minority Muslims and Tartars boycotted and the majority Russians voted. Therefore, to this done deal, even though it was not legal by Ukraine constitution; the West cannot take any action other than protesting with an economic sanction. Since there is no perfect solution, majority has to rule in a democratic process. Hopefully the minority will continue to live peacefully in Crimea.

The Ukraine crisis erupted when anti-Russian opposition forces in Kiev overthrew the country's democratically-elected president, Viktor Yanukovych. This action was also illegal under Ukraine's constitutional law and was not supported by Crimea. However, it was swiftly endorsed by The United States and other European countries. Now Obama refuses to recognize the referenda of Crimea; it seems to be an example of inconsistent Foreign Policy.

The international community largely supports the independence and territorial integrity of Ukraine and condemns Russian's interference and urges a quick solution to end the violence taking place there. Since the annexation was done quickly without Violence, the reaction from the international community seemed to be muzzled, though the positions of the United States and China were closely watched.

Despite of the inconsistent or biased diplomacy regarding Ukraine and Crimea, The strongest condemnation came from the United States, On 6 March, Obama signed Executive Order 13660, Blocking Property of Certain Persons Contributing to the Situation in Ukraine, authorizing sanctions against persons who, being determined by the Secretary of the Treasury in consultation with the Secretary of State, have violated or assisted in the violation of Ukraine's sovereignty. On 17 March, Obama signed Executive Order 13661, Blocking Property of Additional Persons Contributing to the Situation in Ukraine, expanding the scope to include the freezing of certain Russian government officials' assets in the U.S. and blocking their entry into the U.S.

On March 2, China's Foreign Ministry spokesperson Qin Gang stated that "China condemned the recent extremist violence in Ukraine and urged all parties to resolve their internal disputes peacefully. China has always followed the principle of non-interference in internal affairs, and respected Ukraine's independence, sovereignty and territorial integrity. He urged all sides to find a solution through dialogue on the basis of international law and the norms governing international relations". On March 4, China's President Xi Jinping, in a telephone conversation with Russian President, Vladimir Putin, expressed his confidence in Putin's ability to reach a political solution through negotiations with all involved parties. He stated that China supports the propositions and mediation efforts of the international community towards easing the situation.

As Russian was sending troops to the Crimean Peninsula, it seemed the world was watching and taking sides on the Ukrainian issue. The position of China was clearly being watched on the world stage. After the Russian Federation Council authorized the use of armed forces in Ukraine, Chinese Foreign Ministry Spokesman Qin Gang issued a special statement on the situation. "China is deeply concerned about ...," Qin said. He called on "the relevant parties in Ukraine to resolve their internal disputes peacefully within the legal framework." As for external interference in the Ukraine, Qin emphasized that China respects "the independence, sovereignty and territorial integrity of Ukraine" and said that a solution should be found "based on respect for international law and norms."

A Xinhua commentary, however, argued that the West's "biased mediation has polarized Ukraine and only made things worse in the country." The Xinhua commentary had no criticism for Russia's decision to send troops to Crimea, rather it said, "It is quite understandable when Putin said his country retained the right to protect its interests and Russian-speakers living in Ukraine." There is obvious inconsistency in China's stand on the principle of non-interference and yet condoning Russia sending troops into Crimea. While The United States hold a double standard on Ukraine and Crimea, China bends her principles for international politics. Is this the way great nations must play?

Russia eagerly claims that China is backing her. Russian media report, Russian Foreign Minister Sergei Lavrov and Chinese Foreign Minister Wang Yi had a telephone conversation On March 17, wherein they noted "the coincidence of Russia's and China's positions on the situation in Ukraine." Meanwhile, China's Foreign Ministry Spokesman Qin Gang used more diplomatic language in his March 17 press conference. "China upholds its own diplomatic principles and the basic codes for international relations," and he added that "we have also taken the historical and contemporary factors of the Ukraine issue into consideration."

It is clear that China is in a dilemma, backing Russia will make China violating her principles of non-interference whereas opposing Russia will make China appear to be standing with the West while worrying about the West targeting China. Similarly for the United States, accepting the de facto annexation will be a setback to the NATO alliance and the strategic interest of the U.S.; whereas wooing China to take a joint stand against Russia must redefine the Pivot to Asia Pacific policy. Therefore, the Crisis of Ukraine may have raised a significant question on the theory of "China Threat", promoted by Japan and to some degree by the Hawks in the United States; Is China a threat? Or is Russia a real threat? Often the international community perceives "Color Revolution" such as the "Orange Revolution" in Ukraine in 2004 is owing to external interference to change regime, China and the United States as two great nations both must honestly remove their double standards regarding inconsistency of foreign policy and their double talks on human rights in order to deal with real issues of true aggression.

SHOULD THE UNITED STATES BELIEVE OR NOT TO BELIEVE CHINA'S MESSAGE IN KÖRBER FOUNDATION?

—ɯ—

CHINESE PRESIDENT XI JINPING AND his wife Peng Liyuan made a four-nation trip in March to Europe including Netherlands, France, Germany and Belgium. Besides attending the Nuclear Summit meeting in Hague, an Obama initiative, Xi's first visit to Germany as the President of China in eight years marks a very significant event in Germany-China relationship. As China rose to the second largest economy in the world, the trade between Germany and China ranks world's second largest next to US-China trade. With Germany as a key trade partner of China, talks between PM Angela Merkel and President Xi naturally centered around economic issues. The two leaders presided over a string of deals between companies of the two nations. The largest deal includes a 1 billion euro ($1.38 billion) agreement for German carmaker Daimler to expand the production of its joint venture with Beijing Automotive Group. This is the second agreement of its kind, following that of Daimler's rival BMW and its Chinese partner, Brilliance. Another significant deal struck on March 28 was an agreement between the Bundesbank and The People's Bank of China declaring their intent to establish an RMB (Yuan) clearing and settlement center in Frankfurt, which certainly will affect the position of US dollars as a global trade instrument.

Perhaps a more significant event was Xi's invited speech at the Körber-Foundation in Berlin. The foundation is a non-profit organization found by German entrepreneur Kurt A Körber in 1959. As a world citizen, Körber believes that social development calls for critical reflection. The foundation established by Körber takes on this social challenge at a national and an international level. Addressing an audience at the foundation's invitation, Xi stressed again that China had pledged to adhere to the path of peaceful development for a long time and the Chinese people are confident to realize their goals (Chinese Dream) through peaceful development. Xi as the highest leader of China, has selected an international forum to deliver a clear and unambiguous message, which he had delivered in many occasions in China. Xi not only repeats this message but also pleads to the world to believe him (China) rather than to adhere to prejudice, slandering China as a threat to the world. Xi's speech deserves the attention of world leaders and all world citizens.

In plain English, we can summarize and highlight Xi's speech as follows:

1. Five years ago, Xi visited Germany while global financial crisis just broke out, China and Germany had decided then to cooperate to deal with the crisis. Five years later, Europe weathered the debt crisis, economic recovery is on the rise, Germany as the 'safety anchor' of Europe made tremendous contribution and received well deserved praise. Chinese people are happy that Germany and China have accomplished significant results in solving the debt crisis in Europe.

2. At present, China and Germany are at the best juncture to cooperate in breadth and depth for mutual benefits as well as for the economic development and peace of the world.

3. Why have China and Germany achieved such great cooperation? That is because, through long years of interaction and culture exchange, the two countries tried to understand each other, each side's national interests and national system.

4. The recent 30 years of rise in China is not a threat to the world as those who held prejudice would like to depict. Xi took the opportunity to tell the audience that China had insisted on taking the path of peaceful rise hoping the world will understand and believe. China has repeatedly announced to the world her peaceful development and her desire to maintain world peace. China's confidence comes from her history and culture of peace loving nature, her recognition of the realistic condition of her development and her awareness of the world trend longing for peaceful development.

5. Chinese are peace loving people with 5000 years of culture believing in global peace and co-existence. China's goal (and Chinese Dream) is simple, i.e. to double her people's living standard by 2020. To achieve that goal

for her 1.3 billion people, China needs two conditions, internal stability and world peace.

6. History is the best teacher, from the Opium War (1840) to the Japanese invasions (1894-1945) till the birth of the PRC (1949), China was weak and victimized, Sino-Japan wars had cost China 35 million lives. China desires peace just like people desires air, only by taking a peaceful development path can China work with the world to maintain peace, to realize her goal and contribute more to the world.

7. Chinese revolutionary father, Sun Yat Sen, said, a country's development must follow the world trend, today's global trend is peace, development, cooperation and win-win. China doesn't believe in hegemony theory - a strong nation must become a hegemon. Today, colonialism and hegemony are coming to dead ends, so China insists on taking the path of peaceful development.

8. Facts win over debates; in many decades, China has always pursued peaceful development, never interfered in other countries' internal affairs, never supported expansionism, external military bases and hegemony. China's policies dictate this, her system is designed to pursue this and she has consistently practiced her policies. Of course, China will vigorously defend her sovereignty, security and national interests and will never let any other country damage her sovereignty, security and national interests. China says this not as diplomatic jargons but because she has no reason to believe she should act differently otherwise.

9. Last November, China held her 18th third central national conference and laid a blueprint to modernize her country in terms of industrialization, urbanization, agricultural development, and stimulating investment and consumption markets. China's per capita productivity has reached $7000; in next five years, China's import will reach ten trillion US dollars ($10**13) and external investment to five hundred billion US dollars ($5x10**11) with five hundred million (5x10**8) Chinese traveling in the world.

10. Chinese ancient philosopher Lao Tze said, a great nation must have the capacity to absorb the trades and exchanges coming to her. China will never develop her economy by sacrificing other nation's interests. China's goal is to develop her unique Chinese socialist system, to offer her wisdom, to contribute to global development and to take on the challenges of the 21st century that mankind faces.

11. Germany is a great nation with tremendous inheritance and advances in many domains. Germans and Chinese have deep respect and friendship with each other. 21st century is a century of cooperation, Xi believes, 'made in Germany' and 'made in China' can collaborate not only to produce high quality products but also to deliver happiness to the people. The two great economies in the world will certainly make significant contributions to the world economy.

12. This year as 100th anniversary of WW I and 75th anniversary of WW II, the world must remember, history is not a burden but a lesson. The Chinese conscientiously decided to take the path of peaceful development, China hopes the world will believe her and join her to do the same!

The 'China Threat' is a theoretical assumption, promoted by hawks in the media of the U.S. and Japan. Whatever China spent on military budget could be easily understood by her fear of an US-Japan initiated 'Target China' strategy. The US naval pivot to Asia Pacific encircling China and Japan's effort in revising her peace constitution to allow first attack lay the logic grounds of China's repeated 'peaceful rise' message and plea. As said in Xi's speech, "Facts win over debates", it seems that **the U.S. has no reason not believing China** unless the U.S. wants to adhere to a 'hegemony theory' which says a strong nation will never allow another great country to rise to compete even peacefully. Should the United States believe in China's message? I think so, since no country can afford to be a world hegemony!

CHAPTER 25

IS JAPAN'S DEMOCRACY REALLY WORKING

FOR THE JAPANESE PEOPLE?

—◊—

JAPANESE PEOPLE ARE RESPECTABLE PEOPLE with many good virtues. Japanese are polite, clean, proud, respecting knowledge, elders and seniority and extremely obedient and loyal to authorities. The respect for knowledge and education is amply demonstrated in the learning ability of the Japanese in absorbing technologies, industrial practices and skill development, including manufacturing and military training. These virtues have made Japan adaptive and strong in her economic development since the 'Meiji Restoration' era. Despite of her small size, Japan has become a strong nation prior to WW II and even become a second largest economy in the world post WW II. However, these virtues have also made the Japanese people vulnerable to be misled easily by shrewd politicians into a blind alley without consciously questioning the root principles for the welfare of the people. This led to the disastrous Japanese plot of conquering China and other Asian countries. Today, under Japan's Democracy installed post WW II under the supervision of the United States, the Japanese people seem to be vulnerable again to be misled by their ambitious right-wing leaders, creating a dangerous prospect.

Japan, a member of the Axial countries, was a culprit responsible for the Asian part of WW II by waging war against all Asian countries, even attacking the Pearl Harbor of the United States. The Japanese Emperor was absolutely obeyed by the Japanese people. The Japanese Imperial Army working under the orders of the Emperor had developed an invasion plan to conquer the entire China and Asia. The Japanese war leaders misled the Imperial army and the entire country to believe that their aggression to other countries was to save Asia from the colonial occupation by the West. However, the Japanese Army had committed brutal atrocities far worse than the Western colonial countries. Over 25 millions of civilians (over 70% Chinese) and over 6 millions military persons (including 29% Japanese) were killed during WW II. Properties and resources were looted and shipped back to Japan or secretly hidden by killing all workers who labored to hide them. People were tortured and experimented with bacteria and chemical weapons. Women were forced to be sex slaves to serve the Japanese Imperial Army. All of these crimes were covered up from the Japanese people during the war and even to this day they are whitewashed or removed from the Japanese textbooks.

After the Japanese surrendered in 1945, there was a brief moment of joy in the world, especially in Asia, thinking militarism and fascism being finally defeated. A peace constitution was established in Japan where a democratic Japan would be created making Japan a peace loving country never waging war again. The Japanese war leaders should have taken the full responsibility for their war crimes but yet they refused to admit quilt rather insisted that their war atrocities were for the good of the countries they invaded. They would rather sacrifice their lives to protect their Emperor from being tried and punished, exhibiting an absolute loyalty but a blind one ignoring justice and honesty demanded by the facts. Of course, many Japanese civilians had died in WW II when their homeland was finally bombed by the Allies to force the Japanese Imperial Army to surrender. The Japanese civilians never wished to be killed by the war but they never had a choice or chance to voice their own will. Today, Japan's Democracy is supposed to work for the people to prevent the repeat of such a tragic history.

Under the peace constitution, a democratic government system was indeed established in Japan after seven years of occupation by the Supreme Command of the Allied Power (SCAP) led by the United States. Japan was rebuilt with a multi-party democratic government and a two-house parliament with elected representatives. For the past 60 years, with the concern of the spread of communism and the event of Korean War in 1950's, Japan was rebuilt to be an US ally. The Japanese government seemed to work in a democratic way. Japan recovered and eventually rose to be second largest economy in the world, owing to the Japanese people's good virtues (diligent learning, hard working, obedient and loyal to authorities) and the fact that Japan was treated as an US ally rather than as a defeated enemy. However, on a closer examination, one wonders whether Japan's Democracy is really working for the Japanese people safeguarding their desire for peace?!

Similar to the United States, Japan has a multi-party system; the largest is the Liberal Democratic Party (LDP) formed in 1955 and the main opposition party is the Democratic Party of Japan (DPJ) only formed in 1998. The Japanese modern political system has been essentially one party controlling the administration since 1955. The LDP was formed by a merger in 1955 between two right-wing conservative parties, the Liberal Party (1950–1955, led by Shigeru Yoshida) and the Japan Democratic Party (1954–1955, led by Ichirō Hatoyama), as a united front against the Japan Socialist Party. The LDP held majority and power till today, briefly lost her majority in 1993-1996 and lost for the first time in designating the Prime Minister in 2009-2012 (39 months), then the LDP regained control in 2012. In its early days, LDP received help from the CIA of the United States out of its concern of communism spreading to Japan, but that fear turned out to be unfounded, especially now after the Cold War had ended.

The LDP, apart from the goal of maintaining a monarch system and preserving Japanese culture, is backed with **nationalism** and **reactionism** (returning to previous state/glory) lacking a consistent ideology. The LDP leadership was generally emerged from strong or popular individuals with their personal views. Ironically, the formation of LDP under the peace constitution was led by the individuals having intimate ties with the Imperial Japan. For example, Nobusuke Kishi (岸 信介), **the grand-father-in-law of Shinzo Abe, the current Japanese Prime Minister**, was the mastermind in forming the conservative Democratic Party (predecessor of LDP) in 1954. Kishi was one of the top officials in Industrial Development of Manchuria in 1935, later he was accused of exploiting forced Chinese labor. He was appointed as Minister of Munitions in 1941 by Hideki Tojo, the number one WW II war criminal sentenced to death by the International Tribunal. Although Kishi was put in prison after the war but he was released in 1948 and became active politically. Kishi became the party Secretary-General of DP. He then merged the DP and LP to form LDP, the ultimate dominant political party in Japan. He later served as the Japanese Prime Minister (1957-60) with a nickname, Shōwa no yōkai ("the Shōwa era monster/devil") with good reasons.

Today, Shinzo Abe, carries the lineage of political bloodline of Nobusuke Kishi, an associate of Hideki Tojo. Abe exhibits a full spectrum of nationalism and reactionism as evidenced by the following: Claiming "Japan is Back"; Escalating territorial disputes with neighboring countries, notably the Diaoyu Islands; Advocating constitution revision to rearm; Enacting security act; Worshipping the Japanese war criminals (including Hideki Tojo) in Yasukuni Shrine; Demanding further revision of school textbooks to deny WW II history; Comparing Sino-Japan relation to the WW I scenario at the Davos Conference; and Statements made by ministers and NHK board members (NHK, Japanese Broadcasting Corporation) denying Nanking Massacre and Sex Slavery Program ever happened and criticizing the US bombing of Japan during WW II. The above alarming nationalistic behaviors all took place under Japan's Democracy with LDP as its controlling party. Abe is not only misleading the Japanese people with his right-wing agenda but also advancing a dangerous plan to drag the United States into a dilemma. **As American citizens, shouldn't we be concerned? Is 'Japan's Democracy' really working for the Japanese people? Will LDP or Japan become an uncontrollable party wrecking up the US-China Relationship and world peace? Both the U.S. and China must be prudent in dealing with an increasingly militant Shinzo Abe.**

CHAPTER 26

STATE VISIT OF FIRST LADY MICHELLE

OBAMA TO CHINA – 'FIRST' COMMENT

—⚬—

MICHELLE OBAMA IS AN ACCOMPLISHED woman of her own. The fact she is the First Lady certainly adds a halo to her head but being the 'first' black First Lady living in the white house with her own accomplishments simply makes her a very unique 'first' First Lady occupying a spot in the history of the United States. Recently, Michelle Obama making an unusual trip to China on her own as the US First Lady with her two daughters, Malia and Sasha, and her mom, Marian, but without her husband, President Obama, marked a significant diplomatic event in the history of US-China relationship. The significance of her trip to China shall be far reaching simply because of her stature and her influence in the United States in the future. Though partly eclipsed by the mysterious disappearance of Malaysia airline M370, the US mainstream media kept a low profile reporting of Michelle's China trip; however, from a broad observation in the organic media, I believe, Michelle's China trip has a long-term positive effect on the US-China relationship which will be borne out by history.

Michelle La Vaughn Robinson was born on January 17, 1964 in Chicago, right after President Lyndon Johnson declared war on poverty and right before the Beatles' "I Want To Hold Your Hand" appeared as the #1 song in the U.S., a dynamic era of the US history. Ironically, 1964 was the year that the US House Representatives accepted the Civil Rights Act. A landmark legislation outlawed discrimination based on race, color, religion, sex, or national origin. Although there was some controversy surrounding the birth and early childhood of President Barack Obama, there was no question that Michelle was born an American in an era of African-American Civil Movement. Michelle's father was a black labor worker and her mom a black secretary; her mom raised her and her brother with keen emphasis on education. Michelle had been a gifted student, graduated a Salutatorian from Whitney M. Young high school in Chicago in 1981 and received B.A. Sociology from Princeton in 1985 and later received law degree from Harvard in 1988. Not a single US First Lady ever had her academic distinction.

Michelle graduated while Barack entered Harvard Law school in 1988, hence she did not meet Barack in Harvard. It was at the law firm Sidney Austin in Chicago, Michelle first met Barack, an intern at that time, and she served as his advisor. Obviously Barack recognized a smart lady and pursued her. Dating a boss and a Harvard alumnus took courage, the fact they got married in 1992 added a romantic twist to the Obama American Dream. Since their marriage, Michelle has been a great help in Barack's career, as a loving wife, a serious mother of two daughters, and an effective campaign supporter for her husband's bid for the US Senate position and later for the Presidency of the United States. Michelle is not a pretty woman but then her accomplishments on her own academically and professionally as well as a successful person in terms of a model wife and mother, gave her a great personal confidence to be the First Lady of the United States. It showed in her trip to China.

Fourteen First Ladies have visited China in the past. Often the First Ladies' agenda were part of the foreign diplomacy of the United States. Two main doctrines that have been consistently on the US foreign policy towards China are 'Democracy and Human Rights'. The United States have been righteously advocating democracy and human rights but often failed to recognize that democracy is only a method of reaching decisions but not ideology of itself and human rights are rights bestowed by the law or constitution with its historical perspectives. For instance, supporting Dalai Lama's religious right (monk superiority) in Tibet amounts to child abuse and human slavery, whereas the PRC constitution prohibits religious supremacy.

Since the United States only enacted the civil rights act in 1964, a merely 50 years ago and democracy as one person one vote was only granted to women in 1920, less than 100 years ago, why should the United States be so righteous in view of five thousand years of Chinese history? The Chinese started their revolution for establishing a republic only 100 years ago (1911); the revolution is still yet to complete due to many foreign interventions and invasions. Many US First Ladies, including the most recent Hillary Clinton and Laura Bush, have actively criticized China's record on preserving human rights. However, Democracy and human rights do not equate to ideology. Ideology in a plain language is really a civil dream, a dream citizens hope to realize. American Dream and Chinese Dream, not so different, are what we should advocate, rather than a particular form of government. Mrs. Obama on her China trip stayed focused on education and culture are right on. Only education can help citizens understand human rights and practice of democracy. Only education can help citizens realize their civil dream. In today's Internet world, there is more chance now than ever for education to reach everyone if we only place the emphasis on education.

Michelle and Barack Obama are products of American Dream. Education played a significant role in their lives. So Michelle understands the power and importance of education to a family and to a country. She emphasizes education and obviously so in bringing up her own children. She shares in her speech the story of how she overcomes obstacles in setting high educational goals. Her visit to China garnered a billion page views. This impact to the US-China relationship is not only immediate but also has a long-term effect. Currently, there is only 20,000 American students studying in China, (10 times Chinese students in the US) that number must increase for Americans to understand the Chinese and their dream.

In the past, China has no role for a Chinese First Lady, but Peng Liyuan has become the 'first' real Chinese First Lady just like Michelle has become the 'first' black First Lady. As an accomplished singer in China, Liyuan is well known. Ever since her husband, Xi jinping, became the President, she had comfortably ascended to the role of Chinese First Lady. Liyuan travels with her husband to foreign countries. She promotes rural education and campaigns against tuberculosis for the World Health Organization. She even has won a place on Vanity Fair's international best-dressed list in 2013. Her meeting with Michelle made a number of 'firsts' which will have many followers to come.

Michelle and Liyuan, both in their early fifties, have a long bright future ahead of them both in their own countries but also on the world stage. Their common interests in education and health will most likely bring their path to cross in the near future. The bonding they made over this China visit is not only personal but is also inter-national between millions of Americans and Chinese going down in history like the Great Wall Michelle visited.

CHAPTER 27

CONDEMN PITY OR EXONERATE

JAPANESE KAMIKAZE PILOTS?

—ɱ—

IN A RECENT NEWS REPORT, The City of Minami in Kyushu, Japan has submitted to UNESCO's Memory of the World Register (United Nations' Cultural Organization) a collection of Japanese Kamikaze pilots' final farewell letters as world heritage to symbolize the importance of Peace. The submission includes 333 items held at the Chiran Peace Museum in Minami. This action immediately angered China and Korea regarding this submission as against the basic ethics of UNESCO. When I first read the news, I was bewildered, how could the action of the suicide pilots plunging their planes into US ships and harbors with the intent for kill be honored and symbolized as peace loving? Isn't this ridiculous? Then after thinking it over, I think this is again another example that Japanese simply cannot handle the truth about WW II, when the truth places a guilt burden on them. A Samurai culture dictates that admitting guilt is a shame; facing shame one must select death. This culture explains why Japanese would go to a great length to avoiding admission of guilt by persistently denying historical facts. Denying 'Comfort Women', 'Nanking Massacre', 'Human Experiment', etc. are clear examples.

Kamikaze (Spirit wind or Divine wind) were suicide pilots who would fly a one-way mission, flying to the target and plunging the plane into the target. When this is done in a well planned massive program (4000 kamikaze pilots were killed), it is unthinkable even in the name of war. This is the very reason; the 9-11-2001 attack of the New York world trade center by suicide airline hi-jackers had angered the world. Now the world must unite and collaborate to prevent and defend any suicide attackers taking place anywhere in the globe.

The Japanese Kamikaze pilots were recruited from young commissioned and non-commissioned army and navy officers or young air force cadets or officers. Highly thought-out methods of "soliciting volunteers" were used, for example, young officers were blindfolded and asked to raise their hands or step forward if they would volunteer; psychologically this increases peer pressure to say yes and reduces hesitation or cowardice. The recruits were told they were going to serve their country with the highest honor. They were only trained with the basic flying skill, take-off and diving, since their missions are one-way (no fuel for return). They were given what they want before their mission, including having sex with women. It is tragic for these vulnerable young people to commit a suicide but probably never given a day to do some clear thinking. One can imagine the feelings of the parents of these young men and what a nightmare their parents will endure throughout a life time.

Minami hosted the Chiran airfield from which the Kamikazes took off to their death missions. Chiran had become the principal place that Japanese people associate with kamikaze pilots. The Chiran Peace Museum for Kamikaze Pilots opened in 1975 on the site of the former Chiran Air Base, and enlargement of the museum building to 17 thousand sq. ft. was completed in 1986. It is understandable; the Chiran museum is built with a heavy sentiment to commemorate the Chiran Airfield and the Kamikaze pilots. The museum did a very good job in displaying the aircrafts of the kamikaze pilots (1036 from the Japanese Army), their final letters to the loved ones, pictures, uniforms etc. , but no mention of the Japanese Navy Kamikaze pilots or other Kamikaze pilots died (Total 4000). The museum also avoided any judgment of the Kamikaze program such as who were responsible for its implementation how could it be accepted in moral terms, or what positive lessons young people should learn from this museum other than glorifying (a blind) patriotism. It can be seen that there is pain in showing those farewell letters of the Kamikaze letters, but just like the comfort women issue, the museum avoided the guilt question and responsibility accountability and an honest future implication. It is obvious some people in the Imperial army had to be responsible for the 4000-life Kamikaze program, why is it so hard for a museum historian and any government official to admit what exactly The facts are so any emotional feelings can be released? Why is it so hard for the Japanese to handle the truth?

A Japanese movie, called 'Forever Zero', based on a Japanese best seller, (same title) has become a popular film. The story features a brother and sister tracking their grandfather who died in the final days of Pacific War. The end of movie showed a Kamikaze pilot and glorified his bravery and his honor for dying for Japan. It is an emotional movie showing the perspective of WW II from Japanese point of view. In a Chinese article in the US-China Forum (WWW.US-ChinaForum.org issue #31 by Thomas Hann), Mr. Fann commented about this film and his feeling which is very understandable. The author or movie producer chose to avoid the whole truth of Kamikaze. The book and movie should have dealt honestly with 'how Kamikaze came about', 'who was responsible?', 'what methods of "soliciting of volunteers" are used?', why two separate farewell letters were required of the pilots before their mission, one for family and one for government propaganda?', and 'were there any honest letter that revealed the moral issue of the entire Kamikaze program? '

We can understand how Japan yearns for what it sees as its rightful place in the hierarchy of nations. Japan prides herself to be superior than other Asian nations, right or wrong, it is her prerogative opinion. Japan for years has waged a campaign to obtain a permanent seat in the United Nations Security Council, but her continued denial of history (where Japan should bare the guilt and responsibility) just will not win many friends in supporting her. Prime Minister Abe Shinzo's decision to worship at the controversial Yasukuni Shrine, where the "souls" of 14 class-A war criminals from World War II were housed is yet again another example, Japan cannot handle the truth of Japan's war crimes. Japan simply cannot rationally explain herself to the rest of the world.

WW II was a tragedy and Japan committed atrocious war crimes. We can understand there is a tremendous guilt burden falling on every Japanese citizen regarding what Kamikaze did to the world (and to herself). The sacrifice of Kamikaze pilots' lives was wasted in committing war crimes. Only when Japanese citizens understand and recognize that and then condemn what the Imperial Japan had done to the Kamikaze pilots, can the Kamikaze pilots be commemorated with honor. The Kamikazes provoked a fear and revenge in the Allied Forces which led to more severed bombing of the Japanese main islands eventually to President Truman's decision of using the atomic bomb - "When you have to deal with a beast you have to treat him as a beast."

One can never equate Kamikaze madness with peace loving. Calling Chiran Museum a peace museum glorifying Kamikaze pilots without condemning their crimes and creators would not be promoting peace. Hopefully, UNESCO is wise enough to use Minami's submission to deliver a moral lesson to Japan.

CHAPTER 28

DON'T LET JAPAN HIGHJACK THE US 'PIVOT'

POLICY TO A JAPANESE '3FN' STRATEGY

—⚏—

THERE WAS AN ANCIENT CHINESE saying in diplomacy, "Yuan Jiao Jin Gong", which means literally making friends with the states at far distance and attacking the states near the border. In diplomatic language, "Yuan Jiao Jin Gong" strategy can be translated as 'Be Friend with the Far and Be Foe with the Near' (Friend Far Foe Near or FFFN or 3FN) strategy. (This style of acronym takes after another strategy term describing the US-China relation, Neither Friends Nor Foes or NFNF.) The 3FN strategy was often practiced by multiple states occupying a fractured territory. In such a situation, a weak state may have to befriend with the far away states in order to get their support to defend against a close aggressive neighbor, hence friend far is necessary. On the other hand, a strong state with ambition to expand her territory may also befriend with the states at far distance so she can focus on conquering her close by neighboring state first, using a '3FN' strategy for expansion. In the era of late Zhou Dynasty ("Zhan Guo Shi Dai") in the Chinese history, the Middle Kingdom was divided, occupied and controlled by feudal lords forming many states; even though there was a figure head emperor, the separate states had total governance control and independent diplomacy on their own. The '3FN' was developed and practiced in that era. This strategy was also practiced in military war fare and was taught in war theories such as in the famous Sun Zi Bing Fa, which has been a part of curriculum in the world-known United States Military Academy at West Point, New York. In both diplomacy and military affairs, the '3FN' strategy can be used defensively or offensively.

Today, by and large, the world has evolved into nations with legitimate governments barring a few places troubled by self-inflicted or foreign instigated unrest.

Under the umbrella of the United Nations, there are 192 countries being recognized as nations/members with their own history, culture and governance. Under the charter of the UN, member countries must be living peacefully among each other. Hence, the above mentioned '3FN' strategy should never be practiced by UN members. Unfortunately, as we see today, the above strategy not only was never shelved but was vigorously practiced among nations with ambitions. The ambitious and aggressive nations are called hegemony in modern terms, with ambitions to expand territorially, to dominate influence in international affairs and worst of all to prevent other nations to rise to power even by peaceful means through fair competition. The Soviet Union and the United States were branded as hegemony by each other, resulting in a Cold War lasting more than four decades. With the final collapse of the Soviet Union, one would expect the hegemony ambition and practice would stop, but the recent 'Pivot to Asia' strategy initiated by the United States seems to target China as the new cold war (may even lead to a hot war) enemy with Japan not only as an eager ally but also as the principal executioner of the policy in Asia. However, what is more alarming though is Japan's application of the '3FN' strategy for her own purpose.

Japan decided to escalate the territorial dispute with China, the Diaoyu Islands, with calculated measures. Now under the US 'Pivot to Asia' policy, Japan is forming military alliances with nations and territories surrounding China in an attempt to suppress China's rise. The current Japanese Prime Minister, Shinzo Abe, the right wing leader with a right-wing agenda to build up Japan's military strength and to revise Japan's peace constitution to permit Japan to make first attack, is also creating an unproven 'China Threat' theory. Abe has been busy touring and making military and diplomatic alliances with Asian nations surrounding China including the Philippines (the foreign ministers of Japan and the Philippines proclaimed their nations to be strategic partners that would collaborate more in resolving their separate territorial disputes with China, later Japan promised 10 patrol vessels to Philippine's Coast Guard), Vietnam (The two defense ministers discussed measures to elevate defense ties and shared their views on international and regional issues of mutual interest), Malaysia (Japan and Malaysia pledged on to strengthen economic cooperation and bolster security ties, as China heightens its maritime assertiveness in Southeast Asia.), Indonesia (Indonesia and Japan have agreed to increase cooperation in military, particularly concerning military training and exercises, human resources development, defense industry, contra-terrorism, and disaster handling, said Indonesian Defense Minister Purnomo Yusgiantoro), and as far as Australia (Australia will deepen its security alliance with Japan in a new agreement to share military technology. The defense agreement opens the way for Australian access to advanced systems that could greatly increase the power of a new submarine fleet.). Since his PM appointment in 2012 Abe has worked diligently to improve the India - Japan relationship. (This year Japan will join in the naval tri-partite exercises with India and the U.S. The top officials in defense and foreign ministries of Japan and India will begin talks on closer ties. Japan is considering selling India amphibious aircraft and nuclear power plant equipments even though India has refused to sign the nuclear nonproliferation treaty) The Japanese International Cooperation Agency (JICA) has funded the Delhi Metro subway project and just agreed to lend India additional $700 million for the next phase of the Mumbai Subway. This type of financing and new factories opening in India by the Japanese car manufacturers, Suzuki and Honda, and consumer product manufacturer, Panasonic, could be interpreted as fair play in the global economy. However, in view of the above and more bi-lateral military alliances and security web Abe is weaving for Japan, it becomes apparent that the heightened diplomatic relations between Japan and other Asian countries is a result of the Japanese 3FN strategy against China.

3FN strategy explains the behavior and actions of Japan, motivated by her ambition to become a dominant nation in the world. Japan has worked very hard to gain a permanent seat in the UN Security Council for years but unsuccessful and frustrated. Historically, Japan had always targeted China as a prey; hence, it is understandable why Japan would adopt a 3FN strategy against China to pull back her rising, passing Japan as the world's second largest economy. However, the same cannot be said about the United States. China and Japan both are far from the United States in distance; there is no logic for the United States to befriend with Japan only and not to befriend with a rising China who has far more to offer to the United States from economic collaboration as well as from maintaining the world peace. This adds more serious doubt about the wisdom and effectiveness of the "Pivot to Asia" policy or its reinterpreted 'balancing power' policy, discussed openly by many political analysts. Indeed, witnessing recent events related to the US-China-Japan relationship, many astute observers have noticed troubling signs. These signs cast concerns that Japan (through Abe) is trying unilaterally to hijack the Pivot-to-Asia US policy and transform it into a 'Friend Far Foe Near' Strategy against China, fitting Japan's nationalism and militarism which are revived vigorously by Abe's right-wing administration. This is happening too quickly to be left unchecked. Can the United States manage, predict and control the Asian power web of bi-lateral security alliances weaved by Japan? Patrick Cronin et al have raised a serious question in their report, The Emerging Asia Power Web, published by the Center for New American Security (6/2014). The United States must take back her initiative and make immediate assessment on the 'Pivot' or 'balancing' policy before it becomes Japan's 3FN power play. China is no longer a weak country as she was 77 years ago when Japan attacked her. Japan by Allies' mercy was spared total destruction by WW II, but can Japan survive a real nuclear WW III? No, definitely not Japan, neither Asia nor America! If unchecked, Japan's Kamikaze war spirit and her desire to apply 3FN against China and to drag the U.S. into a war might just lead to the total destruction of the Earth! The United States must do something to prevent this from happening!!

CHAPTER 29

JAPAN CAN'T WIN THE DIAOYU ISLANDS

DISPUTE BY INCREASING MOFA BUDGET

—m—

JAPAN'S SANKEI SHIMBUN (5/4/2014) STATED that the Japanese Ministry of Foreign Affairs will increase its budget on international communication ('propaganda') from 4.4 billion to 6.5 billion yen ($43M to $64M), a 48% increase in response to the successful Chinese and Korean effort in the international community in clarifying their respective territory dispute with Japan, namely the Diaoyu Islands (claimed by China, Senkaku by Japan) and Dokdo (claimed by South Korea, also known as Liancourt Rocks, named Takeshima by Japan). The report elaborated on the success of the Chinese and Korean governments in winning the arguments of their claims by taking two different approaches. The Chinese government is focusing on United Nations conferences, world leader summits and other international fora and letting oversea media, think tanks and research organizations repeatedly presenting their ideas and claims about the diaoyu Islands dispute. The South Korean government, on the other hand, is focusing on "local self-governed bodies such as civil society and friends of Korea to launch a variety of activities in the United States and South Korea to clarify Korea's claim. The report implies the above cited budget increase by MOFA of Japan is justified and necessary to counter the Chinese and South Korean's successes.

In advertising, there is a belief that if you kept saying something enough times, it might just get accepted as truth. By this logic, budget allocated for the communication effort is thus very critical. The decision of a budget increase by Japan MOFA is obviously based on this logic. This logic executed as a strategy works well in marketing of products and the Japanese industries do well in that. The

Japanese auto industry has very generous advertising budget and has successfully applied this strategy in establishing its auto brands. When their products indeed are high quality and competitive, this strategy works well, hence, the Japanese cars obtained their reputation and world market share. However, this strategy is no secret to others; it can be applied by anyone. When the Korean and Chinese auto industry began to improve their products and apply the same advertising strategy, the world market share of Japanese cars will be eroded. Indeed, this is happening; the Japanese cars are facing increasing challenge from Korean and Chinese cars. Ultimately, market advertising alone cannot win without product improvements.

Japanese is known to be very good at packaging goods attractively. This is seen in many Japanese consumer products even in foods. However, the territorial dispute such as Daiaoyu Islands cannot be improved nor packaged like products. Hence, increasing MOFA propaganda budget cannot help Japan win the Diaoyu Islands dispute with China. The disputed islands have their historical facts which cannot be denied nor fabricated. They can only be presented or clarified as the Chinese, Korean and the general public has done. Historical facts can only be discovered and established by researching available archived materials such as maps, documents and ancient books. Interpretive documents contradicting to historical facts are simply lies. Truth is like gold, it will forever shine and lies can never be turned into truth. Lies upon lies only make thicker lies which will be eventually proven untrue. This is the very reason that Japan cannot win the Diaoyu Islands by increasing her propaganda budget. Without being on the side of truth backed by historical facts, spending money to distort the truth is doomed to fail. We all knew, "You may fool some of the people some of the time, but you can never fool all the people all the time".

In the cases of Diaoyu and Dokdo Islands, the Japanese claims are based on their (later) interpretation whereas the Chinese and Korean claims are based on (earlier) historical facts such as maps and ancient documents. The sovereignty over Dokdo has been an ongoing point of contention between Japan and South Korea for a long time; Korean claims are partly based on references to an island called *Usan-do* in various medieval historical records, maps, and encyclopedia such as Samguk Sagi, Annals of Joseon Dynasty, Dongguk Yeoji Seungnam, and Dongguk munhon bigo.

The Diaoyu Islands dispute has drawn more international attention recently since Abe Shinzo became Japan's Prime Minister. As a right-wing leader, Abe is using Diaoyu dispute to revive Japan's nationalism and militarism. Abe has managed to make the U.S. to state that their mutual defense treaty is applicable to the Diaoyu islands. The recent maneuver and schemes the Japanese government has made to claim the sovereignty rights of these islands not only angered China but also enhanced China's resolve in defending her sovereignty. The Chinese government has been focusing on bringing out the historical facts and legal proof in her claims and categorically stating that she will take all measures if necessary in defending her rights to Diaoyu Islands. Hence Diaoyu Islands is now a hotspot with possibility igniting a major war.

Of course, no one, all Pacific nations including the United States, would be benefitting from a major war. Unfortunately, the "official neutrality" positions regarding Diaoyu Islands the U.S. has maintained thus far, has not quieted the dispute but rather has emboldened the Abe administration in its ambition to expand territorially. The fusing temperature of the Diaoyu hotspot has been raised too high already and the increase of budget by Ministries of Foreign Affairs and Defense are simply fuels poured over the hotpot. Surveying the mainstream media, plenty of voices are warning 'caution' but few with convincing arguments to reign in the Japanese government's ambition and more importantly to correct the U.S. ambiguous foreign policy regarding the Diaoyu Islands. We present below the arguments to help Japan and the U.S. to come to senses.

Based on the following points, Japan should not wage a propaganda battle and prepare war for Diaoyu:

- The historical facts prior to 1885 clearly showed the Diaoyu Islands, although uninhabited, belonged to Chinese (Qing and Ming government records).
- The Japanese official records around 1885 showed that the Japanese Meiji government conducted surveys and intended to annex the Diaoyu Islands but warned against by her Foreign Affairs Official as an act of invasion against China.
- After a number of Chinese defeats in the Sino-Japanese War, The Meiji government, following a cabinet decision in early 1895, incorporated the islands as booty of war.

- Koga Tatsushiro, the first Japanese citizen to lease the islands from the Meiji government, in his biography attributed Japan's possession of the islands to "the gallant military victory of our Imperial forces."

- Neither Beijing nor Taipei dispute that the Diaoyu along with the entire island of Taiwan were formally under Japanese occupation prior to the end of WW II, 1945. However, per post-WW II arrangements, Japan was required to surrender all territories obtained from aggression and to return them to their pre-1895 legal status.

- The U.S. claims to be neutral but in effect is siding with Japan. The granting of administrative right (1971) of Okinawa and Diaoyu Islands to Japan by the U.S. was based on the San Francisco Peace Treaty (1951) by which the U.S. obtained the administrative rights, but neither the Beijing nor the Taipei government was a party of the peace treaty. Hence, the U.S. has no right to give away rights of territories rightfully returned to the Chinese by the Potsdam Proclamation (1945). (Numeral references support the above points: notably, NY Times 9/19/2012, Nicholas Kristof: "The Inconvenient Truth Behind the Diaoyu/Senkaku Islands" by Han-Yi Shaw, Professor of National Chengchi University and his earlier paper, 'Japan's Dubious Claim to the Diaoyu Islands', in the Wall Street Journal 5/3/2012).

Based on the above points, the United States is obligated to make an honest statement according to the Potsdam Proclamation and *Justice* to clarify the Diaoyu Islands dispute preventing it to be the fuse of a major war.

CHAPTER 30

THE ILLUSION OF CYBER SECURITY AND

PRIVACY PROTECTION FOR CITIZENS

—ɯ—

CYBER SECURITY AND PRIVACY HAS been a controversial issue, flickering in the limelight since Edward Snowden blew a whistle on the United States government engaging in a mass electronic surveillance and data mining program (PRISM launched in 2007 by the National Security Agency (NSA)) on its citizens as well as on governments and companies and their leaders world-wide in the name of national security (under Section 702 of the FISA Amendments Act). The Prism program collects stored Internet communications based on demands made to Internet companies such as Google Inc. and Apple Inc. to turn over any data that match court-approved search terms. The NSA can use these Prism requests to target communications that were encrypted when they traveled across the Internet backbone and stored data that were discarded by telecommunication filtering systems. NSA is known to collect metadata of phone records of the mass and use fake Facebook servers to infect visiting computers with malware.

It is no surprise that the world is very upset. American companies are suffering financially as a result of the allegations of their cooperation with NSA surveillance. Microsoft has lost customers, while other companies like IBM and Salesforce are diverting significant resources to build data centers overseas to assure the safety of their customers' cyber security and privacy. Mike Rogers and Dutch Ruppersberger, the leaders of the House Intelligence Committee, introduced HR 4291, the FISA Transparency and Modernization Act to end the collection of all Americans' calling records under Section 215 of the Patriot Act. HR 4291 stops the mass collection of all Americans' calling records, but the bill's creation of a new order to conduct unconstitutional mass spying on any record created by a communication is still disturbing.

President Obama said he will call for an end to NSA bulk collection and storage of phone records but he wants phone companies, not the NSA, to be responsible for storing bulk phone record metadata making them quickly available, if the government supplies a new type of surveillance court order. Some would interpret Obama's proposal to be a step toward legalizing mass surveillance. In NY Times, Charlie Savage added, "The administration's proposal would also include a provision clarifying whether Section 215 of the Patriot Act may in the future be legitimately interpreted as allowing bulk data collection of telephone data."

Whether these proposed legislations will come to fruition or not are still questionable. The intelligence agencies namely NSA is essentially trying to get the congress to pass a law to allow commercial and private companies to collect and store their customers' cyber data (text, voice, image and video) and make available to the United States intelligence agencies for national security purposes. The rationale behind this effort is that the kind of information, NSA has been collecting or desire to have access to, is the same as the voluntarily divulged information by the consumers to technology companies. Some of that information has been routinely sold to advertisers by technology companies for commercial purposes. If such a legislation was enacted then NSA could stop direct surveillance activities on US citizens simply by counting on private companies to do so legally for them. In this scenario, the NSA can possibly reduce the number of its cyber workers, reducing cyber surveillance budget, and clearing its name from direct spying on American citizens. It all seemed to be a win-win for NSA and tech industries except that the cyber security and privacy of the American citizens (consumers) are not an iota more protected than ever before.

Data collection and analytics are important for businesses, but the train has left the station with no brakes installed. If the US administration had its way in the above proposal, one could only imagine how fast the train might be accelerated. The tech industries will equate data share to market share and equate market share to profit share of their stocks, hence, they will be eager to collect data. The loss will be on the citizens since ample evidence shows that cyber criminals can exploit and create security holes as fast as the IT personnel in the tech industries can plug them. If the current versions of proposed legislation were passed, The NSA would be just capable as the cyber criminals to create any security flaws in order to access and analyze the mass data obtainable by them. So any cyber security and privacy protection for citizens will be simply an illusion.

Fortunately or unfortunately, the above proposed legislation may not pass the Congress. The President does not seem to have his own party's support. Pelosi's understanding of cyber security stops at her own credit card scores. The Republicans have no interest in helping NSA or Obama in cooling off the citizens' privacy concern. In a democratic society, the government or congress is just as good as the citizens want them to be. If the US citizens, as consumers in the market place, really understood the importance of their private data, being identity information, healthcare data, purchasing records or private communications between individuals, they could write to their congress representatives to enact a stronger privacy act to protect them from data snoopers. They could also demand the digital technology enterprises limiting their collection of consumers' private data and prohibiting them to sell the data for profit or not. Naturally, as we are living in a digital world, data helps provide conveniences to us. Trade-offs has to be made. For example, one must weigh the convenience of snapping a photo, sending to a bunch of people and storing at a free cyber storage site versus the possibility that photo of your family got into the wrong hand.

Convenience is the key parameter in the cyber security and privacy issue. The NSA must not be given the **convenience** of making mass surveillance on its citizens simply because the technology is capable of doing so **conveniently!** Likewise, the citizens must give up some **conveniences** to do things even though technology is capable of providing such **conveniences**. As the digital train is speeding in our lives, the citizens need to understand the consequences of a derailed fast train. We need to take precaution to **strike a balance between convenience/speed and protection/privacy**. Legislations are the proper means to strike that balance.

As a provoking thought for us to ponder, perhaps, we should think about laws that will regulate the proliferation of data. For example, marketing calls generate data and intrude on privacy. A commercial entity can purchase a telephone list of citizens (through a commercial activity) and use a phonebot to call the entire list to solicit responses. This mass communication breaches people's privacy and cost people's time. If legislation would require such marketing enterprise to obligate to pay $0.01/second payment to the receiver's phone number account, (this can be easily done with today's technology), multiple benefits were achievable: The caller gets a willing person to receive the call making the call more productive. The receiver can opt out of this type of marketing calls, saving his time and protecting his privacy. Similarly, consumers could be compensated when their data were sold to any enterprise if the consumers would grant the permission to sell their private data. Only by empowering the citizens with this kind of legislations, can the e-commerce and cyber technology world be self-regulated with positive productive business activities. When consumers are really in charge, then the cyber security and privacy will no longer be an illusion!

CHAPTER 31

A WARM BILATERAL RELATIONSHIP IS ALWAYS
BETTER THAN A HATE OR LOVE TRIANGLE
– VIETNAM AND CHINA RELATIONSHIP –

—⚹—

THE RECENT DEVASTATING RIOT IN Vietnam has produced serious destruction, looting and burning of properties and factories (various reports: 2-21 dead, 100-140 injured and over 150-200 foreign companies damaged, Taiwan (120), South Korea (26), Japan(17), China(5), Singapore(3), Germany(1) and Malaysia (1)) Not only the governments of Vietnam, China and the United States were all caught by surprise, all Asian countries were stunned and feared a war eminent. News reports and analyses immediately appeared attributing the riot to a complex sentiment beyond the trigger event - the Chinese $1 billion oil rig sent to South China Sea (Paracel, Xisha Islands) to perform oil exploration encountering Vietnam's objection. The site of the oil rig is located 17 miles from the Chinese Paracel, a legal access for oil exploration, and about 120 Miles from the Vietnam's Ly Son Island and 180 miles from China's Hainan Island. The U.S. expressed concern and called the Chinese exploration provocative and other commentators link the sequential events of Obama's Asia tour (April 2014, Japan, South Korea, Malaysia and Philippines), Chinese oil exploration (early May) and Vietnam's objection with confrontation at sea and the final riot in Vietnam (mid May) as a correlated chain events. Others offered more sophisticated interpretation based on the riot being broadly directed to foreign investments. China had begun evacuating her citizens from Vietnam.

Indeed, the sentiments and reasons of the riot could be very complex in view of the Vietnam history and recent developments. Historically, Vietnam (Annam) was a tributary (suzerainty state) of China centuries ago when China's influence as an imperial nation was far reaching but she did not always intervene (for example, the emperor Hongwu of Ming Dynasty ignoring Annam's attacking Champa (South Vietnam)). The tributary states often behaved like rebels when China had her internal problems. In recent history, Vietnam like China was a victim of the western power, worse than China being colonized by the French from 1884 to 1940's. (France won the Sino-French war forcing China to recognize France's domination in Indochina) Japan invaded Indochina in 1940 and defeated France resulting in a brief Japanese control from 1944-45. During WW II, Indochina was the military supply line for China, hence, Japan was determined to cut that off in order to accomplish her ambition of conquering the entire China then Asia. Vietnam like China was also a victim to the Japanese invasion. When China was forced by the Japanese Imperial Army to retreat to the South West, some military forces retreated to Indochina, ultimately becoming immigrants there till today. Chinese Communist army had ties with Viet Minh then.

The recent developments in Vietnam added more evidence to her past engaged in 'hate and/or love triangle' with other countries. These relationships, aligning with China to fight Japan, or with China to fight France, or with the Soviet to fight the U.S. were necessary to gain independence but nevertheless devastating to the people of Vietnam. Now as an independent country, Vietnam should build warm bilateral relationship to promote her economy and to use it to resolve disputes in a peaceful manner. The following events should serve as lessons leading to the conclusion in the title:

- The Vietnam-France Indochina war (1941 – 1954): North Vietnam fought the French with hit and run Guerrilla warfare and French set up an independent South Vietnam (Saigon government) to resist with help from US financial aid and weapon technology. When Communist China gained control of mainland China and began to help the North Vietnam, they defeated the French resulting in a Geneva Agreement which supported the territorial integrity and sovereignty of Indochina, granted it independence from France, declared the cessation of hostilities and foreign involvement in internal Indochina affairs, delineated northern and southern zones for opposing troops to withdraw to, and mandated unification by holding internationally supervised free elections in July 1956. In 1955, Diem (South) rejected Geneva accord and got elected as the President of Republic of Vietnam. (South) The

Soviet pressured the North to sign the accord. **There were definitely complex love and hate triangular relationships in this period.**

- Vietnam War with the U.S. (1956-1975): French left Vietnam in 1956 and the U.S. assumed responsibility to train the forces. The Vietnam War lasted throughout five American Presidents, Eisenhower to Ford. The last American force left in 1975. A bitter war ended with Vietnam becoming the Socialist Republic of Vietnam. Throughout the war, the communist China was righteously supporting the North Vietnam and the Communist Vietnam took the Chinese revolution as their history lesson. The Soviet initially refrained from getting involved but later stepped in and signed a defense treaty with the North Vietnam in 1965 as Sino-Soviet migrated to a split in the 60's. In 1968, North Vietnam chose the Soviet's over China's aid hence Mao withdrew all Chinese personnel. In this bitter war, the U.S. used the controversial 'Agent Orange' (1962) which had left ecological damage in Vietnam and also gave a tacit approval of a coup deposing Diem and killing him and his brother (1963), but the U.S. also took in nearly one million Vietnamese refugees to the U.S.. **Again there were complex 'love and hate triangles' involved in this period, lots of Vietnamese people died or suffered.**

- After the Independence of the Socialist Republic of Vietnam (1975 - 2000): There was Cambodian-Vietnamese War; People's Army of Viet Nam invaded Cambodia in 1978 and occupied her till 1989 (infamous Cambodian genocide). Then there was Sino-Vietnamese War, Vietnam started to invade Chinese Islands in South China Sea (despite of its official recognition of China's sovereignty over Xisha Islands in 1958), then the Chinese crossed the northern border in 1979; both sides suffered heavy casualties and maintained a sour relationship. Vietnam then favored the Soviet over China, but its economy was in bad shape following the Soviet model. In 1990, Vietnam exit from Cambodia and improved relationship with China (Collapse of the Soviet). Since 1991, mutual visits started and mutually recognized Cambodia. in 1999, China and Vietnam helped each other with admission to WTO owing to a good bilateral relationship at work.

- In the new century (2000 -):

  1. China and ASEAN worked out a process of peaceful resolution and Guarantee against armed conflict (ASEAN did not voice any opinion on Vietnam's recent complaint against China)

2. Jiang Zemin visited Vietnam expanding trade and resolving outstanding dispute.
3. Bilateral trade increased from $32M in 1991 to $7.2B in 2004 and to $25B in 2011, **an obvious benefit of a warm bilateral relationship.**
4. In 10/2011, Nguyen Phu Trong (Party General Secretary) visited China, but on 6/21/2012, Vietnam passed a law placing both Spratly and Paracel under Vietnam jurisdiction which prompted China to denounce it illegal and establish the Sansha City to include these islands. **Is Vietnam engaging in a love or hate triangle again?**
5. 5/2013 Vietnam accused China of hitting one of her fishing ships.
6. Vietnam is seeking assistance from Japan to supply patrol boats.
7. 4/2014 Obama made the Asia tour.
8. 5/2014 China sent an oil rig to Paracel, Vietnam confronted, then it evolved into the riots in Ho Chi Minh City.
9. 5/21/2014 Vietnam and the Philippines announced: will jointly oppose "illegal" Chinese actions in the South China Sea.

It appears Vietnam is falling into another triangle heading to war? It seems that the above events were triggered by the US Pivot strategy targeting China. Is Vietnam falling into a triangular trap? Since Vietnam has not agreed to form a military alliance with the United States nor Japan, perhaps Vietnam is wise enough to realize a warm bilateral relationship with China is better than a treacherous triangle.

COLD WAR I TO COLD WAR II WITH

A CHANGING TRIANGLE

—ɯ—

A WELL WRITTEN AND PENETRATING article, Treacherous Triangle by David Gordon and Jordan Schneider, published in Foreign Affairs (5/22/2014) is one of the few level-headed essays about US foreign policy in relation to Russia and China. It correctly stated that the new Cold War being staged is different from the old Cold War. China is in a position to play off the United States and Russia against each other for her desire and benefit to rise peacefully. The United States is not in a position to play Off China and Russia as happened in Cold War I collapsing the Soviet Union. However, in this treacherous triangle, something needs to be said about each player's new position and what may be a new dynamics. Naturally, no one has a crystal ball that includes Obama (and whoever follows him), Putin and Xi, but it may be wise to speculate and draw out more discussions so that the future dynamics of this triangle may be somewhat guided with reason and wisdom rather than pure emotions and guesswork.

A triangle is a simple geometric figure which can be easily described and comprehended by words, say, three balls connected with sticks. Let's say, the triangle in the first Cold War was formed by the U.S. (with NATO), The Soviet (with Warsaw) and China. The U.S. was clearly the heaviest ball occupying the top tip of the triangle with her weight pressing on the bottom two balls, the Soviet Union, a larger ball on the left and China a smaller ball on the right. The U.S. with her deep rooted anti-communism national policy was applying pressure against the Soviet Union and China. Starting from the 60's, when China had enough of a taste of communism or experimentation of socialism, she developed her strong will to build her nation, thus splitting from the course of the communist camp led by Russia. This weakened the stick holding the two bottom balls together. Even though the Soviet was a heavy weight, but never the less it was no match for the U.S. and NATO. The Soviet Union eventually collapsed in 1990. In the meantime, China was laying low, plotting her own course of economic development quietly and successfully to embrace the new century.

A quarter century later, China has risen to be the number two economy of the world; Russia was weakened but awakened to charge a nationalistic come back plan. The United States although maintaining her superpower position, the expensive and somewhat aimless wars have drained her wealth and energy, now carrying a huge debt with a weak economy. So the new triangle has changed. The three balls do not have much difference in weight anymore. NATO is deflated along with Europe. Russia is struggling to come back from isolation. China has gained sufficient weight and is propped up by the U.S. and Russia and is now at the top tip of the triangle, while Russia is still at the bottom left and the U.S. is at the bottom right. In this new triangle, the dynamics is quite different from the Cold War I triangle, where the U.S. has been able to exert her full weight on the Soviet and China.

For all indications (completely true or not) perceived by the Chinese, the U.S. is building a Cold War II scenario and strategy. The 'pivot to Asia' policy is attempting to create an Asian 'NATO' to surround China, even though disguises were made to cover the real intent by talking about trade and global economy (TPP). In the Cold War I triangle, the U.S. was at the top, she could tilt her weight to the left (more pressure on the Soviet Union) and relax on the right (ease the tension with China), eventually it worked to dissolve the communist union. In the Cold War II triangle, by circumstances, China's economic development and the effort of the U.S. do prop up China to a heavier weight to be on the top tip of the triangle. Perhaps unintentionally, the US policy towards China is stimulating China to build up her military strength. Using Japan in the 'pivot' is a fundamental mistake, since Japan alone cannot be an Asian 'NATO' with her historical baggage. Even if The U.S. were able to wound up an Asian 'NATO', whose relation to China would not be the same as that between the NATO and the Soviet Union. The behavior of ASEAN towards China gives plenty of clues. Sure, it might be possible that with money, weapons and time, the U.S. could cultivate an Asian NATO against China, but time did not seem to be on the US side. China on the other hand would not take chances, hence, was forced to behave more assertively before the Asian NATO really taking form. In the meantime, the 'pivot' strategy is driving Russia to be more aggressive in Eastern Europe and to get closer and warmer to China for mutual benefits. So it is the U.S.'s pivot policy that has created the unfavorable new triangle.

If we could rewind the time back, instead of a 'pivot' strategy, the U.S. could have maintained her attention with NATO and cultivated a somewhat real win-win relationship with China, then Russia would not have taken such aggressive stand and the U.S. and China would have developed a warm great-nation relationship. Under such circumstances, the new triangle would be rotated counterclockwise approximately 60 degree or more with Russia at the bottom carrying the weights of the U.S. and China. In that picture, the US foreign policy would be not only simpler, but more productive and less risky. China would have little reason to accelerate her military strength build-up. Russia would be devoting more energy to her internal economical development. Japan would be less militant and her people less willing to revise their peace constitution. The Diaoyu Islands would not be a hot spot since the United States would not entertain the arguments that Japan had to occupy Diaoyu Islands based on the military strategy in the context of the US-Japan Mutual Defense Treaty to contain China. Japan's territorial ambition towards the Diaoyu Islands would be dashed, since Japan has no legs to stand on from historical facts or from legal arguments. The United States, however, would have an easier task to maintain global peace and prosperity with China positioned on her side in the new triangle.

One cannot rewind the time, but it is never too late to revise an erroneous strategy!

CHAPTER 33

DEMOCRACY IS NOT AN IDEOLOGY BUT A METHOD

FOR ACHIEVING THE GOALS OF IDEOLOGY

—ⱱ—

A COMMON MISTAKE EVEN AMONG scholars is that the word 'democracy' is used as an ideology term rather than a 'method' term for achieving ideological goals. This is often exhibited by phrases such as liberal democracy or social democracy. Liberalism or socialism just like conservatism, capitalism, communism, imperialism or colonialism defines an ideological framework (belief and philosophy) for a human society. In this framework, what and how resources, materials and properties each society member could use, own and share are prescribed, hence, defining a social structure and life style for the society members. Nations as human societies may adopt different or mixed ideologies and employ different methods, such as a dictatorship or a democracy of varying form, to uphold and achieve their ideological goals. In our modern world, members of a society should have (but not always do) adequate political knowledge to define their preferred ideology and to employ an effective method to achieve them.

Democracy is a generic term covering all methods employed by almost all ideological systems and practiced at different levels. Democracy cannot be easily quantified but it can be qualitatively defined in terms of strength. Democracy is the strongest, but most vulnerable (produce divisive and undesirable results), when each society member has the same power and authority in terms of one person one vote for deciding everything. Democracy is less strong, but less vulnerable, when society members have representatives exercising varying degrees of power and authority for them. Democracy is the weakest, nearly nil, in a dictatorship where society members have very little power and authority and the dictator does not want to share authority.

Today, in any country or society, no matter what ideology or multiple ideologies are embraced, the method of democracy is more or less used but practiced fairly differently according to constitutions, laws, by-laws or simply Robert's Rules. Even a government of monarch or a government of communism employs the method of 'democracy' which is operated within its political system with varying degrees of fairness or transparency.

Over the human history, many ideologies have been evolving with time and ideally we hope they can converge to an ideal one acceptable by all people on earth. In the meantime, each country is free to adopt her choice of ideology or ideologies. Democracy as a method existed long ago and in present practice we hope it can be fine-tuned to function effectively in every ideological system.

In ancient China, the emperor has great power; democracy was practiced only in his court. The emperor rarely can arbitrarily enact a law, say taxation, without the consent of the majority of his ministers, but the ministers serve at the emperor's pleasure. So did the practice of democracy in the Roman Empire in its Senate. In modern times, democracy is adopted by nations and defined by their constitutions established with certain assumptions about their national heritage, cultural background and their citizens' aptitude (or knowledge) for democracy. However, the practice of democracy never guarantees perfect results as we have seen recently, regimes collapsed, countries bankrupted and governments disabled all under democracy. The most recent student unrest in Taiwan (supposedly a model democracy in Asia with direct election of a presidency and all administrative and legislative officials) seized and incapacitated its legislative and executive branches of government. In the United States (the pole bearer of democracy with her governments in all levels elected by citizens), however, her two-party system has evolved into rivalry for power, misusing democracy and crippling the federal government and causing many local governments and the Fed to operate under an irresponsible huge budget deficit.

China is essentially a one party system even though her constitution provides her citizens freedom and rights to form other parties. The Chinese Communist Party (CCP) does practice democracy within the party system based on the party's criteria of selecting (and promoting) capable and experienced public servants. Of course, one may question whether the 60 million party members (5% of population) can fairly represent the 1.3 billion citizens? In any democratic representation system, the population is always represented by a small percent of delegates.(For example, only a few hundred federal law makers represent the 350 million Americans). A 5% representation is a large number if it is democratically elected. It seems desirable if the CCP would impose a criterion that its party members must be elected or endorsed by a significant number of citizens in order to be admitted to the party or get promoted to higher offices (rather than an opaque referral or election scheme practiced by old party members), then a single party can be just democratic as a multiple party system in selecting public servants.

Multiple parties are usually created with different ideologies which means the population in a country is divided by different ideologies. Hopefully, the method of democracy will make the parties compromise so that a compromised government can be elected to serve all the people. Ultimately, if the citizens of a country converge to a common ideology, then the multi-party system is equivalent to a one-party system, the democratic election is just a more transparent way of selecting public servants.

Currently, the United States is going through a transformation with forces of different ideologies propelled under democracy. The Americans are divided in ideology by integrating capitalism with liberalism, social liberalism, liberal socialism and conservatism. The convergence to a common or a compromised ideology is very much up in the air depending on the wisdom of American people in defining that compromise. Unfortunately this process seems to be very slow and inefficient.

On the other hand, China is also going through a transformation with multiple ideological forces growing under the one-party system. The CCP party is tweaking to embrace more capitalism (which has helped improving China's economy for the past several decades), modifying socialism (where Marxism has obviously failed), and is gingerly trying to define a Chinese socialism uniquely suited to China to sustain her goal of improving her citizens' standard of living. The Chinese people may ultimately desire to have more democracy (direct one person and one vote, even possible a multiple party system), but they may be wise enough to learn the failures of democracy in other countries and realize that **the democracy is just a method not an ideology and its effectiveness is dependent on the country's**

unique conditions. Only through education, citizens can better understand the trade-off between effectiveness and vulnerability in practicing democracy.

Another political reality hampering the evolvement of a unique effective governing system in China is that she has neighbors who do not wish to see China to become stronger. This can be vividly seen from Japan's behavior in advocating a 'China Threat' and anxiously turning the 'Pivot to Asia Pacific' to a military alliance to limit China's freedom and growth in the region. Japan is nominally governed by multiple parties under democracy, but unfortunately, the Liberal Democratic Party, seemingly to be the only party persistently in power, currently with Abe Shinzo as the Prime Minister, is driving Japan with nationalism and militarism longing for a return to her pre-WW II imperial glory. Whether or not the weak opposition party (Democratic Party of Japan, DPJ) can or will stop Abe's militant agenda is very much in question.

If one would simply compare the economical strength of a few countries, for example, the U.S. China, Japan, and Greece, one could conclude that the different results in national economy are critically dependent on the effectiveness of the government and its leaders in implementing the country's ideological goals. The selection of capable leaders is extremely important but democracy offers no guarantee for a successful selection, more likely, it creates a divided government with divided or conflicting ideological goals.

WILL HILLARY CLINTON WIN THE 2016 UNITED STATES PRESIDENCY? VIEWS OF AMERICANS AND CHINESE AND BOMB SHELL STORIES

—⚏—

THE TITLE TOPIC IS A subject that the mainstream media worldwide will eagerly cover, however, as a presidential candidate to be, Hillary Clinton, as a person with a colorful life and a 'kaleidoscopic' husband, has continuously drawn attention from the organic media, ever since the dawn of the Internet era. Although not officially declared her candidacy, all indications including her effort in publishing her new book, 'Hard Choices', seem to indicate that Hillary is preparing to be a candidate.

American Presidential politics is not only of interest to Americans but also of interest to world citizens, especially China's hundreds of millions of netizens. During the Cold War, prior to the collapse of the Soviet Union, the opinions of certain foreign countries often have an opposite effect on American voters; if China, for instance, expressed negative opinion on an American Presidential candidate, it might actually help the candidate to get more votes when the leadership factor and foreign policy issues were considered. However, in today's world in an internet age, the mainstream media including the official publications may or may not have the final say on a foreign politician. Take Hillary as an example, the mainstream media in the United States has been, in the past, very selective in reporting news or issues related to her, in general, filtering out negative stuff and publishing more positive articles. However, in the organic media especially in the net-world space, it is not always so kind, often digging into her deepest closet on questions probing her personality and private life.

On the other hand, in China, the mainstream media have been portraying Hillary as an unfriendly politician towards China, remembering her poking China on Human Rights issue since 1995 and her siding with Japan in the recent territorial dispute between China and Japan. Hillary is described with a double image; her warm private gestures towards Chinese high officials are contrasted with her public stand, being tough and hostile towards Chinese Administration portraying herself as an assertive and aggressive 'iron lady'. In the Chinese organic media however, the bloggers and vast population of 'weiboers' on the Chinese Internet generally express a good impression of Hillary. The Chinese are very sympathetic to her regarding the Lewinsky affair; they view her as the victim and her handling of her husband's 'indiscretion' admirably. Their impression of her is positive despite of the political pundits' comments on her role as the U.S. Secretary of the State pushing the 'Pivot to Asia' policy with the intent to hurt China. There are more stories praising her as a career woman, pursuing her own goal and a role model in balancing her career and dealing with her 'stressful' marital situation.

In the Internet age, the influence of media on a national election is more powerful and very different from decades ago. Although mainstream media still dominate public opinion but the organic media with viral social (internet based) communication can be detrimental. In the last two American presidential elections, Obama won the election with obvious skill in mastering the Internet media with successful emailing messages and raising funds as well as commanding a well organized web presence. Noteworthy, it has become highly possible that the Internet media can cross national boundaries to influence a foreign election. Therefore, if Hillary begins her presidential campaign, she will have to pay attention to both the mainstream and organic media, domestically and internationally, particularly on China. China is very much on the minds of the American people in their daily lives. Media today, mainstream or organic, can change very fast due to the high speed digital world we live in. Entering the election cycle, it is imperative for any candidate to pay full attention to the media and it is wise for any voter to pay attention as well in order to cast a meaningful vote.

American presidential election is a unique democratic process, an indirect electoral college voting system. Although the election is held as one person one vote, but the victory is not guaranteed by a popular or majority vote. The citizens in each state are really voting for the candidates' electors. The total number of electors is

538, two per Senator representing a state and one per Congressman representing a district plus 3 for the district of Columbia. Electors elect the President and Vice President in the Congress and must vote for the candidate they each represent. All 50 states except Maine and Nebraska, have 'the winner takes all rule', that is, the candidate with highest number of votes will get all the electors in the state to vote for him in Congress. So with multiple candidates, the American President may be elected by a minority of American voters. If more 'comparable weight' candidates would emerge from more than two major parties, an elected American President more likely would have only a minority of supporters.

What is the chance of Hillary Clinton winning the 2016 presidential election then? Presently there are more than two dozen names touted as potential presidential candidates in the US Democratic Party alone and possibly as many in the Republican Party. Hillary is far out in the front from name recognition point of view but she is also the target for spears or smears and bombshells. Her ambition for the presidency was obvious from her 2008 bid and her service as the Secretary of State added some weight to her political credential - First Lady (1993-2001) and Senator (2001-2009 New York). She was low key in her Senate tenure building relations, but as the head of the State Department she was put on a test. As a presidential candidate she will face a number of potential bomb shells throughout her campaign.

Hillary will be 69 if elected to serve the presidency. There were concerns about her health even with 'rumors' of suffering brain damage. Then there was talk about her unflattering personality possibly described in a book to be published by a secret agent. Furthermore, some tabloids are already saying about her being a lesbian, although, some would argue that in today's American culture, it might not necessarily be a bombshell. Rather, it might even help her if she would come out of the closet clearing herself in her new book.

The real significant bombshell perhaps is hidden in Hillary's ability of dealing with foreign affairs. Her handling of the Benghazi incidence had already drawn an investigation from the Congress. It might evolve into a bombshell so might be the charge of her misplacing funds in the State Department. Hillary barely gets a passing grade for her tenure in the State Department even though she suffered through a brutal and aging travel schedule. (See for example, Walter Russell Mead,

Washington Post Opinions, 5/30/2014 and Jonathan Tkachuk, Politics, 2/1/2013). Hillary is an American exceptionalist. She Mixes her belief of the U.S. being the force for progress, prosperity and peace and her emphasis of 'Human Rights', 'Democracy' and 'active support for civil society organizations' in her push for the geopolitical 'pivot to Asia' policy. She has produced an unnecessarily complicated situation in Asia for the State Department and the Obama Administration. China and Russia responded harshly to the 'pivot'. China's neighbors had been overly agitated to inflame the territorial disputes in the East and South China Seas like hot potatoes now tossed to the United States. The situation with China in the coming year is not predictable but it will have an impact on the American presidential election. Barring another crisis in the US economy, the US-China relationship and US China policy may surface to the top of the issue list of the 2016 US presidential election. Even with her experience as the Secretary of the State, she will be debated and drilled in depth on China policy since China is very much on Americans' minds.

WHY AMERICANS NEED TO UNDERSTAND THE REAL CHINA ISSUE? - WATCH THE HISTORICAL VISIT OF ZHANG ZHIJUN TO MEET WANG YOICHI IN TAIWAN

—⚏—

THE HYPE OF 'CHINA THREAT' promoted by some right-wing political pundits in the United States and in Japan has created some serious confusion for Americans. The current Japanese Administration's eagerness in promoting the China Threat theory is unfortunate but an obvious extension from the old Imperial and militant Japanese notion that Japan would be able to stand up on the world stage as a great power only if she could conquer China or at least control her. This notion should have been totally demolished after Japan's defeat in WW II, but the internal split of China and subsequent division of the world by a cold war kept the Japanese right-wing faction of the Imperialists fantasizing a dream to return Japan to her pre-WW II glory and still wishing China to be weak and vulnerable to the Japanese ambition.

The elements in the United States touting the idea that the US domestic problems are somehow caused by the rise of China and her rise would be a national security threat to the U.S. are clearly based on some false assumptions. Their instigation to or alliance with the right-wing Japanese Imperialists in promoting 'China Threat' has caused confusion among American people in understanding and interpreting the US-Japan mutual defense treaty and the US-China relationship. The media seems to be filled more with one-sided reports, projecting China to be an enemy to the American people with no justification and making the real China issue a confused subject to the American people.

As an organic medium, this column will be devoted to the question what is the real China issue to Americans and why Americans need to understand it?

China started a revolution 125 years later than the American revolution to get away from an impotent imperial system to establish a republic nation with western political philosophy. Her first naïve revolution in 1889 failed and her second revolution in 1911 partially succeeded by toppling the Qing Dynasty but failed to unite the factions in China. This revolution is hampered and prolonged by the presence of eight foreign powers in China at the time. In particular, Japan was destined to stop the Chinese revolution and conquer China. Japanese waged wars against China lasted nearly a decade ended in 1945. The United States although was a part of the eight foreign powers in China, her relationship with China was the friendliest among the eight powers due to her sympathetic attitude towards China's revolution. The founding father of the second Chinese revolution, Dr. Sun Yat Sen*(1855-1925), educated in the United States (attended elementary (1879-1882) and high school (1883), later known as Panahou* High School, in Honolulu where Obama graduated in 1979), exposed to Christianity, baptized and developed his Three Principles of People, had a lot to do with getting American support of the Chinese (or Dr. Sun's) revolution. When the eight foreign powers defeated Qing army and looted Beijing including the Imperial Garden, the resulting unequal treaty required China to offer territorial concessions and to pay 450 million ounces of silver (one ounce per one Chinese) to the eight nations (in 37 years). The United States later had agreed to use her share of the money to support Chinese students coming to the United States for studies. This gesture was long remembered by the Chinese through Chinese history books.

After WW II ended, China's revolution continued with the Soviet Union backing Mao and the United States backing Chiang who then lost the mainland to Mao in 1949 and retreated to Taiwan. The recent history of the two parts of China was by no means simple and independent of each other. The mainland China adopted communism as a member of the Soviet Union and experimented with communism. After failing to make progress to raise the mainland from deep poverty, the Chinese Communist Party (CCP) departed from the communist union essentially breaking away from the Soviet Union in 1960's and pursued socialism with partial experimentation with capitalism. Despite of her involvement in the Korean War and Vietnam War, the mainland China had principally adhered to her desire and policy to focus on her own domestic problems and economy. This is evident from the way she exited the wars. Through her decades of hard work, the mainland China has risen in economical strength, remarkably becoming the second largest economy in the world.

The United States had continued in support of the KMT government in Taiwan as part of the strategy of stemming the spread of communism. With the aid from the U.S. and her own practice of the Three Principles of People, Taiwan has emerged as a significant economic power in Asia with a democratically elected government. However, politically Taiwan had a major setback and was replaced by Mainland China in the United Nations. The United States encouraged Taiwan to be independent. However, Taiwan was intrinsically not interested to be totally in-dependent from Mainland especially if the coercion for independence came from a third country such as Japan or the United States, not grounded purely in the in-terests of Chinese people from a historical perspective. The historical incomplete revolution started by Dr. Sun Yet Sen, (who is recognized as the founding father of modern China by both Mainland and Taiwan), and the common cultural inheri-tance of the people are the intrinsic bonding force to move them towards unifica-tion by expecting adjustments in their political systems, resisting vicious external influence otherwise.

Nixon and Kissinger understood the above background hence adopted the one China policy leaving the Taiwan issue vaguely defined. They made the historical visit to China opening a new chapter for the US-China relationship. The result is an ever growing economic tie between the two nations. After the Cold War ended and the Soviet Union collapsed, the US-Taiwan mutual defense treaty strategic for stemming the spread of communism is no longer significant. **The real China issue for the United States today is how to guide the Chinese reunification process** so that the U.S. remains the friendly ally with the United China and together to main-tain world peace and prosperity and together to deal with the nuclear threat, the resurgence of ambitious militant governments and the terror groups, and to culti-vate a symbiotic economic relationship. The 'China blaming' and 'military threat' from China are false theories, really having no place in the US-China relationship. (Meaningless military data quoted by 'Target China' advocates, for example, is the number of aircraft carriers in the world (in service/under construction): US (19/3), India (2/2), Japan (2.1), China (1/2) and S. Korea (1/1))

At the juncture of another historical minister level visit by Zhang Zhijun (Chief, Taiwan-Mainland Affairs (Unification) Office in Beijing) to meet Mr Wang Yoichi (Chief, Mainland-Taiwan Affairs (Unification) Office in Taipei) in Taiwan, the Director of American Institute of Taiwan, Mr. Christopher J. Marut, representative of the United Stated, **should take keen interest and initiative to participate in this event and exert any positive influence possible to the Chinese reunification process** for the benefits of improving the US-China relationship and for the sake of forming a partnership in maintaining a peaceful world.

* Sun Yat Sen and His Education

Dr. Sun Yat Sen (1866-1925) was born in Guanzhou, China. He was sent to Hawaii to live with his elder brother to get an education. He attended the Lolani school (1879-1882) where he learned English and the elementary studies, then attended the Oahu College(1883), a college prep school now known as Punahou High School. Punahou, an excellent school in Hawaii, produced, for example in 2013, 20 National Merit Semifinalists and 5 of 10 Hawaii's National Merit Scholars. President Barack Obama was a graduate of Punahou in 1979 among 26 alumni who went to Ivy League Colleges that year. According to an alumnus report, Punahou's 1979 class eventually achieved 15 PhD, 22 MD, 39 JD, ... An impressive record for the school. Dr. Sun had a great attachment to Hawaii, he once said: "Here (Hawaii) I was brought up and educated, and it was here that I came to know what modern governments are like and what they mean."

Dr. Sun only attended Punahou for one semester and was sent back to China by his brother to get a non-Christian education, but fate had him to complete high school in Hong Kong and pursued medical studies at Canton Boji Hospital (1886) under Director Dr. John Kerr, an American doctor and a Presbyterian missionary to China. Dr. Sun obtained his MD from Hong Kong College of Medicine for Chinese in 1892, one of two graduated among 12 medical students. Dr. Sun accepted the Christian faith and was baptized at the Congregational Church of the United States in Hong Kong. Christianity had a great influence in his life;

he eventually devoted his life totally to the Chinese revolution. His American Christian friends would say that he applied the missionary spirit to his revolution to save China from an unprecedented turmoil.

CHAPTER 36

JAPAN FAST COPYING PRESIDENT OBAMA

IN CIRCUMVENTING DEMOCRACY

—ᴍᴠ—

IN ONE OF MY COLUMNS, "Democracy - Not An Ideology But A Method For Achieving The Goals of Ideology", I have made the point that ideology is more important as a goal and democracy is a tool which may be applied in various ways, from one man one vote to different representation schemes. The constitution defines and protects the ideological goal and the democratic method in safeguarding the constitution and specifying the procedure to make amendments in the constitution. In the United States, a country proud of her democracy, a congress with two houses of representation and the presidency elected by a electoral college is well defined in her constitution. An independent Supreme Court is given the authority to interpret the constitution. Is the American system perfect, probably not, but it worked well for over two centuries. The Presidents (the administration) and the Congress representatives elected by the American citizens served well under the constitution in a balanced power.

Now, we seem to see the imperfections in the democratic system of the United States. On a closer look, it may not be the problem with the democratic system but with the political parties or politicians participating in the system. When the two parties shifted their ideology to two polarized notions, the congress becomes dysfunctional. Legislative process bogs down. The President even elected by a popular vote is stuck with the feuding Congress, two houses controlled by the two polarized parties. In this situation, the President must be exerting his or her leadership and political skills to get the Congress to cooperate or to compromise to get things done. The American constitution has a secure lock to protect the nation and the constitution itself, it requires 2/3 (34) of the 50 states to pass in their legislatures to call for a constitution convention to make amendments or proposals to dissolve any part of the Federal government. This high threshold is necessary to maintain a stable government and a stable constitution.

Obama won his second term as the 57th US President in 2012; this election also helped his party (Democrat) to gain seats in both Chambers of the Congress. However the gain in the Senate, Democrat versus Republican (51+2:47-2) with 2 Independents, and in the House, Republican versus Democrat (340-8:198+8), still presents Obama a challenge to face a Republican controlled House. Out of frustration, Obama had used the recess of the Congress to make his appointments bypassing the Congress; he had declared in a White House strategic meeting that the administration needed to more aggressively use executive power to govern in the face of Congressional obstructionism. "We had been attempting to highlight the inability of Congress to do anything," recalled William M. Daley, the White House chief of staff at the time. "The president expressed frustration, saying we have got to scour everything and push the envelope in finding things we can do on our own. In his Jan 28/2014 address to the joint session of Congress, he essentially said he will use his pen to chip away at his agenda in 2014. Again on June 30th, 2014, he said, "I will bypass Congress to fix immigration." After the mid-term election, both Houses of Congress in the U.S. turned Republican, Obama faces even more challenges in pushing his agenda.

This attitude, behavior and action of the U.S. President have a profound impact on the leaders of other nations, especially Japan. Sure enough, the Prime Minister of Japan, Shinzo Abe, the right wing leader in Japan is fast copying Obama's playbook to circumvent Democracy except that Abe was more vicious than Obama and likely to succeed. This must be explained in detail.

Japan is a democratic country with her constitution very much modeled on the US constitution defining their lower House of Representatives and the upper House of Councilors, similar to the US House and Senate. The Japanese constitution also contains a high threshold for making amendments, requiring 2/3 approval of both houses and a supermajority vote of the people. One unique article in the Japanese Peace Constitution is that Japan shall never wage war or settle issues via military action. The Japanese constitution assures Japan will never fall into the mind-set like the Japanese Imperial Army which invaded China and conquered the rest of Asia resulting in a disastrous WW II with atrocities to this day unforget-table and unforgivable by Asian countries as victims of the Imperial Japan.

Shinzo Abe, a nationalistic conservative became the new leader of Japan's right wing. From his public statements and policies, he appears to be a master of double-faced politician destined to bring Japan back to her pre-war glory. The first image he projects to the United States is that Japan is depending on the US-Japan Defense Treaty for her national security. He is drumming the "China Threat" the-ory and pleading to the U.S. for more weapons and support on Japan's territorial dispute with China. The second image he projects to Japan is that he is the PM to make Japan a 'normal country' again, to build up military strength commencing to her economic power and to defend for herself since the U.S. is weakening – a clear double talk. Abe's double images are not foreign to political analysts in the U.S. and worldwide. As recent as 7/1/2014, A New York Times Article by Martin Fackler and David Sanger, Japan Announces a Military Shift to Thwart China, has essentially covered all the facts leading to the above conclusion.

How does Abe circumvent Democracy then? Whether he is inspired by Obama's speeches or not, he is having a similar attitude except he has the majority of the Japanese Congress under his Liberal Democratic Party. He has advocated to revis-ing the Japanese peace constitution in a wholesale manner to allow building up Japan's offensive military power and to permit Japan to make first strike against other nations. This is such a drastic departure from Pacifism; the Japanese citizens would not support it especially if they had understood Abe's double images. Abe recognizes his obstacles and understands that he will never be able to cross the high threshold for making a constitutional amendment. Therefore, he is inspired (by Obama?) to circumvent Democracy. Instead of pursuing constitutional amend-ment which the Japanese people will not support, he is using his executive power to make the Japanese Congress to reinterpret the Article 9 in the Japanese constitu-tion. Since he has the control of the majority in the Congress, he has just gotten his way of reinterpreting the Japanese constitution. Now Japan is permitted to use its large and technologically advanced armed forces in ways that would have been un-thinkable a decade ago. With this reinterpretation, Japan is able to forge military alliances with other Asian nations such as Philippines and Vietnam to apply more assertive actions in their dispute over Diaoyu, Spratly and Scarborough Shoal in the South and East China seas.

As the promoter of Democracy, any circumvention of democracy will haunt the United States. Any issue not able to cross over the threshold of dissolving the Congress or amending the Constitution must be dealt with under the existing Congress and Constitution. The executive branch cannot bypass the Constitution or the Congress to cheat the people. Obama's endorsing Abe's actions is a huge mistake, disrespect to Democracy and a blind eye to the rising of a dangerous Japan threatening the world peace again.

CHAPTER 37

A STABLE WORLD UNDER THE

THREE-LEGGED DING STRUCTURE

—⟋⟍—

THE 'DING' IS AN ANCIENT design of a container supported with three legs. Various sizes and patterns were made for different purposes such as small wine cups, medium cooking utensils and large urns used in temples for religious ceremony. Any Ding picture is just one example of many different Dings illustrating the fact that a massive brass urn can be stably supported by three legs. A famous Chinese idiom, stability under balanced three legs, was derived from the Ding structure to describe the situation of the Middle Kingdom (China) being controlled by three balanced power, Wei, Han and Wu during the period of year 220-280. Imagine the Ding being a globe (the world) supported on three legs, so long the three legs are similarly strong, then the Ding will be stable. As long as none of the legs was weakened, the Ding could hold huge quantity of goods and its heavy weight would make itself very stable. We may use this Ding as a metaphor to describe today's world in the following discussion.

Ever since the end of WW II, the United States as the leader of the Allies has emerged to be a superpower carrying the mission and responsibility of maintaining order and peace in the world. This mission was partially self-assigned and partially bestowed by nations around the world recovering from the devastating World War II, except those nations adopted communism opposing the ideology of capitalism. Communism as an ideological concept does have its appeal but it is in direct conflict with the free capitalism which the U.S. embraces along with most of the Western European countries, many of them happened to be the more developed nations. The communist countries under the leadership of USSR formed a union, the Soviet Union, trying to develop them under communism. However, parts of communism are fundamentally in conflict with human nature of desiring freedom and control over private possessions. History had borne out; communism eventually failed resulting in the collapse of the Soviet Union. Country like China, which experimented with communism and recognized her failure, had departed early enough (1961) from the Soviet Union and mixed capitalism with socialism for her economical development and nation building. As China has now emerged as the world's second largest economy, it lends a proof that nation building cannot follow a rigid ideology. A nation must adopt and tailor her development to suit the country's historical inheritance and geopolitical characteristics.

The United States, carrying the banner of safeguarding the world peace, has been acting more unilaterally than perhaps she should in dealing with world conflicts and crises. In international affairs or any other business, unilateral actions always produce resentment, even when the cause was just and the end result successful. When the cause was perceived as controversial and the end result was messy, then the resentment would drive a wedge deeper into the differences. The Soviet Union had always taken the position to counter the unilateral actions of the United States, but the two legs (the two camps of the Cold War) just won't support the Ding (world) stably. The instability would create a stressful world. When one of the two legs was getting weaker faster than the other from constant posturing, a situation had made the United States, the other leg, to continue on her unilateral practice in foreign policies to deal with the world problems.

It turns out free capitalism has its own defects and weaknesses as well. Even with the collapse of the communist union, the world has developed many problems manifested as bubbles (energy, financial, real estate, etc) ready to burst, many nations, including the United States, are having unsustainable economy. The United States has her advantage of being able to raise unlimited debt by printing the US dollars and being militarily strong to avoid direct challenge to her national debt financing. However, the world Ding can never be stable under one leg, more so if the leg is also losing strength in a financial sense and the resentment is continuously brewing. This was evident recently from more messes that the United States had to deal with or left behind.

The foreign policies the United States conducted are largely based on the 'carrot and deterrent' strategy, it worked fine when the United States had plenty of carrots and the US military strength held an absolute upper hand over all other nations combined. Deterrent worked most of the time under such conditions. In today's situation, although the United States is still a superpower, she needs to reevaluate her foreign policy seriously for the sake of her future and the world peace. There seems to be three options for the United States to pursue but only one beneficial:

Option I, Continuing the Carrot and Deterrent Strategy and maintaining the role as the sole world order keeper with freedom to take unilateral action. This strategy requires lots of money and a sustainable strong US economy to maintain a superior military. For all indications, this does not seem to be a sustainable strategy, if the U.S. is seriously concerned with her welfare for her future generations. Practicing this unsustainable strategy, the world peace would be in jeopardy.

Option II, Adopting a 'retreat' strategy and disengaging from world conflicts and crises. This strategy may help the United States to mend her domestic problems and to nurse her economy back to health. However, the world is already in an acute mess. Retreating abruptly will create vacuum and dislocations which most likely would cause the world to implode or explode to serious disasters, compelling the United States to step in from the sideline.

Option III, Aligning with two strong partners, namely China and Russia, and creating a stable Ding for the world. The Ding picture may be the answer. By creating three strong legs to support the heavy world burden so the world will be stable. By giving up the unilateral freedom in exchange for sharing the responsibility of maintaining world order so the world will be peaceful. The 'carrot and deterrent' would be still effective with most world problems, if the three legs were balanced with skillful diplomacy. After all, other than the singular issue – different regime structures exist in the three nations, the three legs face a set of common problems: 1. Maintaining a healthy economical growth, 2. Dealing with terrorists threat coming from a common source, 3. Managing nuclear threat and proliferation, 4. Sharing resources (energy and material) for mutual benefits and 5. Avoiding a runaway situation of arms race.

Pondering on the above options, it is not difficult to arrive at the Op III. President Obama had already questioned the viability of Option I; he also had enough info and warning regarding Option II. What he and his peer leaders must do is to develop a thorough plan based on Option III. I urge all think tanks around the world to chime in on this for the sake of the future of humankind.

CHAPTER 38

BIPOLAR (HEGEMONY) AND MULTI-POLAR

(POST-HEGEMONY) WORLD VIEW AND FOREIGN POLICY

—m—

POLITICAL SCIENTISTS AND ANALYSTS, WHETHER or not truly believed in the Hegemony Theory for describing the superpower behavior in the world arena, find the word hegemony a convenient term to use from time to time in the analysis of a bipolar world charged with a Cold War. As the collapse of the Soviet Union supposedly ended the Cold War and possibly changed the bipolar confrontation in the world, there seems to be looming a new Cold War except in a multi-polar confrontation format. This author finds the term, hegemony, to be the easiest short-hand to demarcate the timeline before the Cold War and after, a transition from a bipolar to multi-polar political world. Hence the title was used for this article.

No matter what term is used in the description of the world's affairs, the United States is the principal player either in a bipolar view or multi-polar view. Some would claim that the United States had made her territorial expansion only prior to become a superpower, such as revolution against the British, wars against the Spanish and the Mexicans, or integration absorbing the natives in the US Continent or in the Hawaii Islands. She gained the status of the world's superpower after WW II, her behavior since then was acting as a world order keeper and a defender for Democracy. Post WW II, the communism as an ideology flourished and forged the Soviet Union creating a bipolar political world with the United States and her allies as one camp against the Soviet Union the other camp. However, others would claim that the United States as a superpower acted unilaterally in settling world's affairs like hegemony. She had expanded her influence over the world through establishing pro-US regimes and binding them with military treaties. The United

States had rarely used the United Nation to settle things, rather more through her military intervention and economic and financial sanctions.

Whatever interpretations one chose to believe in, the bare facts of today's world are the following:

1. Cold War ended with the collapse of the Soviet Union. The disastrous economic performance spelled out the doom of pure communism, revisions and transformations became inevitable.
2. The bipolar confrontation was proven unsustainable, not only fatal for the Soviet Union but also exhausting to the United States. Maintaining a 'hegemony' control over the allies is too expensive to be sustainable.
3. Democracy cannot be exported as an ideology. It has to be used flexibly as a method for making decisions under various stable ideological systems. The economical collapse of Greece and troubles in other democratic nations and turmoil of uprisings in many smaller nations in the name of democracy are obvious problems of today's world.
4. The rapid rise of China and the wakeup of Russia, India, Japan, Brazil, etc. have shown that we are now in a multi-polar political world. Supremacy as a single dominating nation (hegemony) is not sustainable nor desirable. The United States, though still the world's number one economy, is seen declining. Nuclear deterrence has limited effectiveness. Pushing democracy has become synonymous with 'creating political chaos and/or economic disaster', witnessing several democratic nations having dysfunctional government unable to function with a heavy national debt.
5. The multi-polar world is forming with more emerging countries demanding voice. The establishment of a BRICS development bank for financing infrastructure projects (competitor to the Washington based World Bank and IMF) is likely to have its headquarter in Shanghai, its first President from India, first Board Chair from Brazil and a regional center in South Africa with an initial capital of $50B equally funded and a contingent reserve of $100B contributed by China ($41B), S. Africa ($5B) and the rest three each $18B.

Based on the above facts and observation, it is clear that the great nations must pursue a new formula in managing affairs in the multi- polar world. In this new formula, the United States still has a pivoting role, however, a single-minded strategy, a unilateral behavior pattern and selecting partners based on 'national security' and US interest only would not work in the multi-polar world. Singling China out as the enemy of the United States is not only erroneous but dangerous. Russia shredded the bondage of pure communism now has a new view of the world especially towards Asia. Japan, no longer content with being a protected and obedient US ally, is perking up an ambition not at all aligned with the interests of the United States or anyone else in Asia or in the world. India, another big nation in Asia, is rapidly emulating China to project her growth. The European Union after suffering from the economic crisis has also emerged quickly with a multi-polar view of the world. Germany, in particular, the fourth largest economy in the world, is quick to recognize China as her most important 'economic' partner in the future.

The United States, of course, is in the midst of these changes and must be acutely aware of what is really happening in the world. However, a troubling phenomenon is that the thoughts of the old school from the bi-polar world and the Cold War era seem to be still dominating the fora of the US foreign policy and national security. In the multi-polar world, the aspiring first tier nations mentioned above will try to hold their poles. The second and third tier nations now have a wider sphere or freedom to select the poles to align with, a very different scenario from the time in the bipolar world. The United States was able to get many countries to join under her flag more or less based on her strategic interest alone, perhaps with a little carrot in the form of "aid" or 'market'. Today more carrots are available in the multi-polar world; therefore, it is not as simple for the United States to fill her camp with the first, second or even third tier nations. More carrots are required to build foreign relations today, but the United States can no longer afford.

One can never overstate the most significant point that the United States can no longer build allies based on her own strategic interest alone. The US national security concern, viewed as coinciding with the national security concern of the second and third tier nations in the bipolar world, may not be accepted easily by the other nations now due to geopolitical considerations. Partnering with a pole-bearing great nation is far more practical in constructing foreign relations with smaller nations. Naturally, the selection of a right partner and sharing a common security concern are critical. For example, in the most important Pivot to Asia strategy, picking a wrong partner, Japan, formulating a false common national security concern and trying to ally with all second and third tier nations against a rising China, their major trading partner, are strategically wrong, likely an idea coming from old thoughts derived from the Cold War in the bipolar world! Hence, it is imperative to bring the new multi-polar world view immediately to the US mainstream media, to stimulate an overhaul of the US foreign policy including the 'pivot' strategy and to right the wrongs for the sake of peace and prosperity in Asia, the United States and the world.

DOES LEADER'S DREAM MATCH PEOPLE'S DREAM?

COMPARING ABE, PUTIN AND XI'S DREAMS

—∭—

LET'S REVIEW THE BIOGRAPHIC INFORMATION of the three world leaders before discussing the subject – does the leader's dream match the people's dream?

Shinzo Abe, 60, the current Prime Minister and leader of Japan's Liberal Democratic Party (LDP), came from a lineage of Japanese political families who were closely associated with the Japanese Imperial Army responsible for the invasion of China, attack of the Pearl Harbor and the WW II in Asia Pacific. Shinzo's father Shintaro was the longest serving Foreign Minister (1982-1986) and a leading member of LDP. His grandfather, Kan, was a house representative (1937-1946) of Yamaguchi Prefecture, a strong base of Japanese conservatives. Shinzo's maternal grandfather, Nobusuke Kishi, Prime Minister (1957-1960), was a member of the Tojo (WW II criminal sentenced to death) cabinet. After being released from prison, Kishi formed the anti-communist Japanese Democratic Party which eventually merged with the Liberal party to become the LDP. So Shinzo came to power owing a lot to his inheritance rather than his own ability. He graduated with a political science degree from Seikei University (1977) and continued studies at the University of Southern California but dropped out in 1979. After three years of work at Kobe Steel, he went into politics and grew like a vine clinging to the LDP. He became the PM in 2006 but his short-lived first PM tenure failed. He became the PM again in 2012 and enjoyed the backing of the extreme right-wing conservatives and the people who were disappointed by Japan's decade long stagnant economy. Abe's dream is to return Japan to her pre-war glory.

Vladimir Putin, 62, the current President of Russia for a six-year term (2012-). He served as the Prime Minister (1999-2000), President of two 4-year terms (2000-2008), the Prime Minister again (2008-2012) and as the chairman of Russian Communist party. In his reign from 1999-2008, Russia's GDP rose 72%, wage tripled (real income 2.5X) owing to a flat 13% tax and the reform of Russia's military, police and the energy policies. Russia is an energy superpower and a developed country today. Putin came from an ordinary family, mother a factory worker, father a navy sailor and grandma a chef. He worked for KGB 16 years gathering intelligence then went into politics from his home state St. Petersburg then to Moscow. A charismatic person who is interested in sports (Sambo and Judo) and exhibits a strong will. Vladimir Putin's dream is to build and sustain a strong Russia.

Jinping Xi, 61, the President of the People's Republic of China, Chairman of Central Military Commission and General Secretary of the Chinese Communist Party, is the son of a revolutionary hero; his father, Zongxun, rose to a high level in the communist party but also was demoted and punished by the party which affected Xi's youth years. He was not admitted to the CCP until 21. His father was eventually exonerated but Xi made his advances through hard work from the bottom, having the experience of hardship and close connection with ordinary people. When Xi was 10, his father was purged and sent to work in a factory in Luoyang, Henan. At 13 (1966), Xi's secondary education was cut short by the Cultural Revolution. At 15, his father was jailed and Xi went to work in Yanchuan County, Shaanxi, one of the poorer provinces in China. He later became the Party branch secretary of the production team. Xi studied chemical engineering (1975-1979) at Tsinghua, a Chinese prestigious university. Xi went through the rigorous selection and evaluation process of the CCP serving at various levels of governments to prove his ability. He has personally endured the hardship and mishap under China's early communism and later reform process. He is keenly aware of the continued transformation the CCP needed. Xi's dream is modest, simply to double the living standards of the majority of 1.3 billion Chinese who still live below the standard of the developed world.

Knowing the background of the above leaders, we can then analyze further whether their dreams match their people's dreams. Abe appears to be brought up with 'brain wash' from his ancestors and their war-time associates. Abe's dream can be revealed from his public statements, notably 'to restore Japan's past glory (his family's honor)'. Hence, not surprisingly, he is denying the WW II history, worshipping war criminals at Yasukuni Shrine and in his book published in 2006 saying that Class A war criminals (who were adjudicated in the Tokyo Tribunal after World War II) were not war criminals in the eye of domestic law. His political goal had always been to build up Japan's military strength. He attempted to revise the Japanese peace constitution to allow Japan to make first strike with Japan's self-defense army. Recognizing that he could not get the needed support of 2/3 of Congress, he cleverly made the cabinet to reinterpret the Article 9 of the constitution instead, essentially giving him the freedom to attack first in the name of defending any of Japan's allies.

Japanese per capita income is one of the highest in the world, the people is living peacefully and contently. The ordinary Japanese is not interested in becoming militaristic or subjecting Japan to war. Despite of Abe's effort in pumping nationalism or his brand of patriotism into Japanese youth, his dream obviously does not align with the dream of peace-loving Japanese, an aging population simply want to keep what they have and live in a peaceful society with job opportunities.

The majority of Chinese people has a similar dream but with a lower expectation due to their worse situation measured by the standard of living. The Chinese had suffered many decades of hardship and they simply want to work hard to improve their lives. Xi had personally lived through the same hardship with the vast majority of Chinese. In his youth, Xi worked with the poorest peasants and was one of them; hence he could identify, understand and share fully with the Chinese people's dream, a dream to elevate them from poverty, to have a little higher standard of living even still far below that of the Japanese or Americans. Thus Xi sets a goal of doubling their per capita income by 2020 as the main thrust of Chinese dream.

Putin as a strong leader, having had a successful record in the past, also understands his people's dream for job opportunity and economic development. He and Xi are realists pursuing practical dreams aligned with their people's dreams; this is different from Abe's dream which is more driven by a family mandate and a right-wing ideology to restore "Japan's past glory" rather than fulfilling the Japanese people's peaceful dream. Putin and Xi seemed to desire political stability (no external influence or crisis) in order to pursue economic development whereas Abe seemed to welcome world crisis so Japan could have an opportunity to build and exert her military strength.

Xi understands that the economic goal of doubling per capita income could not be achieved if corruption would take away all the gain. Hence he must deal with corruption as a first priority. Through Chinese modern history, he also understands clearly that China needs political stability, no external influence or agitation, in order to sustain economic growth to realize the Chinese dream. Hence, his pledge of China will be rising peacefully is genuine.

Following the above discussion and assessing the current events, it seems that the United States, partnering with Japan in drumming up a 'China Threat' war game, is either making a gross mistake or executing a devious strategy playing right into Abe's dream rather than righteously standing behind the Chinese and Japanese people's peaceful dreams. What is the dream of Americans? Igniting WW III? I don't think so!

CHAPTER 40

BAD ATTITUDES IMPACTING THE US-CHINA RELATIONSHIP

—w—

AUGUST 17, 2013 WAS THE date the first issue of US-China Forum was published. August 9, 2014, marks the 52nd issue or the end of the first year of this weekly publication. August 16, 2014 will begin a new year for this forum. Although this column, Mainstream and Organic, did not begin till October 12, 2013, but I felt equally excited to celebrate the first anniversary of this forum along with its founders, a group of dedicated volunteers - American citizens with Chinese roots, devoting their time and energy to the concerns and issues related to the US-China Relationship. Some political analysts have said that the US-China relation is the most important foreign relation (for the U.S. and China) in the 21st century with profound impact to the future of our world. I agree wholeheartedly with that statement.

Today at the anniversary of US-China Forum, I would like to discuss, what I believe, the 'bad' attitudes that will have a profound 'bad' impact on the US-China relationship. Since correcting 'these bad attitudes' may improve US-China Relationship and for the better of the world's future, let us look at the bad attitudes from the points of view of the United States and China separately. If this column would draw further discussions on 'bad attitudes' it will be a good thing.

US ATTITUDES THAT HARM US-CHINA RELATION

1. Hostile attitude towards China now bubbling over to hating the Chinese: It has been commonplace in the mainstream media for right-leaning political strategists to hypothesize China as the target enemy of the U.S. The

effect is devastating to the US-China relationship. Recently, in Fox News, "The Five" program, Bob Beckel in a surprising hate-crime like gesture and mannerism claiming the Chinese people being the single greatest threat to the United States; it typifies what consequences the hostile attitude towards China will fest in the US-China relation. Beckel has no credible reason or proof for making such hatred racial remarks and he deserves to be fired by Fox News as demanded by the Chinese American communities and those Americans having adopted Chinese children.

2. Demonizing Chinese students who are studying in the U.S.: Regardless whether or not some of the students are descendants of Chinese communist party officials. These innocent students are here to be educated. They came with an open heart if not an open mind to appreciate the US culture. It is an opportunity for the U.S. to educate them to become future leaders of a modern China.

3. Different attitudes towards China and Japan in the 'Pivot to Asia Pacific' policy: These attitudes must be fair and sincere to involve China as a partner not as a targeted enemy. Pitting Japan against China is an evil attitude no different from agitating Muslims against Jews or blacks against whites. Cooperating with all major powers in Asia especially China is the right approach not only for a great US-China relation but also for a stable Asia.

4. Conducting military exercises with neighboring countries of China to intimidate China into an arms race or to raise tension in the disputed Islands such as Diaoyu: However, a recent exercise inviting China to participate is a right approach provided it is a sincere gesture to correct the mistake and improve the understanding between the military forces. The collapse of the Soviet Union can't be simply interpreted as the outcome of a successful armed race. To induce China to an arms race is a bad attitude. The outcome of such a new arms race is unpredictable.

5. Influencing and controlling Asian organizations such as ASEAN: ASEAN has ten member countries and ten Dialogue Partners with good reasons. Today, not many countries want to see a bi-polar world forcing them to choose one camp or the other. Keeping open-mindedness towards creating multi-national alliances offers more transparency than having multiple bilateral secret agreements. There is no good reason for the U.S. to create a TPP excluding any Asia-Pacific member, China, in particular.

CHINA'S ATTITUDES THAT HARM US-CHINA RELATION

1.   Close-mindedness towards Western culture: Not everything from the West is degrading moral standards and causing social problems even though sex, drugs and divorces, have been overly perpetrated by the US soft power - media. Open communication and let people raise their awareness and ability to make their own judgment will be good for US-China relation. Let the 'Love America' (people want to come to the U.S. and invest their money there) and 'Hate America' (Chinese remembered being discriminated and humiliated in the U.S. in her early history and to some extent still so today and those dislike to be targeted as the enemy) naturally reconcile by open discussion on the history of the US-China relationship over the past one and half century so that the biased attitudes could be eliminated.

2.   Interpreting WW II and post-war history in a closed world only in Mandarin: Open all state secrets and let the Western world know the truth and the feelings of Chinese being victimized by various unfair treaties (imposed on China by the West and Japan) for more than a century. Let Americans understand the desire of Chinese to recover their losses in respect and sovereignty.

3.   Unhealthy attitude towards the US debt held by China: Stop boasting that China is the largest holder of the US debt. Recalling that China through the 1901 unequal treaty had to pay war reparation of 450 million taels (40 grams) of silver, one tael ($26) per citizen and China paid it. With US GDP, assets and wealth, there is no reason she cannot pay her debts through financial arrangements. Currency war can lead to real war. The new development bank of BRICS should be a complimentary and cooperative bank working with the World Bank to maintain financial stability for the development world.

4.   Complaining openly that the U.S. might not be able to repay her debt to China: China should think creative ways of using the debt money. Recall that part of the war reparation paid to the U.S. at the beginning of last century was used to set up a scholarship trust supporting Chinese students to study in the U.S., the trust money had educated many Chinese to become elite members of the Chinese societies. The U.S. could afford then and was willing to offer the reparation money back to China for scholarships to sow good seeds in the US-China relation and it did. China can also afford to

use part of the US debt money in terms of the treasury notes in her hand to set up scholarships for American students to study in China. The American people need to know more about China such as the atrocities committed by the Japanese imperial Army, the US-China comradeship during the war and the legal implication that the Potsdam Declaration by which Japan surrendered really means. Understanding the facts in history will make issues such as the Diaoyu Island dispute with Japan a non-issue.

Conclusions

Naturally there are differences in the political system and culture between the U.S. and China. When the U.S. assumed the responsibility of governing a post-war Japan, she had made a serious effort in studying the Japanese culture (see The Chrysanthemum and the Sword, Ruth Benedict, written by the invitation of the U.S. Office of War Information, 1946) but towards China, a 5000 years continuous culture, the U.S. has hardly scratched her surface. China has always respected and practiced 'Wang Dao" (being accommodating and conciliating in foreign policy) rather than 'Bah Dao' (acting hegemony behavior and relying on military power). This political philosophy had cost her dearly throughout Qing Dynasty (numerous wars and unequal treaties) as well as during China's early Republic years (devastating wars resisting the Japanese invasions and forgave her after the war demanding no penalty) when China was in Chaos and victimized by the Western Powers. The modern history has taught all of us that hegemony and wars are not the solution to the world's problems. It is best for the two great nations, the U.S. and China to work together to find solutions to maintain world peace and promote human prosperity.

CHAPTER 41

WORLDWIDE TURMOIL VIEWED BY

BRZEZINSKI AND WORDMAN

—ɷ—

MR. ZBIGNIEW BRZEZINSKI (ZB), NATIONAL security advisor throughout President Jimmy Carter's Presidency, was interviewed by Foreign Policy's Editor, David Rothkopf, on the subject of today's worldwide turmoil. The entire conversation was published on FP, July 21, 2014. The key thrust of this interview was: Why a return to global order may rest on the relationship between the United States and China. This interview naturally draws the attention of this column writer, who is eager to understand the "Why" and offer any comment if appropriate.

In the mainstream media, there is the hypothetical 'China Threat' theory that may have been the source influencing the current foreign policy of the United States or the 'marketing tool' for justifying the US foreign policy continued from the Cold War strategy seeking a new enemy target. In this sense, Mr. ZB, a brilliant mind even at 86, a well regarded strategic thinker, a seasoned expert on international affairs, and a prolific writer is in an excellent position (currently not holding any government job) to speak on the issue of world turmoil.

It is clear from Mr. ZB's interview, he is concerned with the United States losing the ability and leadership at the highest level to deal with the world turmoil, resulting in the devoid of will and sense of direction in managing the unstable world. He calls the present situation, "a historically unprecedented instability with huge swath of global tension being dominated by unrest anger and loss of State control", which challenges the leadership role of the United States. Mr. ZB offered an alternative vision, essential for stabilizing the current unrest; a vision calls for the United States and China to embrace one another as the "twin centers of power" to deal with the changing modern world. Following this interview, there are several commentators who have expressed their opinions. One comment under the name, Professor Enki, who wrote a long essay with somewhat scattered thoughts but giving an extremely pessimistic view about the world (hopeless climate change, food, water, fuel and electricity problems) and denounced Mr. ZB's 'two state' leadership solution and blamed the world problems to a dysfunctional United States and an over populated China with severe pollution issue. Many other commentators disagreed with Professor Enki's view and supported Mr.ZB's diagnosis of the problem and vision.

After reading this interview and its reader comments, I am pleasantly surprised, other than Professor Enki's remarks belittling China's rise, there were no 'China threat' argument. However, there are concerns whether China will be willing to side with the United States in taking up the 'Two State' or the "Twin Center of Power" role. The BRICS alliance was mentioned as an example and the competition for superpower between Russia and the U.S. and possibly between China and the U.S. was cautioned. In the following, I would like to offer my opinion.

Perhaps the simpler way to look at the world turmoil is to first examine the regions of the world by 'index of chaos' in ascending order, namely, America, Africa, Asia, Europe and Middle East. America and Africa present the lowest index of chaos. Under the 'Two State' solution, these two regions can be easily managed without leading to higher chaos. China has been extremely active in Africa engaging in infrastructure investment and joint development in agriculture and mining industries. It would be a no brainer for the United States to join hand with China to help Africans to raise their standard of living. In America, chiefly the South America, it was historically the sphere of influence of the United States. Following the trend of the global economy, nations are eagerly exploring business, trade and joint development opportunities wherever possible. It is understandable that China is exploring growth opportunities in South America. Instead of viewing such activities as stepping into US territory, it is a perfect opportunity for the United States to lead a 'Two State' model in guiding the economic development in South America for raising her standard of living. Poverty is the source of unrest and is the cause for the acute illegal immigration problem facing America.

Asia being higher in the index of chaos than America and Africa is somewhat artificial. Over all in Asia, economical development has come a long way. A few decades ago, only Japan was enjoying a developed nation status with GDP being the envy of the world, especially by Asian countries. Then, the four little dragons came up. Now with the rapid rise of China, South Korea, India, and Indochina States in their economies, the prosperity Index should be raising in Asia not the index of chaos. Yet, the tension in the East and South China Sea has been built up making Asia the next serious trouble spot ranked below Eastern Europe and the Middle East. The regional situation has been artificially created and its tension unnecessarily heightened, since the United States announced a 'Pivot to Asia Pacific' strategy. Worse of all, it encouraged the ambitious current Administration in Japan to create a 'China threat' theory, to allow Japan permitting her defense force to attack first and to initiate a territorial dispute with China. The 'Pivot' policy' is being questioned by many political analysts as counter-productive to the long-term interest of the United States. Following Mr. ZB's analysis and my own, I can say this policy in its current form is definitely counter-strategic to the 'Two State' model for dealing with the world turmoil.

In East Europe, Russia's annexation of Crimea Peninsula and the continued unrest in Ukraine is certainly raised to an international level. Denying recognition of Crimea and Sevastopol as subjects of Russian Federation and placing economic sanction against Russia seem to be ineffective, especially without China. As Mr. ZB pointed out that EU is simply unable to deal with the situation and the actions of the United States are simply driving Putin to get closer to China. Will China be willing to mediate the problem in Europe is highly dependent on whether The United States is willing to adopt a 'Two State' model to deal with the Ukraine Crisis.

Mr. ZB was correct in saying that it is the rising of religious identification as the principal motive for political actions causing destructive consequences in the Middle East. The problems there have been in existence for a long time and are spreading widely without solution in sight. I fully agree with his view; the two countries that will be most affected by these disastrous developments over time are China and Russia – especially China with her vulnerabilities to terrorism, dependency on stable global energy market and unrest in Muslin world affecting her minority population. Therefore it makes sense for the United States to work with China (and Russia likely to cooperate) to define a necessary viable precondition for Israel and the rest of Middle East to accept, rather than assuming the sole responsibility for managing a region that the U.S. can't control.

A stable 'Twin Center of Power' of the U.S. and China or a 'Two-State' or 'Tri-State' including a willing Russia, should be a sensible solution to deal with the world turmoil!

CHAPTER 42

WHY DOES JAPAN KEEP DENYING HER WAR ATROCITIES?

- THE NANKING MASSACRE, COMFORT WOMEN

AND UNIT 731 BIOLOGICAL EXPERIMENTS -

—m—

WW I I IS AN aggregate of shameful acts of mankind exhibiting all the evil spirit of human beings in their meanest form. Hitler was responsible for the WW II in Europe and the horrible holocaust which mass murdered several million Jews. More than 50 million deaths occurred in Europe throughout WW II. Japan was responsible for the WW II in Asia, killing more than 30 million Asians and 20 million Chinese alone as well as atrocities including mass murder, sex slavery and biological experiments on innocent humans. Hitler killed himself by suicide when the war ended and Germany had admitted the war crimes committed by the German army. The German people had shown remorse to the Jews and to the world publicly and through offering compensation to the victims. The Germans were able to live with the history and moved on. The world was able to forgive Germany as well. On the contrary, Japan, to this day, is still in denial of her war crimes. The Japanese officials repeatedly deny the Japanese war atrocities committed by the Japanese Imperial Army during WW II. Why? We ask.

Why does Japan keep denying her war atrocities? The Japanese war crimes were clearly documented, including the horrific mass murder, the Nanking Massacre (killing at least 377,000 Chinese), sex slavery program (known as comfort women, forcing Dutch, Chinese, Korean and other Asian women to be used as sex slaves for the Japanese Army), and biological experiments on innocent children, men and women (even with entire Chinese village being secretly fed with bacteria loaded water supply to obtain medical statistics). The repeated denials of these atrocities by the Japanese officials not only anger Asian people but worse they can never heal the wounds. Therefore, the Japanese will not be forgiven by her neighboring countries and some Japanese can not forgive themselves.

Historians have often been puzzled by the 'Why?' in the title question. The answer is not likely a simple one, but as human beings we must seek the answer so we can help the Japanese to live with the history and move on. More importantly, by understanding why, we will never let those atrocities occur again. In the following, an attempt is made to list several plausible reasons that may explain the why question. Hopefully, through an open and candid discussion, a clear answer may emerge.

First, the answer may lie in the Japanese culture, a culture with high regard for honor and loyalty, typified by Samurai or Bushi spirit. Japanese like Chinese have the 'face' issue also (which is quite known to the Western people). For the sake of saving face, the Japanese does not easily admit mistake or guilt. Many of the Japanese soldiers of WW II were very much shamed by their criminal conduct and yet could not muster the courage to admit their war crimes in front of their parents, wives or children. They kept the guilt inside and lived in denial. The same 'face' issue also inhibited the victims, for example, the women suffered from the Japanese sex slavery program, to come out and tell in the open. This fact encouraged the Japanese government to minimize the extent of the Japanese war crime.

Second, the made-up story for justifying the aggression of the Japanese against Chinese may be another culprit for Japan's denial of her war crimes. The Japanese Imperial Army was preaching their invasion to China as a war between civilization, a civilized and modern Japan, against a primitive nation, a backward and corrupted Qing Dynasty. Japan wanted her people to believe, she launched a holy war to save the poor Chinese from misery. This story was so deeply entrenched, when WW II ended and Japan defeated, she would rather live in denial than giving up this false story. This is also a consequence of 'Face' issue. Today, facing a rising China, some Japanese still believe that the large population of Chinese must be saved by Japan.

Third, the biggest mistake responsible for Japan's denial in war crimes perhaps was that the allied command exonerated the Japanese emperor from war crimes.

Hirohito was singly responsible for permitting the Japanese Imperial Army to pursue the aggression plan to conquer China and the war crimes committed thereof. Hitler took his own life - a fact essentially meant he accepted the responsibility of all the war crimes committed by the German Army. Shielding the Japanese Emperor from punishment for Japan's war crimes essentially provided the Japan a way out of admitting her guilt. Hence, to this day, some Japanese officials, especially the militant right-wingers, still want to worship the war criminals at the Yasukuni Shrine, wanting to return Japan back to her 'past glory'. Japanese Emperor Hirohito owed all Japanese citizens and the world a sincere apology and an honest admission of guilt in permitting the Japanese Imperial Army to launch wars and commit such brutal atrocious crimes against Asians in WW II.

Fourth, the Japanese who accept the facts in WWII are a minority in Japan. For example, Professor Saburo Ienaga, who is an author of Japanese textbooks on Japan's military atrocities; he sued the Ministry of Education for censorship barring his books to be used. However, the Supreme Court in Japan only recognized the unit 731 committing crime of performing biological experiments and upheld the censorship of the Ministry of Education. The politicians in Japan can influence their education policy, hence, young people are taught with false history. This is a vicious cycle going on for several generations producing a majority of Japanese living in denial of Japanese war crimes.

Fifth, the world has not been holding the justice regarding Japan's war crimes. The United States had essentially turned a blind eye post WW II to the Japanese war atrocities. Even when a Japanese American Congressman, Mike Honda, of California introduced a bill denouncing Japan's war crimes, it did not make the U.S. Government take any meaningful action to clarify the facts. The U.S. government should release the documents in her possession pertaining to WW II and Japan's war crimes. The huge contrast between holocaust and Nanking Massacre being treated in this country is another reason for Japan to keep denying her war atrocities.

Recently, there are some civil organizations in Korea, China and in the United States raising the awareness of Japanese war crime. For example, monuments have been built in California and New Jersey in memory of Comfort Women. Ironically, the monument erected at Glendale, CA, was challenged by a group of Japanese.

Fortunately, the district court rejected the complaint and the request of removing that monument as frivolous. Apparently the party brought the lawsuit was associated with Japanese right-wing organizations or politicians not having the rights to bring a lawsuit in the court's jurisdiction.

On the question, "why Japan keeps denying her war atrocities?", the above discussion does point out a plausible approach that may help Japan to accept and live with the history and may help the world to forgive those horrible war crimes. The approach is that all countries suffered from the Japanese war atrocities must join hand to bring out all the facts and truth to the world. Through worldwide awareness, it will make Japan to break out from her cocoon to recognize the historical facts and stop fabricating and denying WW II history. 2015 is the 70th anniversary of the ending of WW II, it is a great opportunity for the world, the United Nation, the U.S. and all Asian countries to join hand to conduct a memorial to bring justice to the world and peace to the Japanese people by honestly accepting the WW II war crimes.

CHAPTER 43

"IN THE INTEREST OF THE U.S." – WE WAR!

—◊—

"IN THE INTEREST OF THE U.S.", has been the sacred justification for taking military action against another nation or a terrorist group by the US government. When anyone is violating the strategic interest of the United States, logically, based on her constitutional rights, she can defend her interest and/or strike against the violator. This principle is well-recognized thousands of years ago. For instance, **Sun Tzi Bin Fa**, (by Sun Tzi, The Principles and Laws of Warfare), has cautioned that war should always be the last resort and the phrase, **'Shi Chu You Ming'** (any military action must be launched under a 'proper name'(a cause with sound justification) must be obeyed. This concept is not foreign to military strategists or statesmen in the East or West. The justification must satisfy the following three constituents: the citizens' views, the diplomatic opinions and the reception by the soldiers to be deployed into the war. In addition, the justification should survive the ultimate world opinion as war progresses.

This column's title implies some challenging questions: Is the phrase, "In the Interest of the U.S.", being seriously weighed before taking a military action or being used as a convenient slogan to justify the war activities? Does the U.S. always make proper justification to her people, her soldiers and her diplomatic relations before engaging in a war? According to Sun Tze, the **'justification process'** is vital to a small country fighting against a large neighbor (for example, hypothetically, Japan could take military action again against China using the Diaoyu Island dispute), the consequence could be disastrous if the cause was not well justified to the people, soldiers and diplomatic relations of the small nation. The 'justification process' was sometimes ignored by a large country fighting against a small country. Such action may draw the diplomatic and world opinion against the large aggressor, as exhibited by Crimea taken from Ukraine by Russia.

This old war principle is fundamentally correct and applicable in today's world. The significant differences lie in the technological advances in modern warfare, not in any change of war principles. In ancient times, the communication means were limited (imagine pigeons versus satellite communication), hence, it was simple to justify a war to one's own army or to one's entire citizenry using an inductive slogan. The diplomatic reaction was slow and so was the formation of world opinions. However, the speed of war was slower then, hence, **Shi Chu You Ming (proper justification) was a valid and important principle of war to be obeyed**. Often times, an aggressor was eventually defeated when internal and external elements turned against her when the war was not properly justified.

Today, the technologies are more advanced, mobilization of military forces much faster and power of destruction greater and speedier. These give militarists incentives to launch battles to settle disputes. A wishful thinking often was, the war would be over before the world realized it. However, the communication means today are enhanced and so do the power of media, even across national boundaries. The citizens, soldiers and their command can be informed much faster from internal and external sources, with conflicting messages and so can the world opinion be formed much faster. Before the proliferation of nuclear power, a nuclear superpower may take a military action disregarding justification, but it would be a pure hegemony behavior. Today, it would be foolhardy to take military action without careful justification, especially between nations with nuclear power. **So the 'justification process' for war, is far more important today**.

The past wars, the Vietnam and the Iraq wars, for example, should have taught us how the people's opinion mattered, the diplomatic relations changed and the world opinion influenced in the outcome of the wars. A government may try to manipulate the media to help justify a war plan to its citizens, a deed easily done by an authoritarian government, but surprisingly, often happening in a democratic free-press country as well. Whether such media manipulation works or not is unpredictable, only hindsight can tell for sure. The Vietnam War nearly divided the United States. Hindsight, one could have analyzed whether the war was ever properly justified? Was anti-communism a sufficient justification to engage a war far away from America, dividing the Vietnam into two and subjecting her people in horrible misery for years? Was rivalry with the Soviet Union a justifiable cause for the Vietnam War and **was the war truly "in the interest of the United States"?** We must learn from the past wars and apply to the future!

Presently, the U.S. is implementing 'the pivot to Asia' policy. Although no war has occurred yet, but the creation of a "China Threat" scenario seems to be an obvious PR plot for justifying a military confrontation with China in the near future. Is deploying another carrier, USS Carl Vinson to the Pacific after a Chinese jet fighter getting too close to a US P-8 reconnaissance plane in the South China Sea a justified action "in the interest of the United States"? Isn't surveillance near one's national boundary provocative? Shouldn't we ask a more basic question, is the 'China Threat' a response from China being first threatened by a US-led 'contain China strategy'? Hence, is 'China Threat' really a valid assumption to justify posturing military maneuvers and fortifying bilateral military treaties aiming at curtailing China? Would China be blind to containment or engage in an arms race? **Is "in the interest of the U.S." being casually defined without a serious examination of a right foreign policy and military strategy towards China? The current path, obviously leading to war, does not seem to be "in the best interest of the U.S."!**

The US Administration and the Pentagon do understand the significance of 'justification process'. They do prepare the justification by engaging PR work. **The 'China Threat' Scenario** looks and smells like a PR work with Japan being a willing partner. We must ask: is this PR work "in the interest of the United States"? What is the reason for the U.S., a superpower and well-developed country, to rival with China, an over-populated nation with priority to raise the standard of living for her 1.3 billion people? On the contrary, **we see lots of win-win opportunities benefitting both US and China and the world**.

In general, it is difficult to justify inserting the United States army into any conflict between two parties based on "the interest of the U.S." Take the current turmoil in the Middle East, the ISIS, as an example, the interest of the people and the geopolitical complexity in that region far **outweighs** "the interest of the U.S.". **Thousands of lives** there are at stake; perhaps, the strategic solution is to embargo all weapons going into the hands of the warring parties. Instead of directly getting involved militarily or adding fire power, **the objective of the U.S. should be to reduce the war level in the Middle East** rather than enhancing it. Likewise, **in the Asia-Pacific, increasing military presence of the United States in that region and supplying more weapons there cannot be in "the best interest of the United States" in the long run**.

CHAPTER 44

ROBIN WILLIAMS, DRUG PROBLEMS AND OPIUM WARS

—⁓—

A TALENTED AMERICAN ACTOR AND comedian, Robin McLaurin Williams, died on August 11, 2014 at age of 63. Robin took his own life in a state of depression and suffering from Parkinson's disease and drug dependency. Although I have not been a fan of stand-up comedy which made him famous but I am a fan of his funny movies, which always make me laugh and feel happy at the end. Sixty three is a young age considering the male American life expectancy being 77.2. So while feeling sad about his death, we could not help asking why would a successful performer take his own life? What really drive him to end his life by hanging, not a common and comfortable means of suicide in modern days? Millions of fans were amused by his humor and quick wits; many of them will laugh uncontrollably when seeing his happy face and inviting grin and hearing his little jokes and funny remarks at the right time and at the right place. No one could imagine Robin Williams to take his own life. No, no way!

Robin Williams was born in Chicago, Illinois, on July 21, 1951 to His mother, Laurie McLaurin (1923 – 2001), a beautiful model from Jackson, Mississippi, and his father, Robert Fitzgerald Williams (1906 – 1987), a senior executive at Ford Motor Company responsible for the Midwest region. Robin's great-great-grand father was Mississippi senator and governor, Anselm J. McLaurin, and Williams was a prominent family in Evansville, Indiana. He was raised as an Episcopalian and wrote the "Top Ten Reasons to be an Episcopalian". It was understandable that Robin Williams had a nice childhood and grew up to be a happy person taking up a profession - comedian, but it was never expected that Robin Williams would end his life in a depressed state. It is not right, not right at all!

Robin attended Claremont Men's College and College of Marin and then enrolled at the Juilliard School in New York City. At the great city, he became a friend and a roommate with fellow actor Christopher Reeve. Williams became a successful stand-up comedian in California, held a loving audience in San Francisco and Los Angeles. He began his film career in the 80's and created numerous great movies such as "Popeye", "Good Morning, Vietnam", "Aladdin", "Mrs. Doubt fire", "Night at the Museum" and "Happy Feet". Robin was nominated for the Academy Award for Best Actor three times. He has won the Academy Award for Best Supporting Actor (in Good Will Hunting), two Emmy Awards, four Golden Globe Awards, five Grammy Awards and two Screen Actors Guild Awards. No doubt he was a great actor. He couldn't be depressed by a lack of achievement. Impossible, absolutely impossible!

What then makes Robin Williams depressed enough to take his own life at 63? He did suffer from Parkinson's disease, but was that his primary reason for hanging himself? I rather think not. As a friend of 'Superman' Christopher Reeve, who was paralyzed for life after an accident, thrown off from a horse, it is unlikely that Robin would consider suicide simply because of Parkinson's. Just before Robin's death, he did a wonderful thing for his fan in New Zealand. A beautiful story suggests that Parkinson's cannot be the reason for his suicide. His fan Vivian Waller with husband Jack and daughter Sophie of New Zealand made her bucket list this year after being diagnosed with terminal cancer. She wrote just five items: get married, celebrate her 21st birthday, see her daughter Sophie's first birthday, travel to Rarotonga, an South Pacific island, and meet actor and comedian Robin Williams. The 21 year old Waller was diagnosed in January and married in February, but soon her cancer in her lungs, intestines and liver prevented her to travel to California to meet Williams. A friend of Waller reached out to Williams personally, asking for his help in making the young woman's wish fulfilled. Robin took the time to record a personal video for Waller, joking with her, sending his love to her family and telling her to "knock this off your bucket list." (http://www.legacy.com/news/notable-stories/robin-williams-gift-to-dying-fan/2590/) This video showed how awesome a person Robin was. "There were so many ways and so many things he did for so many people," said Jeff Katzenberg, an Entertainment Executive. It is very hard for us to believe that Robin committed suicide!

Robin Williams did commit suicide. The real culprit for Robin's death is really the drug, cocaine. Robin started to use drugs and alcohol early in his stand-up career. It started simply; before one show, he remembered that he accepted a line of cocaine that someone gave him. Then he could not shake the drug habit despite of committing to rehab many times. It is the drug that has made him paranoid and depressed. I would rather believe that his suicide is an intentional statement to the entertainment industry and to the world that drug is evil. Drug destroyed many great performers, including an idol of mine, Elvis Presley.

Drug is evil and Drug destroyed Robin Williams! While mourning his death, I could not help remembering the infamous Opium Wars between China and Britain (1839-1842, OW I and 1856-1860 OW II). The British brought the Opium to China to trade for silver, silk and spices, essentially with the intent to drug the Chinese people and to drug the entire nation. When the Chinese government recognized the evil effect of opium, they tried to stop the British traders at the ports. They tried to confiscate the opium and burn them. Then the British naval battleships fired and the first Opium War broke out; the Chinese lost and accepted the Treaty of Nanking, an unequal treaty, granting the British an indemnity and extraterritoriality, including opening five treaty ports and the cession of Hong Kong Island. Sadly, the second Opium War took place as the British were not satisfied with her trade relationship with China, namely the British desiring the legalization of opium trade. The British Empire and later requested the Second French Empire, the United States and the Russian Empire to join her in fighting the Qing Dynasty. The Chinese were defeated by the four aggressors, yielding another unequal treaty, The Treaties of Tientsin, opening of 11 ports to Western trade, giving rights for foreign ships to navigate on Yantze river and foreigners to travel freely inland of China plus an indemnity of 8 million taels of silver (~10 million ozt) to Britain and France each.

Today, both the Great Britain and the U.S. have drug problems (but that is not because of China). Is that a punishment for the past sins? Shouldn't we recognize the history and teach our kids about the opium wars and its evil motives? The UN has chosen June 26 as an anti-drug day to commemorate Lin Zexu's dismantling of the opium trade in Humen, Guangdong just before the first Opium War. The observance was instituted by General Assembly Resolution 42/112 of 7 December

1987. Now that the British has returned Hong Kong to China on July 1, 1997, perhaps, China and the world should designate the week of 6/26-7/1 each year as the 'anti-drug' week with festivities in both Human and Hong Kong to raise the awareness of the need to fight the drug trade continuously!

CHAPTER 45

THE US LEADERSHIP TRANSITION AT

2016-17 - MOST CRITICAL FOR US-CHINA RELATION

—⟨m⟩—

THE TENURE OF PRESIDENT BARACK Obama begins in 2009 and will terminate at the end of 2016. He has won two four-year terms. The tenure of the new leader of China, Xi Jin Ping, begins in 2013 and will end in 2022, likely two five-year terms. In next ten years, there is a transition of power in one country during the tenure of the leadership in the other country. From 2025 to 2032, the two-term American Presidency will fall entirely within the tenure of the Chinese leader from 2023 to 2032. Then again the next two term American Presidency from 2033-2040 will fall within the tenure of the Chinese leadership from 2033-2042. You may wonder: what is the significance in these term periods? I would say to you, these two transition points are important, especially the first one being the most important, That is, if you are concerned with the future of the US-China relationship and the welfare of the world.

In the above it is assumed that the leaders will all serve two consecutive terms, which is a safe assumption if they are successful. However, if they are not successful, it usually means a possible change in the nation's domestic and foreign policies mandated by the ballot results. In general, change of policies in one term is not a good thing. It may imply policy failure. The term limit built in a political system is a good thing. If an elected leader turns out to be ineffective, people are able to exercise their rights to change the leadership.

A transition in the top leadership allows significant change of 'national course' since all cabinet positions will be appointed anew. Often times, the consequence of government policies do not show up clearly in one-term. So the two-term limit usually is the fairer and more meaningful period to measure the performance of the commander-in-chief. Therefore, looking at the ten year tenure period discussed above, the 2016-17, (occurring within Xi's two-term, 2013-2022) offers the new US President an opportunity to re-evaluate the China policy after gaining more understanding of Xi Jin Ping; whereas, the 2022-23 transition on the US side (2017-2024) is likely to give Chinese leader to adjust his policies towards the U.S., after knowing the orientations of the new US president. Therefore, if they so choose, these two transition points are significant for the leaders of two nations to move towards a mutually beneficial relationship.

Today, the US-China relationship appears to be on a rocky and treacherous course due to the "Pivot to Asia" policy, which has resulted in a hostile relationship and has brought on an uncertain future. President Obama's foreign policies in relations to the Middle East (ISIS) and Ukraine have been "derided as incoherent, legalistic, bloodless and amoral", by the editors of Foreign Policy. The transition point at 2016-17 may be the only critical correction point for American voters to elect a new President to charter a new course. However, if the new US President (2017-2024) chose to continue a 'hostile China policy', then at 2022-23 transition, the Chinese most likely will elect a leader (2023-32) confronting the US 'hostile China policy' by adopting equally hostile countermeasures against the U.S. Following that, the next US Presidency (2025-32) will have no choice but face the same Chinese leader (2023-2932) and his pre-set unfriendly postures. As the negative spiral continues, at 2032-33 transition, when both China and the U.S. select their new leaders in the same year, the uncertainty of leadership choice may add yet another layer of unknown factor into this hostile environment. The consequences may be very dangerous. Recognizing this possibility, we must regard the 2016-17 US presidential election as extremely critical. As all political analysts would agree, the US-China relation is the most important foreign policy concern for the United States and China, not only for their mutual interests but also for the prosperity of the world.

Of course, whether or not a wise transition could be effected will depend on many factors. In the United States, with over 340 million people of multiple ethnicity (63% white of various European descent, 12.6% African, 9% Hispanic, 4.8% Asian), domestic issues usually take center stage. The election usually also faces a challenge to obtain consensus regarding one desired foreign policy. This challenge places heavy burden on the media, both mainstream and organic. The media must probe the issues, expose the hidden agenda, report the truth and challenge the presidential candidates and educate the public, to make them understand the importance of the US-China relationship and to select the right leader to manage it.

China has 1.3 billion people, and, after numerous failures in stimulating her economy under the communism doctrine, she finally took the "reform and open" route. The reality is China has risen after three decades of hard work and capitalism. When Xi describes the China Dream as a modest goal to lift her population from poverty to above a minimum standard of living, the Chinese people agree with him and support his goals. When Xi repeatedly declares that China will rise peacefully, the Chinese population would not have it any other way.

Throughout the history, the Chinese were apprehensive about foreign invasions. The current US 'Pivot to Asia' policy favoring Japan against China is fundamentally wrong. Creating an external threat simply reminds Chinese people of their painful past and intensifies and cultivates their nationalism. The U.S. gains no benefit to repeat the Cold War by targeting China as the arch-enemy. Post Cold War, the world is ready to welcome rising great nations through fair competition and open trade which the U.S. advocates. New leaders will emerge and they will cast great influence on the world affairs. Foreign policy changes are inevitable. The anti-China policy apparently inherited from the Cold War era and favored by the right-leaning establishments must be called into question. A legacy policy has not worked in the Middle East or Africa and it will fail in other parts of the world if not examined with up-to-date facts. Just like China in admitting her mistakes in the past, the U.S. needs to admit her wrong assumptions about China. The U.S. must re-examine her foreign policies before it became irreversible. If the current Administration fails to change, the next transition point, that is 2016, is the critical decision point for American citizens to elect a new leader to implement a correct, productive China policy. Missing this opportunity, the U.S. and China may walk into a dark tunnel of no return, engaging in arms race and other conflicts, eventually leading to war.

CHAPTER 46

CHINESE AMERICANS SHOULD VOTE

ON ISSUES, NOT PARTY LINE

—ɯ—

UNITED STATES, AS WE ALL know, has essentially a two-party system. Although there are minor parties, but they have almost no influence at elections. In recent years, Tea Party stands out. The tea party started as a movement, concerned with the national debt and the bloated federal budget. The Republican Party, being the party on the right, tried to woo tea party votes. Hence the 2010 congressional election produced a significant number of Republican congressmen with tea party support. However, the Tea Party's momentum does not seem to lead to a third major party formation in view of their recent setbacks in some local primary elections.

Maybe it is not a bad development, since more political parties may not be a good thing in a democracy. More parties tend to divide the nation, resulting in weak and unstable government. The two-party system in the United States has worked reasonably well for nearly two centuries. However, as the world affairs become more complex and many domestic issues beg for effective solutions, the American two-party system seems to show strains in electing capable leaders who can unite the people and carry out effective policies. Likewise, the Senate and Congress have been behaving irrationally with bipartisan bickering, rendering the legislative process impotent and crippling the Administration's ability to take actions.

Since the U.S. is the biggest melting pot in the world, with 340 million people divergent in ethnicities and races, divided opinions and interests are unavoidable. However, with high literacy rate, the United States presumably has an educated voting population, who are capable of making rational decisions when exercising their voting rights to correct a dysfunctional government.

Can this happen? We may recall the 2008 Presidential election; Obama was elected as a young, energetic, wise and tough leader. Many voters voted cross party line to elect a new leader to save the country from bankruptcy and to halt the devastating wars the country was engaged in. Unfortunately, the voters elected a leader who might have been a good social organizer but was inexperienced in foreign policy matters, and who is now trying to conduct the foreign affairs from a lectern, rhetoric and inconsistent. Also unfortunately, the American voters elected a divided Congress immersed in hostile bipartisan fights. Of course, this has to stop or the U.S. is heading to further decline and weakening her ability to perform her role as the world leader.

For ordinary citizens, politics is not science, it is simply viewed as a collection of issues affecting their lives and national security, and it merges into a voting index - economic outlook for the citizens in the contest of the future of the nation. For political activists treating politics like science, politics maybe more complex, arguing about ideologies and principles, stripping down the issues to the barebones, forgetting about the large fuzzy picture the ordinary citizens see.

Unfortunately, the activists with their intellect, organization skills and persistence, backed by huge amounts of money, are able to impose their views on the candidates and ordinary citizens to influence election results. The more money they have, the more mass media time they can buy and the more influence they can affect on the voters and candidates. Sadly, the elected officials, instead of trying to fulfill the real mandates of the ordinary citizens, follow the doctrines of the activists. You would think a smart man like Obama in his second term, facing no future election, could shake away from the grip of activists or money groups, but that seems not to be the case.

I have pointed out previously that the 2016 US Presidential election is very critical for resetting or setting a new direction regarding US-China relationship. If a wrong US leader were elected in 2016, the subsequent leaders in China and the U.S. may enact a series of measures and countermeasures producing a hostile US-China relationship, potentially leading to war. Therefore, for all Chinese Americans, the 2016 US Presidential election is critical, and the candidate's view on the US-China relationship is a crucial factor for them to consider. Every Chinese American must exercise his or her voting right carefully. They should start paying attention now. I will discuss below how every Chinese American Citizen can pay attention to the Presidential election and make his or her vote count.

Chinese Americans, like many other American civil or ethnic groups, may join either Republican Party or Democratic Party, or remain independent. Many politicians and party technicians often think, if an ethnic group is evenly divided in its party affiliations, their votes would cancel out, and they may ignore that group. From Chinese American population standpoint, I can understand how some of them maybe Democrats, some maybe Republicans, based on different issues or their priorities on issues or attributed to generation gap. Let me assure you, your vote and support will not cancel each other out if you do the following:

1. Declare that China-US relationship is the highest priority issue in the presidential election for you, your spouse and your children or your parents.

2. Engage in politics by making small donations. Please always write a sentence on the memo line on your check. (For example: By accepting this donation of $10, you agree to promote friendly relations between the U.S. and China; or write a letter attached to the check with similar message).

3. Send this small donation to the candidate you want to support, and you will get the following results:

I. your check is cashed with or without acknowledgment of your request; or
II. Your check is not cashed with or without an acknowledgment of your request.

Any candidate sending you an acknowledgment is honest and conscientious about the China policy. So, you should vote for the one who cashes your check. If the candidate does not acknowledge your request but cashes your check anyway, you would have an opportunity to watch the campaign development regarding the US-China issue. If the campaign contradicts your request, you could demand explanation, best through media, giving you far more power than your small donation.

If every Chinese American exercises the above political support mechanism (a small affordable donation), the net effect can be huge. The Chinese American voters will be regarded as serious and united, regardless of their party affiliation. This exercise should work for any election on US-China issue or other issues.

CHAPTER 47

CONCLUSION FROM THE U.S.-CHINA

COMMISSION (USCC) MILITARY ASSESSMENT

—᠁—

ORDINARY CITIZENS HAVE LITTLE CHANCE to access top secret military reports. The military news generally consist of either officially controlled press releases with little details on costs and return on investment on weapon spending or unofficial analysis and comparisons on weapons borderline marketing and promotion. Readers can rarely obtain enough knowledge to entertain any strategic questions such as:

1. Is arms race and a particular military direction justified from a long-term strategic point of view?
2. Is weapon development cost effective, sustainable and based on a sound strategy?
3. Is the military strategy guided by a political strategy with sound assumptions?

As an ordinary citizen, no expertise on weaponry, I am more interested in reading meaningful documents related to the above strategic questions. Recently, I came across the Congressional Hearing, "China's Military Modernization and Its Implications for the United States", which was chaired by Senator James M. Talent and Dr. Katherine C. Tobin, commissioners of the U.S.-China Economic and Security Review Commission (USCC). The expert witnesses included Mr. Jesse Karotkin, Senior Intelligence Officer for China, Office of Naval Intelligence; Mr. Donald L. "Lee" Fuell, Technical Director for Force Modernization and Employment, National Air and Space Intelligence Center; Dr. Andrew Erickson, Associate Professor and founding member, China Maritime Studies Institute, U.S. Naval War College; Dr. James Lewis, Senior Fellow and Director of the Strategic

Technologies Program, Center for Strategic and International Studies; Mr. Mark Stokes, Executive Director, Project 2049 Institute; Dr. Roger Cliff, Senior Fellow, Atlantic Council; The Honorable David Gompert, Distinguished Visiting Professor, U.S. Naval Academy; and Mr. Thomas Donnelly, Resident Fellow and Co-Director of the Marilyn Ware Center for Security Studies, American Enterprise Institute. The testimonies of these distinguished experts were available on the USCC website, www.uscc.gov.

This hearing was meaningful which examined the inputs to China's military modernization, including financial resources and China's defense industry, and the current and future capabilities of China's military, and the impact of China's military modernization on the United States and her options. These materials are intended for helping the Congress conducting its assessment of U.S.-China relations and the US China policy. The USCC will produce an annual report for the Congress due in November as it did each tear since 2002.

One objective of a congressional hearing and its publication is to provide citizens an opportunity to express their opinions. After reading through the testimonies, I found little issue with the facts and analysis in each presentation (other than the view about Taiwan expressed by Stoke and Fuell being somewhat out of date), but as an assemble, I discovered a hidden conclusion that was not revealed or articulated by the witnesses. This hidden conclusion, which was so important, would have a profound impact on the U.S. in her military strategy towards China. This hidden conclusion negates the current 'China Threat' theory and the strategy of targeting China as a military enemy of the U.S.

I particularly enjoyed the well written 11-page paper by Prof. Dr. Andrew Jackson, who offered a rational cost analysis on China's military modernization and the corresponding response by the U.S. China's military spending is about 2-3% of her GDP (relatively constant over past decade) much less than what the U.S. spends (~4% US GDP after a 2013 reduction, the U.S. spends 37% of the world's total military spending and contributes only 22% of world's GDP). He argues that far reaching warfare is more expensive than near region defense, hence, for China to wage war away from China would require much more increased military spending on new platforms, weapons, supply structure as well as enhanced training, operations and maintenance. For the same logic (unspoken), that is the very reason the U.S. has difficulty to sustain her military spending to maintain her far reaching military presence. China understood that, hence, she emphasized on defensive technologies to detect invaders rather than building attack platforms and establishing military basis to extend her military presence.

The hidden conclusion I referred to was found in the testimonies of Jackson, Cliff, Fuell and Stoke; namely, China's military modernization is purely a defense strategy, never intended to be offensive, consistent with her national policy, "rise peacefully". The following facts taken from the testimonies support the above conclusion:

1. China emphasizes on defense missiles (DF-21D anti-ship ballistic missiles) not attack platforms (aircraft carrier). She has only a refurbished carrier but lots of DF-21D missiles.
2. China has 875,000 square nautical miles of near sea, she focuses on sensor and satellite technology for detecting invading ships, submarines and air force.
3. China has all her military bases on her coast line and inland, unlike U.S. having military bases all over the world supporting her far reaching naval forces.

Whatever China is strengthening in naval forces seems to be provoked into it by other nations' naval arms race rather than based on an intrinsic expansionist strategy. Ignoring the above conclusion, the U.S. may have made a serious mistake in assuming or interpreting the intent of China's military modernization, hence drawing up a wrong military strategy towards China. Donnelly presented a picture via map presentation illustrating what is needed to fortify the island chain to contain the Chinese Navy within the China seas, whereas Gompert articulated that the U.S.-China confrontation will lead to a potential "missile war" and a potential "submarine war", attributing the confrontation to the U.S. demanding free access in the Asia Pacific while China insisting on an anti-access strategy. Don't these analyses actually reveal the hidden conclusion!? Does the U.S. really believe she will provoke China by choking China's sea lanes and orchestrating air sea battles with China at long distance in the Pacific so to force her to engage in a Naval Arm Race and bankrupt her (like Russia)? Firstly, it is very doubtful that China will bankrupt before any other nation, including the U.S. Secondly, as revealed by the testimonies, China's defense based military modernization is far more economical than maintaining an offensive military. Jackson cited a DF-21D smart missile costs about $5-11 million but a Ford class carrier's cost can produce 1127 DF-21D missiles. Go figure! Any one played air sea battle electronic game will tell you unless you have an indestructible carrier, you lose under a shower of missiles.

China's military spending could very well be correlated with external provocation. As a rising great nation, China spends a defense budget in proportion to her GDP is fairly normal. While being embargoed, China diligently seeking new technologies to develop her nation is understandable. All under-developed countries (Asian nations, including Japan) did it, but they would comply to international IP law after they became developed nations. In fact, China realizes that copying technologies stifle innovation, not a process to be sustained. Japan is a historical example of that, eventually she had to get off the copy mode.

The hidden conclusion from the USCC hearing is actually not so hidden. China was not hostile towards the U.S. but is worried. Recognizing this conclusion, the implication for the United States becomes very clear:

1. The U.S. should not engage in an arms race with China; the monies saved will result in a sustainable comfortable national defense budget for both countries.
2. The U.S. and China should collaborate in technology, optimize in trade and join force in helping developing countries.
3. Under a stable and friendly relationship, they can deal with any world issue such as climate change and other crises effectively.

CHAPTER 48

FROM NIXON-KISSINGER TO

OBAMA-RICE ON US CHINA POLICY

—⚏—

US-CHINA RELATIONSHIP IS A UNIQUE one from historical perspective comparing to other western nations' relationship with China. While China was a closed nation to the West, the United States was a new rising great nation advocating Monroe Doctrine opposing the colonization in North and South America by European nations. However, while the European countries were encroaching China in the name of trade, the United States was a participator with a gentler heart. The unique US-China relation, perhaps perceived more unilaterally by the Chinese, is attributable to some Americans' role played in the Chinese revolution led by Dr. Sun Yat-Sen*. In 1911, the Qing Dynasty was finally toppled and a Republic was established. Dr. Sun, recognized as the father of the republic China, was educated in the United States (Sun and Obama attended the same Punahou* high school in Hawaii) and had many American friends lending help (including financial support) to his revolution. Dr. Sun and his followers regarded the U.S. as a role model which was vivid in his book, Three Principles of the People. Unfortunately, Japan's ambition to conquer China from the first Sino-Japanese War (1894) to numerous invasions leading to WW II (1937-1945) hampered China's revolution to emerge as a united country. The war drew Chinese and American people closer as allies in fighting the Japanese, even though the governments had distances. Although as allies, the U.S. had a shallow understanding of China and her people; they shared very little in pursuing China's goal in building her to be a modern nation. Two strong Chinese leaders, Chiang Kai-Shek and Mao Ze-Dong, influenced and supported by the United States and the Soviet Union respectively throughout eight years of Sino-Japanese war and WW II, led China into a bitter rift, an internal war, after winning WW II. Sadly for the Chinese people, China (and the U.S.) wasted the golden opportunity of (helping) uniting and building a modern China.

The U.S. had been preoccupied by her persistent anti-communism principle, treating China's internal battle as a 'pure' communist struggle to convert China into a 'pure' communist state. It was certainly a possible goal from Stalin's perspective. However, the China policy the U.S. is adhering to is to support an anti-communist government as first principle rather than cultivating a policy to assist China to unite and develop her into an independent modern state. Similar philosophy was applied to Japan after her defeat. To Japan's fortune, the collapse of the militant Japan was rapid and Russia's influence on Japan with communism was minimum during the war, hence the post-war 'rebuild Japan' policy of the U.S. was successful in keeping Russia out of Japan and in recovering Japan back to a strong economy, making Japan a complete and united nation despite of the fact that Japan was the brutal aggressor in WW II. Unfortunate to China, the U.S. never had a coherent policy to 'rebuild China' post WW II even though she was a loyal ally of the United States in defeating the Japanese. Some would claim that it was less to the interest of the U.S. to rebuild China than it was to rebuild Japan. However, judging on the recent development in Japan, starting from "Japan Can Say No To The U.S.", "Japan Is Back" to her past glory and "Japan Should Become A 'Normal Country'" with constitution revised or reinterpreted to allow Japan to use military to strike first, it is not entirely clear that Japan would forever accept a subordinate position to the U.S. under a US-Japan Mutual Defense Treaty. Some would claim that the 'not to build China' policy was a contradictory foreign policy with false logic (when compared to 'rebuild Japan' policy), based on long-term strategy consideration and humanitarian grounds.

The US China policy had little change in more than two decades post WW II, rejecting the government of People's Republic of China (PRC), governing close to a billion people in mainland China and supporting the government of the Republic of China (ROC) in Taiwan, historically a small province of China. A policy based more on military strategic reasons complimenting the US Japan policy rather than on long-term geopolitical reasoning. This policy was fundamentally questioned when Nixon became the 37th President of the United States. Nixon should be credited for his vision and bold action to develop a new China policy against the State Department's two-decade persistent position on refusing to recognize (with intent to isolate) the PRC. Kissinger, a brilliant man with vision as well serving as Nixon's Principal Assistant on National Security, was able to help Nixon to turn a new page on the US China policy. It took them nearly the full term of the 37th US Presidency to accomplish the feat that Nixon was the first American President ever visited Beijing, conversed with Chairman Mao Ze-Dong and Primier Chou En-Lai and declared the most significant 'Shanghai Communiqué', recognizing Taiwan as a part of China.

Nixon's China trip shocked the world. Nixon-Kissinger opened up China to the world and removed trade embargo to China. PRC was eventually admitted to the UN and its Security Council. The U.S., China and Soviet had begun a delicate triangular world politics, though more complex but far safer for the world. Although it wasn't until 1979, the 39th Carter Presidency, the U.S. formerly recognized the PRC establishing a diplomatic relation with China on Jan.1, 1979; the change, though a devastating blow to the ROC Government, was the correct step to reinforce a proper US-China relationship, as announced in the communiqué: the U.S. recognizes only one China (treating China as a sovereign country with no intent to divide her) but continue commercial, cultural and unofficial contacts with Taiwan (to be guided by the Taiwan Relation Act). Reviewing the history of the US China policy, it seems to suggest that the US State Department through its bureaucracy and some institutionalized lobbying efforts tend to maintain certain foreign policies through legacy; even a visionary President may be hampered to make changes. The Nixon-Kissinger effort in changing the US China policy was a clear case. The Taiwan issue is a classic example.

After Carter, through Reagan, Bush Sr., Clinton and Bush Jr., the US China policy had been essentially stayed in a legacy mode, again. Over the past three decades, China has miraculously risen to be the number two economy in the world. Her ability to serve the world as a great nation in a still existing triangular world politics is far stronger than 30 years ago. While Nixon-Kissinger recognized so early the merit of regarding China as a rising player with stabilizing value in a triangular geopolitics, the current administration, Obama-Rice could not be blind to the fact that a healthy US-China relation is not only to the advantage of the U.S. but also in the interest of maintaining world peace. Unfortunately, the current "Pivot to Asia Pacific" policy seems to be driven by a legacy obviously contradictory to the Nixon-Kissinger vision. The current US China policy, turning backwards, being hostile to China again, and driving her closer to Russia, is dangerous and wrong. The Obama-Rice team is at a juncture similar to Nixon-Kissinger in history; a vision and bold action must be taken to turn a new page in the US China policy. This action may just define Obama like Nixon was defined as a great statesman in American history regardless what else happened in his Presidency. Time is the essence on Obama's watch to turn the new page.

* Sun Yat Sen and Punahou

Dr. Sun Yat Sen (1866-1925) was born in Guanzhou, China. He was sent to Hawaii to live with his elder brother and get an education. He attended the Lolani school (1879-1882) where he learned English and the elementary studies, then attended the Oahu College(1883), a college prep school now known as Punahou High School. Punahou, an excellent school in Hawaii, produced, for example in 2013, 20 National Merit Semifinalists and 5 of 10 Hawaii's National Merit Scholars. President Barack Obama was a graduate of Punahou in 1979 among 26 alumni who went to Ivy League Colleges that year. According to an alumnus report, Punahou's 1979 class eventually achieved 15 PhD, 22 MD, 39 JD, ... An impressive record for the school. Dr. Sun had a great attachment to Hawaii, he once said: "Here (Hawaii) I was brought up and educated, and it was here that I came to know what modern governments are like and what they mean."

Dr. Sun only attended Punahou for one semester and was sent back to China by his brother to get a non-Christian education, but fate had him to complete high school in Hong Kong and pursued medical studies at Canton Boji Hospital (1886) under Director Dr. John Kerr, an American doctor and a Presbyterian missionary to China. Dr. Sun obtained his MD from Hong Kong College of Medicine for Chinese in 1892, one of two graduated among 12 medical students. Dr. Sun accepted the Christian faith and was baptized at the Congregational Church of the United States in Hong Kong. Christianity had a great influence in his life; he eventually devoted his life totally to the Chinese revolution. His American Christian friends would say that he applied the missionary spirit to his revolution to save China from an unprecedented turmoil.

CHAPTER 49

IS WAR BETWEEN THE UNITED STATES

AND CHINA INEVITABLE?

—⟡—

THE SUBJECT QUESTION HAS BEEN in debate in media for some time, a few appeared in 2014: Robert Farley (The National Interest), Aaron Friedberg (International Security), John Mearsheimer and Zachary Keck (The Diplomat), Joseph S. Nye (World Affairs) and Paul Craig Roberts and Jeff Steinberg (Press TV). The question is of course very important for the U.S. and China but also for Asian nations, particularly Japan (Currently behaving like a pawn in Chinese chess ready to cross the border to fight). Although the question begs a yes or no answer, but people are interested in the rational thinking and arguments supporting a definite conclusion. Partaking in this debate in this column, a reasoning will be presented before offering a conclusion.

Among nations, there are always many conflicts, for example, territorial (political), trade (economic), cultural (religious), even small disputes (civil, like two fishing boats collided). However, disputes generally do not lead to war unless under the following three scenarios: (I) One or both countries are premeditating a war against the other for whatever reason, a premeditated war plan, (II) One country has misjudged the other country's military strength believing a dispute can be resolved simply by winning a war, a miscalculated action, and (III) A war is triggered by an accident such as a clash of military planes or ships in the public space, an impulsive decision. By analyzing the US-China conflicts along these lines, we can draw a conclusion.

(I) A Premeditated War

There is a hegemony theory claiming that a rising China is threatening the hegemony position of the U.S., however, we doubt either country is premeditating a war. The U.S. is a democratic country with her leader elected by all citizens of voting age. Since American citizens by and large are not warmongers, the American leader is most likely a compromising leader or balanced by a compromising Congress. Even though the defense department usually maintains war studies, their elected commander-in-chief is not likely to take a premeditated war path as a China policy to start off the Presidency. Americans remember very well the consequences of the two Asian wars (Korea and Vietnam) - a superpower got stuck for years gaining no apparent benefits. The current US economy and a shrinking federal budget with defense spending cuts just do not support a premeditated war plan against China. Launching a war at a far away distance is very costly. A wise US President would focus on US economy than waging a war against China.

Looking at the China side, a premeditated war against the U.S. can also be ruled out. Historically, the Chinese people dislike war even more so than Americans. Even though China is rising very fast economically, she still has a long way to go to catch up with the standard of living of the developed nations. China's military spending is only about 2-3% of her GDP, not a sign of premeditating a war. Examining China's military development, clearly she is focusing more on defense rather than offensive platforms and weapons. China's modernization of military forces is for deterrent purposes and is consistent with her desire to rise peacefully to achieve a modest goal of China Dream.

Therefore, we believe neither the U.S. nor China is premeditating a war against the other.

(II) Misjudgment Leading to War

The U.S. is a superpower with the greatest military might in the world. No matter how hawks in China, the U.S. or elsewhere are drumming, there is no way China will underestimate the military strength of the U.S. The fact that China is modernizing her military is largely motivated by her insecurity facing border and sea lane troubles from her neighbors. Russia, Japan, India even Vietnam had waged wars against China aiming at her land and sea. Japan's recent behavior led by a right-wing leader seems to suggest a possible rise of a militaristic Japan. However, although the U.S. has used Japan to strengthen her presence in Asia

Pacific, but she has no illusion that an aging Japan will become the leader in Asia. Neither China nor Russia would allow it.

Even though Japan has a strong navy, but her forces are really controlled by the U.S. China hadn't been as transparent as the U.S. in revealing her military establishment, but recently she was demonstrating her new weapons development apparently for two purposes: 1. To deter outside threats and 2. To export as the U.S. had been doing. The U.S. has a good understanding of China's military hardware; by inviting China to participate in joint military exercises she gains further understanding of China's battle capability. It is fair to say that the two nations have an accurate assessment of each other's military strength. No one holds a winning card over limited warfare and both realize that an all out war leads to mutual destruction.

Launching a war in the South China Sea with Air Sea Battle (ASB) or in Mainland China is a very expensive proposition. The U.S. and China both understood that. China accelerated her development of inexpensive missiles to counter the costly US attack platforms (likely provoked by the 'Pivot to Asia'), but China had no illusion she could wage a war against the U.S. and Japan and win. China is concerned more with a possible militant Japan rather than a rational U.S. The U.S. has been calling China to take on more world responsibilities as a great nation presumably based on a good assessment and judgment on China's military intentions.

Therefore, we believe the U.S. and China each have a proper understanding of each other's military strength and both will not wage a war to settle conflicts.

However, a warning must be said, the present Japanese Prime Minister, Abe Shinzo, a descendent from a lineage of Japanese imperialists, might be a variable. Hopefully, Japan cannot shake off the control from the U.S., hence, not foolish enough to take on China alone.

(III) Accident Leading to War

Accidents by definition are neither planned nor predictable. The likelihood of accidents is real, if the U.S. continues to exert her presence in South China Sea without any dialogue with China. The recent encounters of a US naval guided missile cruiser and a reconnaissance plane with the Chinese over South China Sea were peacefully resolved. The modern military gear all have sophisticated communication equipment, hence, accidents are less likely to occur than poor judgment calls. Developing a protocol regarding military encounter will sure prevent any accident. An open communication channel and frequent dialogue will be enough to avoid accidents and resolve issues. China's declaration of an air defense identification zone (ADIZ) in the East China Sea might have angered Japan but the U.S. accepted its value for air safety reasons. It is clear that China and the U.S. need better understanding in their mutual conduct to avoid accidents and to set the game rules for other nations such as, Japan, Philippines, Singapore, Vietnam, etc. Both the U.S. and China are fully aware that their relationship will govern the conduct of other Asian countries.

Therefore, we believe both China and the U.S. would not wish to have accidents leading to war.

There are many conflicts between the U.S. and China, but based on the above analyses, we believe war is not inevitable between them. Mutual accommodation will ultimately prevail. Otherwise, the damage would be too great. With the US-China relation on a friendly balance, Russia will play ball, Japan will accept her place (barring a militant Japan) and other Asian nations will contribute to the world prosperity and adopt a new order. A US-China war will sure lead to WW III with suicidal consequences. Who with a rational mind would want it?!

CHAPTER 50

COMMON INTEREST, OBJECTIVE AND UNDERSTANDING (IOU) POLICIES MAKE THE U.S. AND CHINA WIN-WIN

—⁓—

MEDIA COVERS OBSERVATIONS, ANALYSES, EVEN theories and recommendations about the US-China relationship and their foreign policies. US mainstream media devote volumes to China issues seemingly tilted to a hostile attitude at the moment; whereas the organic media especially blogs, comments and emails offer a wide spectrum of opinions in billions of bytes on US-China issues: friendship, conflicts, history, ideology, trade and vision positioned from extreme right to extreme left. China shows rather restrained expressions through her mainstream/official media generally defending her foreign policy and interpreting that of the U.S.; whereas her organic media exhibit trillion of bits via Weibo (Twitter like) and blogs venting the citizens' confusion, complaints, frustration and patriotism. Occasionally some "deep-thought" articles would circulate to make a salient point about the US-China relation.

Obviously, the two great nations, the U.S. and China can never isolate their relationship into a pure bilateral one. Whatever they say and do have implications to other nations in the world. Conversely, whatever major events happening in the world will complicate their relationship. Hence, we see daily headlines tying current events to the U.S. and China; ranging from politics, economics, military conflicts, health, energy, space, etc., even earthquakes and storms. So long as the world is complicated; the US-China relationship cannot be simple despite of wishing otherwise.

Dealing with a complicated relationship, understanding the issues are the key, as marriage counselors or business arbitrators will tell their clients. Relations between nations are no different. Chinese idiom, "Know yourself and know the enemy thoroughly, You would win one hundred percent of the time", originated from Sun Zi Bin Fa (The Art of War by Sun Zi), means that if you understand your opponent and yourself thoroughly, you will never fail in dealing with your opponent; a logical statement widely accepted by military strategists as gospel and by all walks of life as well. When two nations practice this doctrine, logically, both should not fail, hence, a compromise or a win-win solution must or can occur. Thus, the author wishes to propose an 'IOU' policy, based on this logic, for developing and managing the US-China relationship.

IOU, a catchy acronym in American English means "I Owe You", typically a note stating money, objects or interest owed to someone. The IOU issuer pledges to pay the IOU holder, who in turn understands exactly what to expect to receive. Here, as a US-China policy, IOU stands for "Interests, Objectives and Understanding". Under this policy, each country should declare honestly its national interests, describe clearly its objectives on issues and understand earnestly each other's claims. We believe, the U.S. and China will be able to manage their relationship in harmony and create win-win situations. In the paragraphs to follow, I illustrate how IOU may work using a few specific issues currently blasting on the media's TV screens, such as, ISIS in the Middle Ease, Ebola spreading from Africa, Global Warming affecting the world, tension in arms race, trade relation and space research. Taking one issue at a time, we state the interests and objectives each nation has, then through comparison and understanding, we arrive at a common interest and objective, on which a policy surfaces.

ISIS is the result of a complicated ideological conflict in the Middle East; the conflicts existed for decades and won't go away by brutal wars. The element of Muslim fostering terrorism is a common threat to the world. Both the U.S. and China have a common interest in the oil energy there and a common objective to have the oil flowing freely to the markets of the two nations. Therefore, the U.S. and China have a common objective to reduce the turmoil in the Middle East. Both nations are vulnerable to Muslin terrorists in their own homeland. Understanding that, the U.S. and China should have a common and sharable policy regarding the Middle East and ISIS. It makes no sense for the U.S. to agitate any unrest among Muslim minority in China or for China to refuse cooperation with the U.S. to thwart the threat of Muslim extremists.

The forth coming APEC meeting in Beijing would be an excellent venue for Obama and Xi to develop an 'IOU' policy regarding this hot-potato issue.

Ebola spread is a serious world problem, an issue both the U.S. and China can reach a common interest and common objective. The two great nations probably have the greatest number of international flights in the world and they both hold a keen interest in Africa from economical development, trade and humanitarian viewpoints. The US medical technology and the large number of Chinese agricultural and business people living in Africa together would be a powerful resource to deal with Ebola. Understanding that, Xi and Obama can easily develop an 'IOU' policy on the Ebola Issue to stop its spread and claim a deserved credit.

Global Warming is a scientifically characterized problem. The U.S. and China are two largest CO_2 emitters. Each nation has its own internal constraint to commit to reduction effort as driven by the Kyoto protocol. On this issue, again, the U.S. and China do share a common interest - to reduce global warming, and a common objective - apply technologies and internal policies to reduce pollutants. Understanding this, it would make great sense for the U.S. and China to develop an 'IOU' policy regarding pollutant emission and Global Warming, They should share or trade clean energy technology and resources, for example, US clean gas and China's solar energy products. Doing so, they could set a positive role model leading the entire world on this issue. Recently, Obama met Zhang Gao Li, Vice premier from China at the UN Climate Summit, I hope an ' IOU' policy on this issue can be quickly established. (Note: See Chapter 54, Significance of APEC-Beijing and Post-APEC Agreements between the U.S. and China regarding climate change agreement between the U.S. and China)

Similarly, on issues of reduction of arms race, collaboration in economic development in Africa and South America, and even sharing of R&D expenses in Space exploration, I believe, the U.S. and China can find a common interest and a common objective there. As I am limited in writing space in this column to get into more in-depth discussion on each of these issues, I shall, based on the logical thinking outlined above and earlier examples, make the following conclusions:

It is not difficult to understand at all why insecurity drives each other to more weapon development and arms race. It is also understandable from Growth of

GDP and world economy point of view why both nations hold a keen interest in the economical development in African and South American nations. As for space research, an expensive endeavor, it is fairly easy to understand that great nations wish to push the human frontier to space, but cooperation in space exploration under a common interest and a common objective makes the greatest sense here. Therefore, I believe, the U.S. and China should develop an 'IOU' policy regarding these issues quickly. Both the United States and China stand to gain and the world stand to benefit from these 'IOU' policies.

CHAPTER 51

USE SPACE COOPERATION TO UNITE THE EARTH

—᚜᚜᚜—

SIX MONTHS AGO, I WROTE an article, "Can Jade Rabbit (Yutu) Help Win The Space Exploration For Mankind?" (See Chapter 22), when China sent the space lab code named Jade Rabbit (Yutu) to the Moon. I commented that the U.S. mainstream media kept silent on that event, deliberately buried the news under the media rug. I also called for international cooperation on space exploration, since the endeavor is challenging for any single nation. I was thinking then a joint project in space science may focus mankind's energy on collaboration than squabbling over Earth problems, such as the dispute over Diaoyu Islands. However, In view of the U.S. foreign policy - Pivot to Asia, targeting China as a new Cold War enemy and tension with Russia over Ukraine, I was pessimistic about such a grand international cooperation project. However, the United States, Russia and China are the principal players in space research; China made significant strides despite of being a late comer and isolated from a U.S. led international space research.

Yutu, the Chinese Moon Rover was carried by Chang'e 3 and landed on the moon on 12-14-2013. China is the third nation to make a soft landing on the Moon, a significant accomplishment by the Chinese space researchers. Yutu was designed to explore the lunar surface and to perform a number of experiments powered by solar energy. In March, 2014, Yutu had problem positioning its solar penal but then the latest news revealed that Yutu was still alive and able to release a panorama view of the Moon surface just in time before the Chinese world-wide celebrating the Moon Festival.

In August, 2014, China's State Administration of Science, Technology and Industry of Defense Department announced that a recoverable moon orbiter will be launched before the end of the year. Flown from Beijing to Xichang, Sichuan and transported to the Xichang Satellite Launch Center, this orbiter would be the test model for the new lunar probe Chang'e 5, whose mission is to land the orbiter on the Moon surface to perform unmanned sampling and to return back to Earth. The breakthrough challenges are takeoff from the moon surface after sample encapsulation, ducking with the orbiter and high-speed earth reentry. No doubt, this mission should make further inspiration in space travel, if everything went well.

On September 4th, China successfully launched her Long March 2D, a 13 story rocket, carrying two satellites, Chuan Xin 1-04, each weighing 90 kilograms, into orbit. These satellites are a series of small satellites to form 'store and forward' communication architecture in low earth orbit. The first satellite of the series, CBERS-2 Earth Observation Satellite, was launched in October 2003 and the next two were launched in 2008 and 2011 respectively. As a store and forward satellite, the CX 1-04 can receive data packets from remote ground stations such as weather station, water-level monitoring devices or sensors on electrical grid or pipelines, store them in their onboard memory and then downlink to a ground station for distribution. Long March 2D can launch payloads up to 3500 kilograms. This launch was China's 4th orbital mission of the year and third in the last four weeks, a clear indication that China has a viable transport technology for space travel.

The U.S. was the first country landed human (Neil Armstrong, Mike Collins and Buzz Aldrin via Apollo 11) on the moon on July 16, 1969. National Aeronautics and Space Administration (NASA) has demonstrated a long list of glorious achievements over half a century. From the first Mercury astronauts to the present, over 300 people have travelled into orbits on U.S. spacecrafts. Well said in a history book by NASA, "The first astronauts went along stuffed into capsules barely large enough for their bodies, eating squeeze-tube food and peering out at Earth through tiny portholes.... flights lasted only hours. Today, ... launch seven people at a time to spend a week living, working, and exploring aboard the Space Shuttle. .... crew members from various nations keep a permanent human presence aboard the International Space Station (ISS)". This is a proud history for Americans but also for the whole mankind. Space technologies have been advanced to extend space travel in range and sophisticated human operations in space. These advances inspire us to entertain a dream: "a permanent human presence off Earth". The challenges ahead are beyond rockets, takeoff and landing, we need to learn how to travel comfortably in space and how to stay and live there.

The ISS was first launched in 1998 and it has been continuously occupied and visited by spacecrafts from 15 nations since 11-2-2000. As of 9-11-2014, 214 individuals and 358 spaceflights have made to ISS with Americans and Russians being the dominant parties. Notably, China was not a partner of ISS but China launched its first experimental space station, Tiangong 1, in September 2011 and officially initiated her permanently manned Chinese space station project. In 2007, Chinese vice-minister of science and technology Li Xueyong said that China would like to participate in the ISS. While European Space Agency (ESA) was open to China's inclusion, the U.S. was against it concerning over the transfer of technology ended in military use. The U.S. had similar concern about Russia but they were overcome; Russia brought in substantial technologies and astronaut experience. The funding of ISS is committed by the U.S. to 2024 and by Russia to 2020. The recent Ukraine crisis has cast doubts on the Roscomos (Russian's space agency) ISS funding beyond 2020. President Barack Obama declared a mandate that U.S. astronauts would no longer rely on Russia for transport. NASA, in a recent historical announcement of privatization of space travel with ambition to land humans on Mars, the agency awarded Contracts of nearly $7 billion to Boeing and an upstart SpaceX to carry astronauts to the International Space Station by 2017. These changes certainly put ISS, the most ambitious international collaboration project, in uncertainty.

China has expressed interest in joining the ISS project and China's manned Shenzhou spacecraft could dock at the ISS barring political objection according to American observers. Presumably China is willing to contribute funding and share her technologies with all partners. Why is the U.S. managing the most significant international cooperative project under the umbrella of world politics rather than treating ISS as a noble, valuable and common goal for all mankind beyond politics? Today, the global economy dictates all global corporations (and nations) to think as a global entity. Why can't ISS be managed like a global corporation to achieve its intended goal?

As a key organizer partnering with the Association of Space Explorers (ASE, an international nonprofit organization of over 395 astronauts and cosmonauts from 35 nations), China's Manned Space Agency is hosting the landmark gathering in Beijing from September 10-15 to talk space cooperation. The conference theme is "Cooperation to Realize Humanity's Space Dream Together" with a goal to encourage open discussion about international cooperation in human spaceflights in the future. The U.S. should take a lesson from CEO 101 to redefine her strategy with ISS and her space programs to support the human dream. Focusing on space cooperation together rather than scheming over limited Earth resources in the Pacific is for the best interest of the U.S. and the Earth.

CHAPTER 52

Who is More Stupid to Engage in Arms Race and

Repeat the Cold War? is the U.S. or China?

—∭—

COLD WAR STARTED AT THE end of WW II. The U.S. and the Soviet Union engaged in it (1947-91) for a total of 44 years. The Western bloc led by the U.S. and the NATO alliance and the Eastern bloc led by the Soviet Union and the Warsaw pact engaged in an arms race prepared for a scenario of WW III. Although there were several military conflicts and regional wars but the Cold War ended with the collapse of the Soviet Union without the eruption of a world war. The Berlin blockage (1948-9) and the Korean war (1950-53) were short-lived but the Vietnam war lasted 20 years (1955-75) resulting in a defeated South Vietnam (backed by the U.S.) and the split between the Soviet and China (1968-) changing the dynamics of the Cold War.

During the Cold War, the first conflict close to America was the Cuban Missile Crisis (1962) when the Soviet Union was attempting to build a missile base in Cuba. President Kennedy took the risk of erupting into a nuclear war by facing down the Soviet to back off from Cuba. What we learned from the Cuba Crisis was that one, the U.S. would risk going all out when her home base was threatened and two, the nuclear weapon is an effective deterrent to global war barring its proliferation into slippery hands. Hence during the Cold War era, the U.S. and the Soviet Union engaged in an arms race with the development and stockpiling of nuclear weapons on one hand and playing containment, détente and counter-measures on the other hand. The collapse of the Soviet Union is not due to her deficiency in military technology, especially nuclear weaponry, but due to her weakness in economy. The Soviet Union, though a large exporter of energy, was unable to sustain a costly arms race. The U.S. was somewhat fortunate under Reaganomics to have a recovery of her economy but did incur an increase of the budget deficit of more than 50%.

China's defect from imperial communism changed the dynamics of the world economy. The past quarter century witnessed the rise of China's economy to $9.5 trillion, ranking number two in the world. This is not a bad thing for the world as it clearly indicates that fast growth is possible for an underdeveloped nation if she focuses on economical development. However, instead of analyzing and re-producing such a rapid nation development model, the world media seems to be focused on the arms race between the U.S. and China. The international voices are split between the U.S. (and Japan as a partner) drumming up a 'China threat' theory to justify military expansion versus China and her third world friends de-fending against a hegemony behavior and a possible revival of military imperial-ism in Japan. (with the U.S. looking on) A most recent article, one and half page spread in the Wall Street Journal (October 25-2014) entitled, "'Deep Threat' and 'China's Submarine Gambit'", by Jeremy Page, clearly painted a picture of naval competition between the two nations. Sifting through the rhetoric arguments in the media, one wonders whether the military rise in China is a response to the U.S. Pivot strategy (fortifying a first and second island chain containing China with choke points) or the U.S. Pivot strategy is a response to the military rise in China (threatening her neighboring countries).

No matter how one interprets the rhetoric, the US China policy appears to repeat a new Cold War scenario that may not lead to a peaceful outcome as the previous one. As a concerned US citizen without intimate knowledge of national defense secrets, the only sensible thing one can do is to ask some rational questions and hope to get some rational answers that may guide us to a logical conclusion. Hopefully such a conclusion can be presented as a citizen's opinion on the US China policy influencing it into a logical path avoiding an all out war.

We have learned from the previous Cold War some basic principles such as: A. When a nation's homeland and her livelihood are threatened, she will react even risking engaging in an all out war; B. Arms race especially nuclear weapon race does not provide solution to any conflict; and C. Arms race is costly requiring a strong economy to sustain it and risking crippling the economy and leading to an eventual economic collapse. Based on these principles, we may ask the following questions about the 'China Threat', the US Pivot strategy and China's military rise:

1. If the U.S. as a nation with military might were so concerned with a Soviet missile base in Cuba, why wouldn't China as a rising nation be nervous about the first island chain and second island chain the U.S. is designing to contain China? The logical answer is: She sure would.

2. As an example, despite historical evidence and WW II Potsdam Declaration supporting China's claim of the Diaoyu Islands, the U.S. is encouraging and siding with Japan in the Diaoyu Island dispute under a pretense of staying neutral; why shouldn't China be concerned with the US motive and the obvious ambition of Japan in territorial expansion? The logical answer is: She is forced to take a more assertive stand to settle the dispute than her previous position of postponing the settlement indefinitely.

3. When Okinawa people was protesting against the US Military base there, why shouldn't China be worried about the US intention in upgrading and expanding her military base there to fortify her island chain strategy against China? The logical answer is: China has no choice but strengthen her military base and naval forces to break the island chain.

4. While China is saying that she is not stupid to repeat the mistake the Soviet made in draining her treasury by arms race during the Cold War, why is China accelerating her military expenditure? Could China's military strategy be a simple response to the US 'Rebalancing' strategy - by deploying 60% of her naval forces in Western Pacific targeting China as an enemy? The logic answer is: It does not make sense, the military strategies must be wrong.

Jerremy Page's long article, although titled as "Deep Threat", fails to articulate the threat to be real. The U.S. is not only maintaining superiority in her naval forces but also can control the narrow straits (choking points) where the Chinese subs must pass to get to the Pacific and Indian Oceans. The Chinese Navy although has four boomers (ballistic missile submarine), five nuclear powered subs and at least 50 diesel powered attack subs, but the U.S. Navy has 14 boomers and 55 attack subs. The Chinese boomers are noisy hence detectable whereas the US navy is confident that her deployment of subs in the Pacific is "untracked by anyone" according to Philip Sawyer, the commander of the US submarine forces in the Pacific. Under this condition, it is hardly logical for the U.S. to promote an arms race with China (whose economy is still growing with a 7.5% GDP growth per annum) knowing her own defense budget is being cut projecting a specific reduction of her attack subs to 41 by 2028. As for China, she is fully aware of her military burden (and the cause of the Soviet's collapse) hence planning a reduction of her army personnel. Shouldn't a concerned citizen ask: **Who is more stupid to engage in arms race and repeat the Cold War?**

CHAPTER 53

APEC PAST, PRESENT AND FUTURE SPROUTING

OF THE TWO GREAT NATIONS RELATIONSHIP

—ᴍ—

APEC (ASIA-PACIFIC CO-OPERATION) IS A summit conference and international forum established by leaders and business executives in the Asia Pacific region to promote economic growth and co-operation in trade, investment and development. Over the past 25 years, APEC has evolved to gain prominence by having national leaders of 21 economies participating every year. This year is APEC's 25th anniversary; the host China is not only making it a festive occasion but also a milestone event to energize the members to focus on new growth for Asia Pacific. While the 2014 APEC conference just came to an end, it is very appropriate for me to devote this column to discuss the Past, Present and Future of APEC.

THE PAST

The origin of the APEC idea was attributed to Bob Hawke, former Prime Minister of Australia and its first meeting was held in November, 1989 at Canberra, Australia with 12 founding members, Australia, Brunei Darussalam, Canada, Indonesia, Japan, Korea, Malaysia, New Zealand, the Philippines, Singapore, Thailand and the United States. China, Hong Kong-China and Chinese Taipei concurrently joined in 1991, followed by Mexico and Papua New Guinea in 1993, Chile in 1994, and Peru, Russia and Viet Nam in 1998. The APEC now has 21 full members representing about 53 percent of the global gross domestic product (GDP) and 44 percent of international trade. To former United States President Bill Clinton's credit, in 1993, he established the practice of an annual APEC Economic Leaders' Meeting to provide greater strategic vision and direction to cooperation in the region. This has since bestowed importance, value and expectation to APEC as an annual conference.

The 25-year history of APEC and its accomplishments may be briefly summarized by the following key words in a long chain: Establishment (1989 Australia), National Leaders Meeting (1993, United States), Bogor Goals (1994, Indonesia, free trade for developed economies by 2010 and for developing economies by 2020), Osaka Action Agenda (1995, Japan, framework for meeting Bogor goal), Manila Action Plan (1996, Philippines, outlining liberalization measures for Bogor goal), Early Voluntary Sectoral Liberalization Proposal (1997, Canada, 15 sectors), EVSL 9 (1998, Malaysia, agreed on 9 sectors), Paperless (1999, New Zealand, paperless trading for developed economies by 2005 and underdeveloped economies by 2010), E-IAP, electronic individual plan (2000, Brunnei Darussalim, Triple Internet Access in APEC), Shanghai Accord (2001, China, broadening APEC vision and clarifying Bogor), Trade Facilitation Action Plan (2002, Mexico, counter-terrorism and Secure Trade in APEC Region), APEC and WTO (2003, Thailand, re-energizing WTO Doha Development Plan, Security and Health Security), Statement on WTO Doha (2004, Chile, Sets Target Date), Busan Roadmap (2005, Korea, Well Met Mid-Term Bogor Goals and Privacy Framework), Ha Noi Action Plan (2006, Vietnam, Actions and Milestones for Bogor, Capacity-Building Measures, Reform Working Groups and Strengthening Secretariat), Declaration on Climate Change, Energy Security and Clean Development (2007, Australia, Closer Regional Economic Integration and Reducing Trade Transaction Cost A Further 5% by 2010), Social Dimension (2008, Peru, Reducing Gap between Developing and Developed Members, Statement on Global Economy/Financial Crisis), Balanced, Inclusive and Sustainable Growth (2009, Singapore, Senior Trade & Financial Official Met Addressing Economic Crisis, Supply-Chain Connectivity Framework), Yokohama Vision (2010, Japan, Long-Term Growth Strategy, assessment of Bogor Goals, Structural Reform), Honolulu Declaration (2011, United States, Steps to Seamless Regional Economy, Reducing Tariff on Environmental Goods to <5% by 2015, reducing aggregate Energy Intensity by 45% by 2035, Good Regulatory Practice by 2013), List of Environmental Goods of Green Growth and Sustainable Development (2012, Russia, Leaders Endorsing Transparency Model for Trade and Investment), Push To Conclude "Bali Package" at 9th WTO Ministerial Conference (2013, Indonesia, Enhanced Regional Connectivity, 1 Million intra-AP University Students Per Year by 2020).

The above chronological listing of achievements is very significant, interested readers can visit APEC website for further details. The initiation of national leaders meeting added impetus to APEC to set vision and goal as well as to define specific action plans. APEC has been a democratic organization and each member economy feels accountable to APEC resolutions. Over the past 25 years, tremendous progress has been made in facilitating trade and investment in the region with conscientious effort towards the development of green growth and sustainable development.

The Present

China is the host of the 25th anniversary of APEC Summit. China as an APEC nation has enjoyed a sustained growth over the history of APEC, proudly emerging as the world's number two economy. China is not a founding member of APEC but her development is an enviable example of all Asia Pacific economies. Apparently, the leaders in China are putting a lot of efforts in the planning of the 25th anniversary of APEC, including forcefully presenting a blue sky over Beijing during the week of the meeting. A city of 21 million people and 6 million cars registered with Beijing city license plates is faced with a tremendous challenge in controlling its air pollution. The Chinese leader Xi Jinping in his address to APEC attendees humorously acknowledged that the blue sky over Beijing during the conference period has been called APEC blue, but stressed that China would continue making efforts in pollution control to keep the skies blue, mountains green and waters clear.

The theme of the 25th APEC is to unlock New Growth. The multi-tier conference agenda of the 2014 APEC in Beijing consists of:

I. Senior Officials Meeting on November 5-6: It finalized a package of new growth enhancing measures.
II. Ministerial Meeting on November 7-8: It decided new actions for deepening Asia-Pacific partnership to navigate the changing regional and global landscape and boosting economic recovery. The meeting concluded with a statement of 103 points.
III. CEO Summit on November 8 -10: It welcomed 1500 economic leaders and CEOs to deliberate the key issues facing the development of the

Asia-Pacific economy - "Advancing Regional Economic Integration", "Promoting Innovative Development, Economic Reform and Growth" and "Strengthening Comprehensive Connectivity and Infrastructure Development".

IV. Economic Leaders Meeting on November 10-11: It was hosted by China's leader Xi Jinping. It had declared the Beijing Agenda (2014, Beijing) for an integrated, innovative and interconnected Asia-Pacific.

The leaders' declaration, of course, is the highlight of every APEC meeting. The 22nd Declaration outlines new far-reaching measures for advancing regional economic integration, promoting innovative development, economic reform and growth, and strengthening comprehensive connectivity and infrastructure development expecting an expanding and deepening of regional economic cooperation, and attaining peace, stability, development and common prosperity of the Asia-Pacific.   *(View the 22nd APEC Economic Leaders' Meeting Declaration – http://www.apec.org)*

THE FUTURE

APEC has gained a respectable position as an organization and annual event to plot the future of Asia-Pacific. Prior to the meeting, national leaders not only look forward to participation but also seek opportunities to meet with other leaders to have a meaningful dialogue to improve foreign relations and economic cooperation between economies. For example, Abe Shinzo sought after a meeting with Xi Jiping during APEC to thaw the icy relation between Japan and China. The Sino-Japan relation took a dive ever since Abe visited the Yasukuni and chanted a nationalistic slogan to restore Japan's past glory. Abe's behavior reminded the Asian countries the atrocious past of the Imperial Japan. Xi did agree to meet with Abe at APEC after Japan had agreed to a four-point declaration to respect the past historical agreements and moving forward with peaceful actions.

The leader of Chinese Taipei Economy, Ma Ying-Jeou, on the other hand, could not obtain a meeting with Xi at APEC since the relationship across the Taiwan Strait had deviated from the direction the two sides agreed on back in 1992. China apparently in her diplomatic relations has been firm and consistent in staking her positions. The Russian leader Putin had met with Xi and in his speech stated that Russia and China would do business using RMB and Ruble as trade currency. In this APEC conference, Xi appeared to be confident about realizing the China Dream to raise the prosperity of the Chinese people but he also called for an Asia Pacific Dream in his speech, a greater aspiration.

Obama, the leader of the U.S., in his speech, claimed credit for helping China to join the international community and would welcome the rising of a prosperous and innovative China. He said in his speech: "The relationship of China and the U.S. is important; the world benefits from a great relationship between the two largest economies", which received a thundering applause. Obama's and other leaders' open statements all point to a possible rosy future for Asia Pacific. In APEC, China has essentially demonstrated to the U.S. what 'two great nations relationship' really means and how China can step up to the plate of world responsibilities. Of course, world politics depends on personalities and domestic politics. At the time of this writing, Obama and Xi are announcing post-APEC agreements regarding climate change, military exercise protocol, broader visa accord and investment, all showing that the 'Two-Great-Nations-Relationship' is sprouting and working.

The loss of the Democratic Party of the U.S. in the 2014 mid-term election may spell uncertainly about the leadership in the U.S. in 2016; however, in the remaining two years of Obama's tenure, perhaps, he has an opportunity to tune down the US China policy of 'Target China' – increasing arms race in the South China Sea and pitting TPP against FTAAP – to a more accommodating policy of 'Embracing China' - engaging China to deal with world hot spots and crises such as ISIS, terrorists, nuclear proliferation as well as economic recovery, Ebola and global environment. An immediate positive stand the U.S. could take is to support the Asia Infrastructure Investment Bank (AIIB) that China and several other nations are promoting. The goal of the bank is definitely in line with the APEC declaration this year. An early involvement of the U.S. in AIIB will be a win-win opportunity for the U.S. and all APEC members. The world definitely can use more than one World Bank.

History often has turning points which may or may not be all predictable. Watching the APEC events unfold, one cannot help but feel that the APEC Beijing (2014) may be a turning point in the global history or at least in the Asia Pacific history. What the U.S. and China will do together in the next two years, will define precisely how promising this turning point will turn out to be!

(Another article, The Significance of Post-APEC Agreements between the U.S. and China, published on the website, www.us-chinaforum.org, is included below as chapter 54)

SIGNIFICANCE OF APEC-BEIJING AND POST-APEC

AGREEMENTS BETWEEN THE U.S. AND CHINA

—m—

APEC BEIJING HAS JUST BEEN concluded. As the 25th anniversary event, it is understandable that the 2014 APEC showed a bit more of extravaganza than prior conferences. China as the host did a fantastic job in welcoming the top leaders, ministers and business executives of the 21 Asia Pacific economies with manicured accommodations, services and personal gifts, awe-inspiring, lavish and sumptuous State Dinner, and splendid, impressive and entertaining art performance. The Mayor of Beijing, by administrative measure of traffic and air pollution control, even managed to offer the APEC guests blue sky during the week of their stay. Beijing citizens rarely could see blue skies, hence pleasantly called the color of their sky APEC Blue during the November month. However, the grandiose happenings in Beijing were not the real significance of 2014 APEC. The significance is in the expectations and goals that are created by the APEC leaders and the immediate post-APEC agreements that have been reached between the U.S. and China.

The 68-point leaders' Declaration made in the 2014 APEC was not only a continuation but also the expansion of the scope and pace of reaching the goal of Free Trade Area of the Asia Pacific (FTAAP). The leaders set the following focuses:

1. Advancing regional economic integration,
2. Promoting innovative development and economic reform and growth, and
3. Strengthening comprehensive connectivity and infrastructure development. The emphasis is to bring vision to reality on FTAAP.

The significance of 2014 APEC was first demonstrated by the fact that the key economies, the U.S., China, Japan, Russia and India, all had been cordially making commitment to the APEC goals. The competing (and distracting) topics such as Trans-Pacific Partnership (TPP) did not come up openly during the APEC meeting; they might not even have occurred in private discussion since there was no post-APEC grapevine report on them. The 21 economies had appeared to be on the same page in charting the economic course of Asia Pacific.

Prior to APEC, the Japanese PM, Abe Shinzo had made concessive agreement to recognize the historical accords regarding territorial disputes between Japan and China in order to obtain a meeting with China's leader Xi Jinping. This is a significant development for Japan and China to thaw their icy relation ever since Abe visited the Yasukuni Shrine to worship the WW II war criminals. Another significant break-through was that the South Korean President Park Geun-Hye and China's President Xi Jinping agreed to sign a free trade agreement (FTA) (which had been in negotiation for two years) at the APEC summit. Immediately following APEC, the U.S. President Obama made a formal State Visit to China; what is surprising and newsworthy was that Obama and Xi held long personal talks lasting two hours beyond their scheduled two and half hours private meeting. Obama claimed he had for the first time learned so much about the Chinese Communist party and its governing philosophy from Xi. The most significant outcome, which surprised the world, was the agreements they announced.

While the news media were busy reporting on the details of APEC meetings, President Obama of the U.S. and President Xi of China took the spotlight again immediately after the APEC summit. Post-APEC during Obama's state visit, the U.S. and China announced the following significant agreements:

1. Climate Change - The United States would cut between 26-28% of the level of her carbon emissions set in 2005 by 2025, and China would regulate her carbon emission to peak before 2030, a welcome surprise to the world and to the International Climate Conference to be held in Paris next year.
2. Military Protocol - Rules of conduct regarding military encounters and exercises to avoid accidents to occur. This agreement certainly will reduce the tension in Asia Pacific Air and Sea. (See Chapter 49)

3. Visa Requirement - Both countries will offer broader and longer visa to their business people and citizens to facilitate easier interaction and cultural exchange.

4. Tariff Reduction - Drop of tariffs on a range of tech products possibly covering $1 trillion in trade, a significant agreement to be ratified by WTO in Geneva next month.

The climate change agreement, containing several action plans to achieve the goal, is a big deal, since both countries have groups opposing any effort in reducing emission and climate control, in the U.S. for fear of losing economic competitiveness and sacrificing life style and in China for fear of limiting her economic development and hampering her citizens' desire of higher standard of living. The fact that the efforts do not solely depend on government agency (EPA, in the U.S.) as much as private enterprise efforts in research and development and implementation of green energy initiative, is also significant. The agreement will transcend beyond Obama's tenure to 2016 (facing a possibility of Republican taking over the White House) and even beyond Xi's tenure to 2022 when PRC is likely to change her top leadership.

The world must congratulate the APEC leaders for making a broad declaration and the leaders of China and the U.S. for making the above agreements. The world stands to benefit. However, the real significance of the events taken place pre-APEC to post-APEC is the fact that the U.S. and China finally engaged with each other in a two great nations relationship. China has voiced before her desire to enter such a Two-Great-Nations Relationship with the U.S. when Xi visited Obama at the Sunnylands, Rancho Mirage, California, but the U.S. had not figured out what did that mean. Throughout the APEC conference, China had acted as a confident host, not only as the world's second largest economy but also had taken charge of the responsibility of a great nation. Prior to APEC, China initiated the idea of establishing an Asian Infrastructure Investment Bank (AIIB), implemented an anti-graft proposal, announced a $40 billion Chinese-financed fund to improve trade links among Asian economies as well as approved a plan to open Chinese stock markets wider to foreign investors by linking exchanges in Hong Kong and Shanghai. During APEC, China, in addition to being a gracious and generous host, was able to bring forward her ideas into implementation plans as seen by the adopted action plans to strengthen comprehensive connectivity and infrastructure development and advancing regional economic integration. China has exhibited her confidence in realizing her China Dream by calling for an Asia Pacific Dream.

The Post-APEC agreements made with the U.S. further provide evidence that China is now acting as a great nation cooperating with the U.S. in facing the world challenges together. The intimate interactions between Obama and Xi had clearly revealed that the two leaders now had understood each other much better and the U.S. had come to realize what did the two-great-nations-relation really mean. From Obama's speeches, it seems that the understanding, respect and trust between the U.S. and China have opened a new page, that is, when the U.S. and China work together, the world stands to benefit! So one can say the most significant impact of APEC and Post-APEC events is that the two great nations relation is now understood and working.

Of course, two great nations will always have differences and each has its own legacy. In diplomatic relations, protocol and face (West and East all have face issue, it was never an East monopolized characteristics) are always critical; it is more so for two great nations. Interpreting the APEC impact from a two-great-nations-relation point of view, it may be said that it is a win-win situation for the two nations. China has succeeded in demonstrating her confidence as a rising great nation, capable and willing to assume more world responsibilities, certainly able to start from Asia Pacific. China's status as a great nation has been demonstrated and will be there whether other countries recognize it or not. She has brought her ideas to APEC and promoted them into action plans. She has made the 21 Asia-Pacific economies to realize that China is a great nation in AP and her success will be the success of the entire AP region. On the other hand, the U.S. has demonstrated that as a super-power, she has always carried the world responsibilities and she is a pragmatic great nation. After being absent for two APEC meetings, Obama has recognized the value of APEC and the damage from being absent. By participating again with vigor, the United States has demonstrated that she is a part of AP. She has been able to influence China to respect the world order and the existing rules that have governed international relations. **Both the U.S. and China can claim credit to the evolvement of 2014 APEC resolution; and indeed, only when they can work together, then Asia Pacific benefits and the world benefits.**

As an observer of APEC from afar, I can see all the positive effects pointing to a bright future for the two great nations, the Asia Pacific and the world. Hence, I am optimistic about the two great nations being able to work together and handle whatever differences there may be. The other economies will play in this new order so long as the two great nations are willing to honor the two-great-nations relationship. In fact, **many Asia pacific countries do not wish to take sides; they rather see the two great nations work well together!**

CHAPTER 55

IS CHINA SO DIFFICULT TO UNDERSTAND

BY THE WEST? WHY? WHY NOT?

—⟋⟋⟋—

WHENEVER THE TOPIC OF US-CHINA Relation comes up in a conversation among Americans with varied background, inevitably the discussion moves to interpreting current events involving China and the U.S. The fact that more and more people are interested in China-US affairs is a good thing, but very often one only heard these interpretations in a third person voice, namely quoting the media or hearsay. If there were Chinese Americans present, they were expected to engage in the discussion but expecting a first person opinion or knowledge. Unfortunately not all Chinese Americans, especially second or third generation Chinese Americans, who may have physical Chinese features but rarely they can express their opinions convincingly in a knowledgeable manner with a first person tone. Nothing wrong with this phenomenon except the discussion tend to end with puzzles and question marks to the issues in discussion. This is not a good thing. The end result is that China is hard to understand by the West.

Occasionally in group conversation, you have Chinese people who possess reasonably good knowledge about China but then they have not been in the West long enough to understand why China is so difficult to understand by the West? Or they don't have a reasonably good knowledge about the West, especially the views of mainstream media which dominate the mass. Or they have a language handicap in English to deliver their opinions in a convincing sound bite manner. Therefore, these Chinese people, being American citizens or residents or recent immigrants very much wanting to express their opinions, cannot convince their friends to accept why China is not so difficult to understand?!

Of course, it is not any single person's fault the title questions exist among Americans or westerners and to some extent for many people in the entire world. China is a large country with more than 3.7 million square miles of land not counting her islands and seas. China has the biggest population in the world, evolved from many races over thousands of years. This population consists of a principal language, a central Chinese culture and an uniquely blended Chinese philosophy but it also contains multiple dialects, different customs, rich variation of cuisines, all sorts of religions (despite of an atheist constitution limiting promotion of religion in contrast to a religious American constitution now being challenged to remove its religion base by some people), long economic and political history and very different life styles expanding many centuries. This characterization of China alone is enough a challenge for Chinese to understand China completely and you sure can appreciate what is like to Americans.

In a digital world today with Wikipedia, Weibo, Twitter and abundance of search engines in the Internet cloud, there is no lack of raw data and information about China and the U.S. but what is missing is some honest interpretation of facts with no bias. Unfortunately, to the title questions, the five millennia of Chinese history (a huge literal challenge) and the recent centuries of anti-communism ideology (a constant intellectual brain-rinse) have created obstacles or biases preventing turning the zillions of data and information (including the Chinese classic literature) to fair and honest knowledge about China. Hence, the metaphors such as a rising China, an awakening lion or a flying dragon have been created and interpreted to represent a mystical China and a future threat to the West.

Many people don't believe that, especially the Chinese Americans who have a good understanding of the Chinese history and culture. What can or shall the Chinese Americans do regarding the title questions then? I would like to take an optimist's view to say, it is simple, or at least not difficult, to do a logical analysis on the title questions and tell anyone who cares to listen to your answers. Here is my version of the analysis for the readers of this column with the hope that it will draw many plausible versions to demystify 'China' and prove that China is not difficult to understand.

CHINA IS NOT A MYSTERIOUS COUNTRY

China is not more mysterious than Japan or India. Americans often say that on a personal level, Chinese is not difficult to get along or become close friends. Generally, Chinese are hard working employees, devotees to children, considerate in personal relationship or being a boss and generous when becoming close friends. Yes, they may have some English language handicap or they may appear to be more reserved or conservative but they are more than willing to receive an extending hand of friendship, nothing mysterious at all. China as a country is not mysterious either recognizing the facts mentioned above: big country, large population, multiple dialects, religion neutral, different inheritance and long history of prosperity but century of misery due to the invasion of the West including Japan. There is no real mystery if one logically analyzes China from the above aspects. Yes, China has too many philosophies, some with opposing assumptions, for example, one believes that humans are born 'good' with a kind and compassionate heart, but environment and upbringing will contaminate and lead them to be evil; another believes that humans are born 'evil' with all bad traits such as being barbaric, selfish, greedy, etc, only education and good upbringing will make them good people. Is there anything wrong with these philosophies? Anything really mysterious? No, one simply has to understand that both may be true. The Chinese people brought up in Chinese families exposed to multiple philosophies do develop a central universal philosophy though, that is, be kind to oneself, others and the environment. Yes, love the environment is deeply ingrained in Chinese philosophy. On this point, It is nice to see that the U.S. and China signed a Climate Change agreement recently.

Let's continue the analysis by asking what about China's economic, political and legal system? Aren't they different from ours and threatening our systems? Here is my view below.

ECONOMIC SYSTEM

I would say China's economic system might be different from the western economic system, but it would be neither mysterious nor threatening. West civilization evolved late but fast, more materialistic than spiritual, easily visible and admirable; hence since 19th century, the West had developed an attitude of being superior, which formed a bias and persisted in the United States throughout WW II as the U.S. emerged as the superpower in the world. China, despite her prosperous past in her long history, suffered greatly in the 19th century owing to the West invasion. In the first seven decades of 20th century, she became extremely poor owing to her devastating past (unequal treaties imposed on her by the invading powers) and a treacherous revolution (trying to establish a republic and experimenting with socialistic communism). However, in the recent four decades or so, China has adopted reform and pursued the western style of economic development as manifested by her advances in infrastructure, technology and modernization of life style. Capitalism was employed in this reform process, but as a concept, capitalism has not been foreign to Chinese at all in their history. Money bank (Qian Zhuan), Pawn shop (Dang Pu), and private enterprising had been in practice in China for at least a couple of millennia resulting in examples of wealthy merchants richer than the emperor. The fast development in the recent few decades may be envied by many other countries; but it is actually costing China a lot in compromising her deep traditional culture as well as going backwards in spiritual civilization. Corruption has always accompanied with money and riches. Corruption was tolerated for the sake of harmonious peace in ancient Chinese history by emperors who would only take some cleansing measures when corruption had become so severe, either choking the nation's economy, threatening governance or hampering people's survival. Therefore, one should not be surprised that China had launched a serious anti-corruption program after recognizing that many of her successful state enterprises were deep in corruption.

POLITICAL SYSTEM

Politically, China has long been an imperial system. With her advanced economic and cultural development, the Chinese emperors firmly believed that China was in the middle of the world, geographically centered to lead the world, hence the dynasties in China practiced a foreign policy of 'suzerainty' or 'tributary relation', rewarding any suzerainty with gifts and aids even marriages with Emperor's daughters. This policy worked most of the time except some ambitious foreign leaders exploited the situation. The three dynasties, Jin, Yuan and Qing are the result of such foreign invasion. This part of history was the principal motivation for Japan to try to conquer China after Japan had succeeded in her westernization process (Meiji Restoration). The Chinese revolution against a corrupt and weak Qing dynasty was a treacherous route interrupted by the Japanese invasion (WWII) and the Western powers' intervention, namely, Russia backing a communist revolution group (Mao Ze-dong) and the United States backing a national revolution group (Chiang Kai-chek). Mao eventually won and established the People's Republic of China in the mainland while Chiang's Republic of China retreated to Taiwan. Mao succeeded in revolution but failed in experimenting with communism leading to a break up with the Soviet Union in 1968. The subsequent reform in China initiated by Deng Xiao Ping had led to the four decades of rapid economic development moving China's economy to be closer to the second largest in the world, which lent tremendous credit to the unique Chinese one-party governing system. Democracy is practiced within the party and the exclusion of other political party assures the unity of the nation. The current leader, Xi Jinping, rose to the leadership position only after serving the party and the country successfully in many challenging positions. Now he is facing the challenge of sustaining China's economic growth while dealing with a complex world with several hostile and envious neighbors. Obviously, the failed and antique 'suzerainty' foreign policy could not be employed anymore. So it is no mystery that China is learning from the United States in strengthening and conducting herself. This explains China's assertive attitude regarding any territorial dispute and her desire to be recognized as a great nation. China's proposal of two-great-nations relationship with the U.S. should not be interpreted as a threat but a sincere desire to work with the U.S. together to maintain a peaceful world. Unless the U.S. believes that she alone and only she alone can maintain the world order, otherwise, engaging China in a two-great-nations relationship appears to be a logical win-win policy.

LEGAL SYSTEM

The legal system in the West is a corrective system, assuming innocence then correct mistakes or criminal acts with legal actions. This system seems to have philosophical roots in 'people are born good' discussed above. This legal system is by no means perfect, for example, regarding freedom of speech, an abuser of freedom of speech, making slanderous attack on someone else, may be prosecuted, convicted even punished, but often the end result is still unfair to the innocent with his or her reputation ruined by the bad publicity associated with the trial. Another example is sex crime committed by a sex offender; in protecting the offender's right for a trial, the victim's privacy and human dignity often get destroyed. These types of examples give a bad impact to the society. Whereas in the East, the philosophy of 'people are born evil and education is needed to drive away the devil' seems to exist in the legal system in China; 'assuming innocence' is balanced with a bit of 'assuming evil', hence there are more restrictive and preventive laws limiting people's freedom especially in the area of moral subjects such as sex crime, pornography, and freedom of speech, etc. Again, there should be no mystery why the Chinese society appeared to have less liberty in some ways and more permissive in others.

RELIGION

A Christian society or nation worships one God; various denominations of Christianity more or less have a common root. China, with a long history existed before Christ, is basically an inclusive society when comes to religion, hence Christianity, Buddhism, Islamism, Taoism, etc all exist in China. Since China is rich with philosophy, some people will regard religion like philosophy or vice versa, for example, Taoism is often contrasted with Confucianism. Chinese had long recognized the power of religion, its ability to do good as well as its ability to do evil, hence, in China, religious freedom is curtailed to protect the rights of non-religious population as well as to maintain stability in society, assuming promotion of religion especially at the expense of other religion or even at the rights of atheist can cause instability. In view of the problems with Islamic terrorists today, perhaps one would not interpret China's laws regarding religion mysterious or too repressive.

MEDIA

Media rights are sacred in the U.S. in contrast with China where there is tighter control in newspaper publications, radio and TV broadcast. With the same logic as in the legal rights and religious rights, China believes that media can do good as well as do evil causing instability in society. It is understandable why China is ultra sensitive to society stability since she had suffered nearly a century of instability, punished with unequal treaties and lost territories, Hong Kong, Macaw, Taiwan, etc. to foreign countries. This concern of instability is deep in the minds of the Chinese communist party. The fact that Hong Kong students' demand of direct nomination* of the Hong Kong Chief Executive by the citizens is dealt with extreme care is a clear example. Another example is that terrorist activities infiltrating into west China's Muslim populated states is naturally making the Chinese government nervous. The 9-11 event and continued terrorists threats are making the U.S. nervous as well. The National Security Agency is seeking power to monitor the U.S. Citizens' communication data like phone records and the right to demand media and Internet companies to turn over their customers' privacy information are actually based on the same logic and fear. Therefore it is not difficult to understand why there are stronger media controls in China. Putting these political-oriented security concerns aside, the media freedom enjoyed by hundreds of millions of Chinese citizens through the Internet is actually amazing as exhibited by the activities of weibo and blogs in China so long they are not targeted to cause instability of society.

From the analyses above, I can say the title questions are not difficult to answer. One can find other similar explanations. The US media has a legacy or a bias against communist countries, hence always painting them an evil face. However, since the end of Cold War, communist regimes including Russia had taken up transformation. China is particularly unique in her transformation incorporating modern capitalism with her ancient philosophy. I hope the above analyses can serve as a building block for you to frame your answers to the title questions to any doubting Thomas in the West.

*The nomination process of the U.S. Presidency evolved over decades into a state by state primary election system to endorse candidates nominated by major parties and never entertained a national direct nomination by citizens - a good lesson for the Hong Kong students to study.

CHAPTER 56

WHY APOLOGIZING TO JAPAN?

—⚏—

IN THE OPINION PAGES OF NY Times (October 30th, 2014), Dr. Paul Krugman, wrote an article, "Apologizing to Japan", which caught my attention. Paul Robin Krugman is an American economist, a Nobel Laureate in Economics (2008 for New Trade Theory explaining the patterns of international trade). Dr. Krugman is also a Professor at Princeton University, the Centenary Professor at the London School of Economics, and a distinguished Scholar at the Luxembourg Income Study Center at the CUNY Graduate Center. Unquestionably, he is an expert on international economics and probably the most influential economics thinker in the U.S. In his article, he said he and Ben Bernanke ought to apologize (to Japan) not because their economic analysis were wrong but because the West did not learn well from the 'Japan problem' of reacting too slowly to the slide to deflation and too eager to raise rates at the first hint of recovery. Krugman blamed Germany for insisting hard money and austerity and raising rates in 2011 sending EU back to recession. He also blamed the US government policies for failing to abandon the conventional wisdom of balancing budget and firmly fighting inflation. He further blamed the deep division in the US society namely the conservatives blocking efforts of the liberals in fighting high unemployment.

Dr. Krugman said in his opinion to the NY Times from Tokyo: "I'll be writing more soon about what is happening in Japan now, and the new lessons the West should be learning." This teaser statement has made me as a reader felt extremely hungry. After reading his article, I did understand what he meant by 'apologizing to Japan' but I am not sure that phrase has any significance except being a catching title for an article written while in Tokyo. Japan made mistakes on her own on her economic policies, which often were coupled to her foreign policies. For example, Abe's aggressive stand on encroaching the rights to Diaoyu Islands had alienated Japan's large trading partner China making Japan's current economy gloomy with no prospect of return to a healthy growth. Therefore, no one owed Japan any apology on her economy. As why the West had done worse in dealing with its economic crises and why the West did not become wiser from the Japanese experience, Krugman offered some simple answers basically supporting a 'common sense principle' which a layman like me can understand. **The common sense principle** is that economy is never independent of politics. Krugman cited Japan's long term failure and Germany's policy contributing to EU recession, but did not dwell deep enough on the national and international politics to explain their influence on the various economies.

I am not a scholar in economic theory nor rich and famous; my interest in economics and economic theory simply came from a common folk's point of view and curiosity. A common person generally interprets facts and observations with common sense. Economy can never be independent of politics and politicians are not regulated like economic science Nobel Laureates are common sense. An economist is awarded a Nobel Prize because of his or her long career of scholarly work devoted and contributed to economic science with significant findings. If a Peace Nobel Prize were awarded to a politician (excluding true peace workers who sacrificed their lives for world peace), it usually would produce more smell than halo. That is also common sense.

Economy cannot be divorced from politics simply because politics decide policies which then affect economy. Politics are played within a political system and under a political culture unique to a country. Japan is a 'democratic country' essentially created post WW II by the U.S., yet her politicians never were purely coming from a democratic background or revolution. On the contrary, many Japanese politicians had roots in the imperial and militaristic Japan. Several Japanese leaders came from the lineage of political families in the era of Imperial Japan which dictated Japan's war ambition and operation. Nobusuke Kishi is a well known example (Prime Minister 1957-1960, original name, Sato Nobusuke, served as minister of commerce and industry in the war cabinet of Hideki Tojo, an executed war criminal); he is the maternal grandfather of the current Japanese Prime Minister, Abe Shinzo. Japan, as a small resource limited island nation, historically has exhibited ambition to expand through aggression. (Okinawa and Diaoyu Islands are clear historical examples) Japan is super sensitive to inflation since she is always vulnerable to shortage of supplies, food, energy and raw materials. Japanese people are diligent and disciplined; Japan would rather tolerate a stagnation even deflation for a long period of time rather than accepting a high inflation. So it was a common sense explanation why Japan had resisted the West's recommendation and would not allow her economy to become inflationary, for fear of high food and energy prices and/or a devaluation of the Japanese Yen (shrinking buying power).

Again, it might be common sense that Germans would insist on austerity and would not bail out the Southern Europe during the EU crisis. Germany depended import of raw materials, food and energy as well. Both Germany and Japan do not have the luxury of letting their currency slide and still be able to buy or spend as much as they need or want from the world market. The United States could because she had control of the printing press of the dollar, the currency for international trade. The political psychology is very different in the U.S. versus that in Germany, Japan or Sweden who recently raised her interest rate. The only country besides the U.S. seems to be able to use stimulus policies to sustain her economic growth is China but then her political system and political culture are uniquely different from the U.S. and other countries.

China is a large country ranked number two in world economy; her economy is not yet fully extended through an internal consumption based economy. Hence, it is a very different situation from Germany or Japan. China holds a vast amount of US treasury bills which supported her somewhat similar political psychology as the U.S. has; that is, to deploy massive stimulus measures to pump the economy. Japan and Germany also hold substantial dollar reserve as well but they have to use them for buying imports rather than freely spending it for building infrastructure or easing or stimulating the economy. However, prudent conservative politicians do worry that kind of 'political psychology' influencing economic policies. Hence, in the US political system, the conservatives are against the liberals opposing deficit spending, quantitative easing and ever increasing national debt. Similarly in China, the conservatives have similar concerns hence urging prudence and taking measures gingerly in managing her economy as well as protecting her currency (RMB) by negotiating more trade exchanges on RMB, fearing the devaluation of the dollars they possess.

Whether the economic measures practiced was derived from the common sense principle or not, they do not offer guarantee of success for sure. The fact, the world economy is so vulnerable to political events, such as, the stability of energy supply in the coming winter, the U.S. Foreign policies, in the Middle East (ISIS) and Asia Pacific (Target China), the stability of the Japanese government surviving corruption scandal, Abe's right-wing agenda focusing on restoring Japan's past glory instead of current economic problems, Russia's relationship with EU and the U.S. (Ukraine) as well as China's aggressive internal cleansing of corruption and her international financing endeavors (FTAAP and AIIB), all showing the dependency of economy on politics.

Dr. Krugman's promised writing on Japan's current economy and lessons to be learned, undoubtedly hinged on China-Japan-US relations, should be more valuable than his liberal remarks blaming American voters being wrong in giving the Republicans a mid-term election victory. After all, the stability of world economy depends on the world leaders **to learn from history** to be prudent and sensible in steering their economic policies **with due consideration of common sense**.

CHAPTER 57

AMERICAN TV SHOULD PROVIDE LIFELONG
LEARNING IN AN ENTERTAINING MANNER

—ɯ—

ONE GREAT VIRTUE OF AMERICANS is their humor and carefree jokes about everything from political leaders to mother-in-laws. This is very much reflected in American television shows which are especially popular and entertaining when the contents are delivered by celebrities and/or about celebrities. These shows can run very late into the night still commanding a big audience often including intellectual or educated audience. Unfortunately, the learning content in these shows are minimal perhaps revealed by their not so intellectual names such as The Tonight Show, Late Night, Late Show, Late Late Show, etc. Recently in the mainstream media, a very much talked about news is the announcement of David Letterman (who, living in my neighboring town, inspired me to start a weekly TV show in retirement, Community Education – Scrammble Game Show, nicknamed Dr. Wordman Show) to retire from his Late Show in 2015. Early in the year, Jimmy Fallon, 39, took over from Jay Leno NBC's The Tonight Show and Seth Meyers, 40, filled Jimmy's spot in NBC's Late Night show, both are young and have had the imprint of the Saturday Night Live, a program premiered October 11, 1975 filled with funny live shows but apparently losing it according to TV. COM reviewers.

The changes in NBC talk shows naturally put a lot of pressure on CBS and Letterman, since show business including TV talk shows, don't believe in evergreen. Letterman, 67, has to retire and be replaced by a younger host. The announcement named Stephen Colbert to be David's replacement. Although Colbert, 49, is about ten years senior of Fallon and Meyers, he made his name with his political satire about conservatives on his show, The Colbert Report, on cable's Comedy Central weeknight show. Attracting young viewers is a job performance goal CBS certainly hopes Colbert to accomplish with the Late Show. Colbert surely will put Colbert in the Late Show. The question of speculation (and a wish of mine) is what (some) changes Colbert can make in the CBS Late Show with his talents?

There are three competing late hour shows airing at EST 11:35-12:35pm, namely Jimmy Kimmel Live (ABC) hosted by Jimmy Kimmel (47), Late Night (NBC) hosted by Jimmy Fallon and Late Show (CBS) hosted by David Letterman soon by Stephen Colbert. To compare these three, I will put my money on Colbert to fulfill my wish to put some learning content in an entertaining way in TV shows. Specifically my wish is that some of the late shows should include more current events into their skits to offer lifelong learning in a funny manner to do some real good to American television for American people. There are intellectuals even young ones out there as potential late hour viewers, they need to connect the serious stuff they should care, economy, jobs, politics, global competition and international affairs, with wise and funny comments to relax (and learn) at the end of the day. In the digital world, TV is hanging on its favored status competing with other media. Sometimes even an eighth grader may multitask at late hours, doing homework, searching info and watching TV at the same time. Should they keep a late show open on their screens catching a bit of humor and learning some serious current events? Sure they should. All the networks want their shows to catch younger and younger audience, but then they won't come by surveying the older people what they like. The young Americans potentially could be lifelong audience of great and useful TV programs, shows delivering some lifelong learning contents in an entertaining way. Is this wish too much to ask the networks to fulfill?

On that wish, I first gave up on Jimmy Kimmel. If you recall an incidence on one of his shows with kids on a table talking adult questions (which could be a lifelong learning theme), an innocent six year old kid answered: "You came the other way round and kill everyone in China." to Jimmy's question, "America owes China a lot of money, 1.3 trillion dollars, how should we pay them back?" Jimmy handled the situation miserably as an adult and a host of a national TV program. He not only missed the opportunity to teach the kids right from wrong, he chuckled and said it was an interesting idea then after the kids answered 'Yeah' to his question, "should this country be forced to pay our own debts?", he brought the kids back to the 'violence' concept (which appears too much on TV) by asking, "Should we allow the Chinese to live?" and the kids answered: "Yeah, No!". This episode brought on a serious protest from Asian Americans to ABC and himself, thus I had to conclude that Kimmel is either ignorant or insensitive to serious political and moral issues. Therefore, I don't think Jimmy Kimmel is capable of offering any lifelong learning content on his shows. I think not many people seeking learning within entertainment (and I hope not many youngsters) will watch his shows unless he wises up from the above incidence and puts in some serious efforts in studying what lifelong learning through entertainment means, definitely not the 'Scandal' stuff he created to gain ratings.

As for Jimmy Fallon, he hasn't been long on The Tonight Show, but his interviews disappoint viewers for lack of depth or penetration. I hope he will read this article to ponder the question, can TV shows deliver lifelong learning in an entertaining way? Being funny with 'learning content' is a challenge, it requires hard learning on the host part to keep up with current events and broad knowledge such as what is the American 'Pivot to Asia' policy, is it right or working effectively, and what do the political analysts debate about, can you interview them on the show to make it both entertaining and informative? I have no idea whether Fallon can venture into this meaningful area or not. Hence I reserve my judgment on Fallon as well.

Colbert is an American political Satirist (The Colbert Report), a writer (Example: I am America (So Can You!), 2007), and a comedian (Comedy Central) in one. As the Late Show host, I hope (and I think) he can include more political current events into his shows with some depth and humor. I bet he will have some good and funny answers, if you ask him about the China-Japan Diaoyu Island Dispute, what is Abe Shinzo up to with his right-wing agenda or what does Putin hope to accomplish after Cremia? Letterman has a 'Top Ten List' in his Late Show, a great format for lifelong learners. In one episode produced after 9-11, Letterman was so emotional, sincere, informative and entertaining; the audience (young and old) learned a great deal about the attack, New York City and Mayor Giuliani. That was a great episode for lifelong learners and a mini example of lifelong learning/entertaining TV show.

The world is getting more complicated, America is losing competitive edge, unemployment is hovering on a high rate, blaming China or creating a 'China Threat' story is not the answer to our domestic and international issues. Learning is the answer, skill upgrade is the answer, shouldn't CBS do something to help America in lifelong learning, starting with the Late Show which generates at least $20 million profit every year? Dr. Wordman Show is producing it weekly through public access TV with his $100 annual budget! Wordman would be honored to have Letterman as a consultant to his Show with an honorarium at a thousand times of Wordman's pay; this line if told by Colbert skillfully might just bring the Sullivan Theater down. No, don't tell it, NY does not want to lose the Late Show to LA!

CHAPTER 58

WHY DO PUTIN AND XI CLING TO THE THEME

OF PATRIOTISM BUT NOT OBAMA?

—〰—

IN TODAY'S COMMUNICATION WORLD, CELEBRITIES get tremendous attention. Many reporters make a living under the umbrella of journalism but produce many tabloid articles in cohort with paparazzi. Celebrities often hire security personnel to protect themselves from snooping photographers and reporters. The world leaders, of course, are celebrities, but they generally have sufficient security protection keeping the paparazzi away. The news reports about world leaders by and large are either from official sources or political commentators concerned with their thinking, behavior and policies which affect the world. Reports on world leaders are generally found on the mainstream media tied closely with official news sources.

Occasionally, when a world leader's behavior touches the negative boundary of moral principles, then the paparazzi descend on him or her directly or indirectly. The "Not Sex" scandal of the **Clinton-Lewinsky** affair in the White House is one such example. Even though, the mainstream media, especially in the U.S. is restrained in reporting that affair, plenty of stories were told in tabloids throughout the world. Another example is the "chambermaid assault" story of the Managing Director of the International Money Fund, **Dominique Gaston André Strauss-Kahn** of France, who was accused by the chambermaid for sex assault while he was visiting New York City. Both stories were muffled in our mainstream media. We mention these examples here simply to remind readers the mainstream media do have constraints when comes to reporting world leaders.

In this column, the topic of interest is 'world leaders and patriotism', which touches the positive (not negative!) boundary of moral principles. This subject should have no constraints in the mainstream media; it is important enough to deserve your attention.

One took for granted that citizens ought to be patriotic and our leaders did not have to remind us on patriotism. However, if we observe the most important leaders of the world today, namely Obama, Xi and Putin, we see very distinctive differences in their thinking, behavior and policies which of course will have profound impact on their nations and the whole world. These differences can be captioned with one word, 'patriotism'. Both Putin and Xi are vigorously beating the drums of patriotism but Obama does not. Before we get in deeper on this subject, we need to first make a distinction between patriotism and nationalism; a fine line between them which can be blurred and twisted as shown by Nazism, Japanese Imperialism and Stalinism.

Nationalism and patriotism both show the 'loyalty character' of an individual towards his or her nation. **Patriotism** is a cultural attachment to one's homeland or devotion to one's country. **Nationalism** denotes a strong association of individuals and groups with a national identity and national interest. The word 'national interest' is often ill defined by leaders to transform patriotism into a sentiment of superiority and aggression toward other countries – making Nationalism a cause of war and imperialism.

Putin, the President of Russia and an outspoken leader, has recently taken the spotlight due to the Ukraine crisis. His action, Russia's annexing Crimea, has raised an uproar and strong reaction in the West with the U.S. advocating an economic sanction against Russia. On the world stage and through media, Putin is drumming patriotism and using it to defend his actions. Putin is supporting his drive of patriotism with three main arguments. First, he cites history. He acknowledges and accepts the collapse of the Soviet Union but brings back the history of how the national boundaries are changed and how Ukraine is formed. He claims that Russia is recognizing history and honoring people's desire. He cites Crimea's referendum, an overwhelming majority vote, not only legitimate but also a clear voice of the people. The annexation is based on patriotism not nationalism. Second, he wants patriotism to drive Russia's economy. Whether dealing with productivity, austerity or external sanctions, patriotism, requiring sacrifices, is an important element. This concept is hardly touted in the United States. Thirdly, he believes Russians must be patriotic in dealing with the hegemony behavior of the United States. The unilateral military actions of the United States and her pumping arms into the Middle East, especially into the hands of mercenary soldiers who fights and switches sides for money, are not solutions but causes to the problems.

Xi, the President of China and a deep thinker, is also drumming patriotism not only on national but on world stages as well. Firstly, one thing in common with Putin, Xi is very well versed in history and he firmly believes that China cannot live as a weak nation under the shadow of the unequal treaties cast on her in the past. Secondly, he believes patriotism is the fundamental element for the Chinese people to realize their China Dream – raising the standard of living. Patriotism is the driver for China's economic development, a central faith for everyone whether as a factory or government worker, a farmer, a soldier, or a scientist. Patriotism is even called upon in the fight against corruption. Thirdly, he clearly differentiates patriotism and nationalism. He denounced Abe's 'Japan is back' and his military expansion as the right-wing nationalism. He controlled Chinese people's anger in protests against Japan when Japan made the comic purchase of the Diaoyu Islands which were historically parts of China. Fourthly, he believes that Chinese patriotism will not become nationalism. His foreign policies are firm and clear. China demands respect from her neighbors and the world for her past, present and the future in the world. In the recent APEC meeting, Xi made it clear China was wishing co-prosperity with Asia Pacific nations. He is confident about the China Dream and he extends the China Dream to Asia Pacific Dream while agreeing with the United States in climate change control, calling for Chinese people to be patriotic, sacrificing, and contributing to the national environmental goal.

Obama, the overwhelmingly supported first black president of the United States, somehow diminished his political fortune in his tenure of past six years. He has been called an 'apologetic' American President. His demeanor of not saluting to the flag, preferring a golf game to a memorial ceremony, his bowing to a Saudi King, etc. etc., have cast him an unpatriotic image nationally. His domestic policies seem to be divisive for the nation and are reflected in the results of the mid-term election. His recent unilateral executive order of giving blank amnesty to five million illegal immigrants can hardly be labeled as a patriotic act even though some of the illegal immigrants have been law abiding and tax-paying residents for years. The long-term ramifications of this immigration order on the U.S. Economy and national security are far from clear. Will the U.S. attract more illegal immigrants in the future or will she officially usher in more terrorist elements by this executive order? Knowing that the national debt of the U.S. is crippling her economy and hampering her ability in maintaining world order, why doesn't she reset our priority? Why doesn't Obama let the citizens know that national prosperity calls for patriotism and patriotism calls for sacrifices?

At the XI session of the Valdai International Discussion Club, Putin gave a speech under the theme, The World Order: New Rules or a Game without Rules, and entertained extensively questions raised by the audience. There were rhetoric statements in Putin's speech but there were also significant truths about how the world was deteriorated to today's situation, even some good advice for the U.S. on new rules for the world order. After reflecting on the entire video recording, one could not help but ask why Putin and Xi are drumming the theme of patriotism but not Obama? Does the United States substituting Nationalism for Patriotism believe superiority offering license to play the world game by her own rules? I hope not!

CHAPTER 59

SIGNIFICANCE OF OKINAWA, TAIPEI

AND HONG KONG ELECTIONS

—︿w﹀—

TAIPEI'S MAYORAL ELECTION ON 11-29-2014 is big news in Asia overshadowing the Hong Kong two-month long "occupy Central" protest demanding a direct election of the Hong Kong Executive Administrator. These Asian events certainly have the attention of Washington DC. On December 3rd, the Congress held a hearing on the Hong Kong Affair as well as on the Taiwan issue in view of the fact that the Taiwan local election did not please Washington as her favorite 'blue' party (KMT) suffered a major setback. The opposition 'green' party (DPP) although captured more local legislator and mayoral seats but did not win Taipei, a city ranked administratively above other local cities. A clever physician turned politician won the Taipei Mayoral election by smartly organizing a youthful group taking advantage of the continuous rift between the 'blue' and 'green' party voters jostling in election campaigns occurring biennially. This new Mayor, Dr. Ko Wen Je, won by also employing a trendy campaign tactics fully utilizing the Internet power and its social media tools.

Although Washington has been denying she had any hand in the Hong Kong student protest, but the fact that the Congress just held a hearing on Hong Kong (Daniel Russel, Assistant Secretary of the State Department, Bureau of Eastern Asia and Pacific Affairs testified) and the fact the British parliament wanted to send an investigative delegation to Hong Kong but was rejected by China saying "Hong Kong is now a sovereignty of China and her affair is a Chinese internal affair", basically buzzing off the British Lords - none of your business. There are definitely opposite diplomatic positions between the West, Washington and Downing Street, and the East, Zhong Nan Hai of Beijing in dealing with matters like protests.

You would never hear that the People's Congress in China would hold a hearing about the protest of 'Occupy Wall Street' or the referendum on the independence of Scotland or the recent black protest against alleged police brutality killing Eric Garner in New York City and earlier against police shooting killing Michael Brown in Ferguson, Missouri. Such ideas of the East meddling the domestic affairs of the West would be ridiculed on American comedy or late night shows, but yet the American Congress is dead serious in holding a hearing on the Hong Kong protest and Taiwan election. In reality, the Chinese government has either gotten more skilled or more confident in dealing with her internal affairs such as the Hong Kong student protest or the Taipei election. Observing from afar, I would say the Chinese Government is now wiser, commendable for dealing with her internal and foreign affairs calmly. Perhaps China is justified also to tell Washington to mind her own business.

In fact, there is a recent Asian election that does have a serious impact on the U.S.; that is the gubernatorial election in Okinawa held on November 16, 2014. Of course, an Asian election in principle is not the Americans' business, however, in Okinawa, where we have a military base, said election does indeed affect the U.S. The new Governor, Takeshi Onaga, "comprehensively defeated incumbent Hirokazu Nakaima" in the Governor's election. Takeshi is an opponent of the U.S. base relocation plan, a controversial proposal in Okinawa. The incumbent agreed last year to support a plan to move the Futenma air base to the north of the island for exchange of getting some grant money from Tokyo. However, there is a strong local opposition to the plan. Takeshi wanted to have the base removed altogether and he won his election on that basis. He and the Okinawa people may have a very good reason to oppose the U.S. air base. They see that the military base is a security threat to their peaceful and quiet living rather than sharing with the Tokyo view: The presence of American military in Okinawa is boosting Japan's defense and fulfilling the responsibility of the U.S.-Japan Mutual Defense Treaty. Takeshi declared, "I will do my best to cancel and withdraw the plan as I stand side-by-side with the people of Okinawa."; local media said Mr. Onaga defeated his rival by about 360,000 votes to 260,000, a huge margin.

Okinawa has a unique history. She was an independent country many centuries ago maintaining a peaceful relationship with China as a suzerain nation, depending on China (Ming and Qing Dynasties) against the aggression from Japan. At that time, Japan behaved like barbaric pirates on the open sea. In 1850, Japan had a taste of the West power in demanding trade and began to transform herself leading to the famous Meiji Restoration (1868-1912), taking lessons from the western countries' industrial revolution and adapting their ethics and colonialism. Japan went through a rapid development and militarization and pursued an imperialistic expansion. In 1872, Japan invaded Liuju Guo (known as Okinawa today) and captured her King. In 1874, Japan invaded Taiwan, 1894 invaded China over control of Korea. As a result, Japan also seized Taiwan for 50 years (1895-1945) until she was defeated in WW II. Okinawa was under the U.S. administration after the War but the U.S. gave the administration right to Japan in 1972 along with oceanic territory including the Diaoyu Islands (Japanese named them the Senkaku Islands). Some Okinawa people were unhappy and they preferred to be independent.

Taiwan had also been a U.S. Military base under a U.S.-Taiwan Mutual Defense Treaty. These military alliances are important part of the U.S. Pivot to Asia strategy. This strategy inherited a legacy from the Cold War targeting communism as the archenemy. Since the collapse of the Soviet Union in 1992, the world has changed. Communist countries are adapting their transformations to embrace the free market economy whereas the capitalist countries are implementing social programs finding compromise within democracy. It is no surprise that Today, the people, with availability of advanced communication technologies, opportunities of global interaction and richness of social and historical information, would want more say about their lives than adhering to some military alliances cooked up by out-of-date strategists. These Asian election results simply manifest that people now understand more about real security issues from their individual and personal point of views. The Okinawa people do not feel the threat from China as depicted by Abe Shinzo or the Hawks in the U.S. Likewise, the Taiwanese folks may have finally realized that the entire national threat issue might just totally disappear if politicians would stop making charades. Why would China attack Taiwan? Or Why would China attack Okinawa? If Abe Shinzo would stop chanting the China Threat theory, there could be a very different Pivot To Asia strategy from the U.S., a strategy could create a lot more win-win opportunities and far less arms races and military confrontations.

CHAPTER 60

THE NEAR-TERM FUTURE OF THE U.S. AND CHINA

—w—

PREDICTING INTERNATIONAL AFFAIRS AND WORLD events is not a smart thing to do as seasoned political analysts swear to you. However, as an 'unseasoned' columnist, to review the past and to predict the future at year end seems desirable; after all that is how analysts get seasoned. Thus, I would beg your indulgence in letting me presenting this yearend forecast, capping the crystal ball with the phrase, 'near-term', for obvious reasons.

Thinking about the future of the U.S. and China, the two largest economies, is essentially thinking about the future of the world; even their domestic affairs will have an impact to many nations. The past events bore evidence to that effect. For instance, from the US military actions in the Middle East to her domestic executive order legalizing the illegal immigrants all have impact to the world! Likewise, from China's hosting a grandiose APEC Conference for '21' Asia Pacific economies, casting an Asia Pacific Dream, to her domestic 'reform', vigorously cleansing corruption and easing economic growth, have all been on the world's TV screens! Were the U. S. and/or China to sneeze, the world might just reach for a thermometer to check body fever. Under this metaphor, crystal balling the two countries in near-term, should be a worthwhile exercise.

First, let's look from China's perspective to extrapolate from the current events to her near-term future. The list below is not ranked by 'probability of occurrence', but the comments associate with them offer readers some food for thought to draw conclusions:

1. Transformation of economic model – China's intention to shift more from manufacturing to a consumption based economy is serious going forward.

In the process she will upgrade low-tech to high-tech manufacturing with fierce emphasis on innovation (創新) – a possible positive outcome in the near future dependent on China's tuning of her job and wage policies.

2. Shifting infrastructure development from domestic to abroad – An intimate marriage of China's domestic economic development with her foreign policy is striving for mutual economic prosperity (Win-Win) – a strategy that will be elevated to more actions in the near future with Asian, African and South American countries.

3. More assertive in contributing and influencing world economy - stabilizing currency, pushing operation of Asia Infrastructure Investment Bank (AIIB), opening up her stock markets, and driving more of her enterprises to go global – a clear agenda in the next two years.

4. New Silk Road Policy and High Speed Railroad Technology Export – fulfilling the new Silk Road Strategy to bring mutual economic prosperity to countries along the proposed silk route. The world's longest 8,111 miles rail run from Yiwu to Madrid paves the way for more intense China-EU interaction from next year on. The export of High Speed Rail Technology will be enhanced in the next two years despite of Mexico's renege on a signed development contract. China to build and operate a high speed railroad for Britain, inked by David Cameron and Li Keqiang, will demonstrate an on-time completion legion in the railroad business.

5. Pacific-Indian-Atlantic maritime route - this is a serious contention between the U.S. Pivot to Asia strategy and China's strategy of securing free passage in these ocean ways vital to her commerce and energy supply. China will continue her assertive non-violence approach promising mutual benefits from co-development versus retaliation for hostile obstruction. A 'choke' strategy from the U.S. and/or Asian countries will increase tension in the South China Sea but a corroborative position will lead to Asia Pacific prosperity – Here the crystal ball shows a cloudy future.

6. China's Anti-Corruption Drive - the vigor will continue with more visible results on punishing the Tigers and the Flies. The wolves and foxes in the middle will witness those punishments and reflect. Will the anti-corruption drive continue beyond next two years depending not on the speed of government prosecution in the legal system but on the speed of political (communist party self-cleansing) and economic (engaging more international enterprising game rules) reforms.

7. China's concern for Muslim unrest – the increasing not diminishing Muslin terrorists activities has a potential influence on China's Muslim population. In the near-term, China is expected to engage more anti-terrorists efforts with the international community. The recent bombing of the Charlie Hebdo magazine in Paris committed by Jihads - Al Qaeda terrorists sent a shock wave to the world and China. It is understandable that China had been annoyed by the human rights slogans touted by the West to Muslims in China; now is the moment, China and the United States may work together in the near future to find practical solutions to stop Muslim terrorism.

Looking from the perspective of the U.S., forecasting her near-term future is less crisp than that for China and more difficult and yet simpler at the same time – **an oxymoron situation**. It is all because of the 2016 Presidential election. In principle, the unknown next President of the U.S. should not affect the U.S. current foreign and domestic policies; in reality, the lame duck President, Barack Obama, facing pressure from his Democratic Party and a Republican controlled Congress, will be ineffective in initiating major policies but resigned to prescribing his presidential legacy. Let's look at the US near future in terms of international and domestic issues:

A. International

The Pivot-to-Asia strategy continues with self-contradictory execution - On this issue, Obama can win no brownie point with a Republican controlled Congress. Even Hillary Clinton, a potential Democratic candidate for 2016 presidency, will have to deal with this difficult issue. Many signs point to faulty assumptions and ineffectiveness of using the 'Pivot' to curtail China's rise, creating more unnecessary tension in AP than benefits for the U.S. and other Asian countries in the long run. The long talk between Xi Jinping and Obama post-APEC has indeed influenced Obama's world view. Obama is likely to collaborate with China, be it on North Korea's nuclear threat or recent hacking to Sony to thwart the movie 'Interview', an assassination plot against Kim Jong un, or stamping out terrorists, or on dealing with Russia and ISIS.

The effect of sanction on Russia as a punishment to Putin's behavior hinges more on China's attitude and position. Putin has played the patriotism card successfully so far. The U.S. and NATO sanction may hurt Russia's economy but not necessarily Putin's grip of power. Obama has no choice but to get China on board or risking driving China and Russia closer in trade and military alliance. To get China on board is harder than to get China staying neutral. Being a lame duck with a disagreeable Congress, taking on tasks not accomplishable in two years is not smart. Furthermore, Europe has to be soft to Russia for her energy needs every seasonal cycle; therefore, a sanction will be painful on both Russia and Europe.

The restoration of full relations with Cuba is a significant change in the U.S. foreign policy, one to be Obama's legacy. This may not be related to Russia, but it speaks the Obama administration's mind: Sanction was not effective in changing political system in Cuba or China but we will do it to Russia anyway. Ironically, the conservative Republicans spoke against Obama's new Cuba policy on anti-communism (Castro) basis rather than criticizing his lack of an effective negotiation in forging a mutually receptive relationship.

On ISIS and Middle East, Obama is equally hamstringed by 'pledged' cease-fire on the one hand and increasing battles against violence spreading around the world linked to Muslim terrorists. Based on the history, the conflicts in the Middle East will continue and the U.S. will continue to participate in firefighting and bandage solutions, hence, no peace in the near-term in the Middle East.

B. Domestic Issues

The U.S. Economy is on the mend with a modest economic growth and job increase (thanks to the global oil and gas price drop and U.S. effort in increasing her own energy production). No drastic improvement is foreseen since no drastic domestic policies are in place. The Obamacare will not be scrapped by the Congress for fear of turning it to be the 2016 election liability for Republicans than for Democrats, hence, lots of bickering will be heard but no major legislation will get through Congress and the White House in the next two years.

Another hot domestic topic is the immigration reform. The legality of Obama's executive order, granting illegal immigrants legal status, will be debated and argued in the media, but long-term policy or solution to guarantee a healthy sustainable immigration program is difficult to come by. So long as Americans do not wish to take up low wage labor jobs, illegal immigrants will come across the borders. Any enforcement measure will be infringing on citizens' liberty. 9-11 and terrorists threat have produced a 'patriot act' but illegal immigrants with links to large voting blocks of legal immigrants will cast immigration reform as a dilemma for the near future.

Regardless whether or not we have a clear or cloudy projection for the future, the world will be always eventful. The Paris bombing (1/7/2015) at Charlie Hebdo killing 12 including the editor started the year 2015 with a big bang. This terrorist act, even though, far away from Washinton DC and Beijing, it will have impact to the US-China relation in the sense of drawing them together as two great nations to deals with world crisis together. As world citizens, we must stay tuned not only to the mainstream but also to the organic media.

NOTES AND REFERENCES

—ᗡᗡ—

Chapter 1 Why An Uninhabited Island May Draw The U.S. into a War

Where Are The Diaoyu Islands? What Are Their Geographic Features?

Diaoyu Islands consist of 5 uninhabited islands and 3 rock formations with a total area of 6 square kilometers. Diaoyu Islands are located offshore northeastern Taiwan, an extension of Datun mountain range. Together with Taiwan they belong to the island group of the continental shelf in the East China Sea with water depth less than 200 meters. Further to the east is the termination of the continental shelf with bathymetry reaching 2500 meters known as "Hei-Shui-Gou", or "Black Water Trench" (also known as Liuqiu (Okinawa) Trough), which is not the Taiwan Strait; and it separates Diaoyu Islands from the Ryukyu Islands on the other side of the trough. Historically ever since Ming and Qing Dynasties till today, China has always viewed the "Black Water Trench" as the boundary between China and Liuqiu (or Ryukyu), which was a China's tributary state with local sovereignty.

Japan unilaterally claims Diaoyu Islands (renamed as Senkaku Islands in 1900) as her territory with the intent to extend westward a sea territory to include the "Black Water Trench" and Diaoyu Islands as her Exclusive Economic Zone (for fishing and other rights). The disputed region bounded by the Chinese and Japanese defined boundary lines is equivalent to an area of 6 Taiwan. The loss of such a giant size territory and its economic rights would be a devastating impact to the national defense, economic development of resources and the livelihood of Chinese fishermen who have been living by these waters for centuries. After capturing Diaoyu Islands, Japan would be able to block off all fishing boats from Taiwan and coastal provinces of China and use the islands as a jumping board to launch attacks to both Taiwan and Mainland China since the separation would be only a narrow strip of water.

What Does History Say About Diaoyu Islands In Relation To Chinese People?

Chinese as far back as Ming Dynasty has named Diaoyu Islands. Since 1372, when Ryukyu began to pay tribute and seek protection and blessing from Ming emperors, the Chinese diplomat delegations sent by the Emperor had traveled by Diaoyu Island and recorded it in their navigation diaries. There were also several defense maps, which had recorded Diaoyu Islands within the defense territory. Since 1683, Qing Dynasty Emperor Kangxi had included Taiwan in Qing's sovereignty and formally designated the "Black Water Trench" as the boundary between China and Liqiu (Ryukyu). In the same time frame, there were many local governmental records (such as the *Gazetteer of Taiwan Prefecture* and the *Revised Gazetteer of Fujian Province*) had documented that Diaoyu Islands were under the governance of Yinan County (then called Kavalan County) of Taiwan. Besides these Chinese documents, many nineteenth century maps produced by France, Britain and America had also clearly documented that the Diaoyu Islands are part of Chinese territory. Based on so much Chinese and Western historical documents and the fact that numerous Chinese fishermen lived by and fished in the ocean region of Diaoyu Islands, ample evidence shows that the Diaoyu Islands were not only part of China over six hundred years, but more as inseparable and integral part of the Chinese people.

Today, Japan, ignoring the vast amount of evidence, purposely sought for certain individual maps or documents, which did not include Diaoyu Islands or did not print the word "Chinese Territory", to deny the legitimate Chinese claim on Diaoyu Islands. It must be pointed out that not all historical documents can be expected to be complete or in anticipation of thievery centuries later, hence, it is laughable that Japan can ignore the majority of historical evidence to single out the incomplete pieces of documents to serve her purpose of stealing Diaoyu Islands. Most importantly, it can be further pointed out, many of the Japanese or Liuqiu (Ryukyu) historical documents at that time all indicated that Diaoyu Islands plainly belonged to China and had nothing to do with neither Japan nor Liuqiu (Ryukyu).

Reference: https://groups.yahoo.com/neo/groups/baodiao/info

Chapter 2 True American Exceptionalism

American Exceptionalism is attributed to Russian President Vladimir Putin in his letter to the NY Times.

Reference: NY Times Op Ed, 9-11-2013.

G-2: The **Group of Two** (**G-2** or **G2**) is a proposed informal special relationship between the United States and the People's Republic of China. Since initiated in Foreign Affairs by C. Fred Bergsten, Director of the Peterson Institute, as primarily an economic relationship, it began to be adopted by foreign policy experts as a term recognizing the importance of the U.S.–China relationship. As the two most influential and powerful countries in the world, advocates suggest that creating a G-2 relationship the two nations could work out solutions to global problems together, preventing another Cold War.

Robert J. Samuelson is a columnist for The Washington Post, where he has written about business and economic issues since 1977, and is syndicated by the Washington Post Writers Group. He was a columnist for *Newsweek* magazine from 1984 to 2011.

Charles Murray is a political scientist, author, and libertarian. He first came to national attention in 1984 with the publication of *Losing Ground*, which has been credited as the intellectual foundation for the Welfare Reform Act of 1996. His 1994 *New York Times* bestseller, *The Bell Curve* (Free Press, 1994), coauthored with the late Richard J. Herrnstein, sparked heated controversy for its analysis of the role of IQ in shaping America's class structure. Murray's other books include What It Means to Be a Libertarian (1997), Human Accomplishment (2003), In Our Hands (2006), and Real Education (2008). His most recent book, *Coming Apart* (Crown Forum, 2012), describes an unprecedented divergence in American classes over the last half century.

Chapter 3 US-China Relationship and A Dangerous Xiaosan

Xiaosan is a social term widely used in China referring to an intruding third party wrecking a marriage.

G-2 (See notes in Chapter 2) refers to the U.S. and China.

Mark Leonard is co-founder and director of the European Council on Foreign Relations, the first pan-European think tank. His areas of expertise are in European foreign policy, China, EU-Russia relations, transatlantic relations, EU institutions, Public diplomacy and nation branding, UK foreign policy. He created the 'Chimerica' term.

Deng Xiaoping (22 August 1904 – 19 February 1997) was a Chinese revolutionary and statesman. He was the leader of China from 1978 until his retirement in 1992. His doctrine of focusing on economical development with reform and low-key style was credited for bringing up China's economy.

Chapter 4 True Conflict in US-China Relationship

The Trans-Pacific Partnership (TPP) is a proposed regional regulatory and investment treaty. As of 2014 twelve countries throughout the Asia-Pacific region have participated in negotiations on the TPP: Australia, Brunei, Canada, Chile, Japan, Malaysia, Mexico, New Zealand, Peru, Singapore, the United States, and Vietnam. The fact that it excludes China makes it questionable as an effective treaty especially in view of the progress made in the Asia Pacific Economic Conference.

Reference: http://www.ustr.gov/tpp

Chapter 5 A New Model for US-China Relationship

Rosa Brooks is a professor at the Georgetown University Law Center, where she teaches courses on international law, national security, constitutional law, and other subjects.

Reference: Foreign Policy, It Was Nice While It Lasted – Reflection of the End of America 10-16-2013.

Chapter 6 ABC TV's Mistake Reflects Americans' Insensitivity To US-China Relationship

Jimmy Kimmel Live is an American late-night talk show, created and hosted by James "Jimmy" Kimmel, and transmitted on ABC. The nightly hour-long show made its debut on January 26, 2003, following Super Bowl XXXVII. *Jimmy Kimmel Live!* is produced by Jackhole Productions in association with ABC Studios.

Reference: http://entertainment.time.com/2013/10/29/ poll-jimmy-kimmel-leaves-90-of-chinese-angered-saddened-and-on-guard/

Chapter 7 Caroline Kennedy's Historical Mission

Caroline Bouvier Kennedy (born November 27, 1957) is an American author, attorney, and the current United States Ambassador to Japan. She is the only surviving child of U.S. President John F. Kennedy and First Lady Jacqueline Bouvier Kennedy and a niece of Senators Robert F. Kennedy and Ted Kennedy and an older sister to John F. Kennedy, Jr. Caroline Kennedy is the new Ambassador working under the new US Secretary of State, John Kerry who succeeded Hillary Clinton.

Abe Shinzo is the current Japanese Prime Minister (See notes in Chapter 11 and Chapters 15, 25, 29 and 36)

Gary Locke, US Ambassador to China, resigned in Early 2014; Max Sieben Baucus succeeded Gary Locke serving from 2-21-2014.

Chapter 8 Right Cyberspace Strategy And Policy For The U.S. With Respect To China

Edward Joseph "Ed" Snowden (born June 21, 1983) was an American computer professional, a former system administrator for the US Central Intelligence Agency (CIA) and a counterintelligence trainer for the US Defense Intelligence Agency (DIA); later he worked as a contractor for Dell in an outpost of NSA. In

June, 2013, he decided to expose the US cyber intelligence activities which caused much embarrassment to the U.S. and a uproar of the international community.

Reference: http://www.theguardian.com/world/2013/jun/09/edward-snowden-nsa-whistleblower-surveillance

The National Security Agency (NSA) is a United States intelligence agency responsible for global monitoring, collection, decoding, translation and analysis of information and data for foreign intelligence and counterintelligence purposes (a discipline known as Signals intelligence, SIGINT. NSA is also charged with protection of U.S. government communications and information systems against penetration and network warfare. The agency is authorized to accomplish its mission through clandestine means, by bugging electronic systems and allegedly by engaging in sabotage through subversive software.

Abraham Newman received his BA in International Relations from Stanford University and his PhD in political science from the University of California, Berkeley, currently a professor at Georgetown University. His research focuses on international political economy, with a special interest in global regulatory issues. He is the author of Protectors of Privacy: Regulating Personal Data in the Global Economy (Cornell University Press: 2008). Henry Farrell is an Irish-born political scientist and an associate professor at George Washington University. Martha Finnemore is a prominent constructivist scholar of international relations, and a University Professor at the Elliott School of International Affairs at George Washington University. Thomas Rid is Professor of Security Studies at King's College London. Rid's work covers a broad spectrum of security questions. His influential most recent book, *Cyber War Will Not Take Place* (Oxford University Press/Hurst 2013), is a comprehensive analysis of political computer attacks, driven by events, technical detail, and political theory.

Reference: Foreign Affairs 11-6-2013 and FOREIGN Affairs November/December/2013

Chapter 9 Imperfect Diplomacy Evidenced by China's New AZID in East China Sea

The Air Defense Identification Zone (ADIZ) is an airspace over land or water in which the identification, location, and control of civil aircraft is required by international agreement in the interest of civil air travel safety as well as national security. ADIZs extend beyond a country's airspace to give the country more time to respond to foreign and possibly hostile aircraft. The authority to establish an ADIZ is not given by any international treaty nor prohibited by any international law and is not regulated by any international body. The first ADIZ was established by the United States soon after World War II.

Chapter 10 US Secretary John Kerry's Legacy to Be

John Forbes Kerry (born December 11, 1943) is an American politician who is the 68th and current United States Secretary of State succeeding Hillary Clinton. He was a US Senator served as chairman of the Senate Foreign Relations Committee. Kerry was the presidential candidate of the Democratic Party in the 2004, losing to incumbent President George W. Bush.

Aaron David Miller is currently the Vice President for New Initiatives and a Distinguished Scholar at the Woodrow Wilson International Center for Scholars. Between 2006 and 2008, he was a Public Policy Scholar when he wrote his fourth book The Much Too Promised Land: America's Elusive Search for Arab-Israeli Peace (Bantam, 2008). For the prior two decades, he served at the Department of State as an advisor to Republican and Democratic Secretaries of State, where he helped formulate U.S. policy on the Middle East and the Arab-Israel peace process, most recently as the Senior Advisor for Arab-Israeli Negotiations.

References: Newsday Op Ed 10-29-2013, Foreign Policy 11-18, 2013

Chapter 11 Should Obama's Administration Re-examine the U.S. Asia-Pacific Strategy?

Shinzō Abe (born September 21, 1954) is the Prime Minister of Japan, re-elected to the position in December 2012 since his short first term from 2006-2007. Abe is also the President of the Liberal Democratic Party (LDP) and chairman of the *Oyagaku* propulsion parliamentary group. Hailing from a politically prominent family associated with WW II, he became Japan's youngest post-war prime minister. Despite of the stagnant economy in Japan, his policies are more visible and controversial in national defense and foreign policy. He advocates revision of the Japanese peace constitution to allow Japan to make first strike, strengthening Japan's military defense and formulating military alliances with other Asian nations targeting China as a 'China Threat', all under a nationalistic slogan – 'Japan is back' (to Japan's pre-WW II glory).

Center for Strategic and International Studies (**CSIS**) is a public policy research institution dedicated to analysis and policy impact. CSIS is the only institution of its kind that maintains resident experts on all the world's major geographical regions. CSIS is a bipartisan, nonprofit organization headquartered in Washington, D.C. The Center's 220 full-time staff and large network of affiliated scholars conduct research and analysis and develop policy initiatives that look to the future and anticipate change. CSIS is where Abe Shinzo delivered his "Japan is back' speech.

Chapter 12 What Are the Intentions behind the Foreign Policies of the United States and China?

Nicholas Donabet Kristof (born April 27, 1959) is an American journalist, author, op-ed columnist, and a winner of two Pulitzer Prizes. He has written an op-ed column for *The New York Times* since November 2001 and *The Washington Post* says that he "rewrote opinion journalism" with his emphasis on human rights abuses and social injustices, such as human trafficking and the Darfur conflict.

Reference: NY Times Op Ed 12-4-2013

Chapter 13 New Year New Hope and New US-China Relationship

Li Keqiang (born 1 July 1955) is the current Premier of the State Council of the People's Republic of China. An economist by training, Li is China's head of government as well as one of the leading figures of Chinese economic policy. He is also vice chairman of the National Security Commission and second ranked member of the CPC Politburo Standing Committee next to Xi Jinping, the *de facto* highest decision-making body of the country. Li rose through the party ranks through the Communist Youth League. From 1998 to 2004, Li served as the Governor of Henan and the province's Party secretary, and then the Liaoning party secretary. From 2008 to 2013, Li served as the first-ranked Vice-Premier under then-Premier Wen Jiabao. During this tenure, Li's official portfolio included economic development, price controls, finance, climate change, and macroeconomic management.

Bo Xilai (born 3 July 1949) is a former Chinese politician. He came to prominence through his tenures as the mayor of Dalian and then the governor of Liaoning. From 2004 to November 2007, he served as Minister of Commerce. Between 2007 and 2012, he served as a member of the Central Politburo and secretary of the Communist Party in Chongqing city. Bo was considered a likely candidate for promotion to the elite Politburo Standing Committee in CPC 18th National Congress in 2012. His political fortunes came to an abrupt end following the Wang Lijun incident, in which Wang sought asylum and allegedly disclosed sensitive political information related to Bo and his wife at the American consulate in Chengdu. Bo was removed as the party chief of Chongqing in March 2012 and suspended from the politburo the following month. He was later stripped of all his party positions and his seat at the National People's Congress. Bo was eventually expelled from the party. On 22 September 2013, he was found guilty of corruption, stripped of all his assets, and sentenced to life imprisonment.

Chapter 14 From Mandela To Diaoyu Islands – A Lesson For World Leaders

Nelson Rolihlahla Mandela (18 July 1918 – 5 December 2013) was a South African anti-apartheid revolutionary, politician and philanthropist; he served as

President of South Africa from 1994 to 1999. He was South Africa's first black chief executive, and the first elected in a fully representative democratic election. His government focused on dismantling the legacy of apartheid through tackling racism, poverty and inequality, and fostering racial reconciliation. Mandela served as President of the African National Congress (ANC) from 1991 to 1997.

In Johannesburg, he became involved in anti-colonial politics, joining the ANC and becoming a founding member of its Youth League. He was repeatedly arrested for seditious activities, but as a lawyer with the ANC leadership, he was not convicted in the Treason Trial from 1956 to 1961. Mandela was influenced by Marxism and Mao's thoughts; he secretly joined the South African Communist Party (SACP) and co-founded the militant Umkhonto we Sizwe (MK) in 1961, leading sabotage campaign against the apartheid government. In 1962; he was arrested, convicted of conspiracy to overthrow the state, and sentenced to life imprisonment in the Rivonia Trial. Mandela served 27 years in prison and was released in 1990 after an international campaign lobbied on his behalf. Mandela joined negotiations with Nationalist President F. W. de Klerk to abolish apartheid and establish multiracial elections in 1994, in which he led the ANC to victory and became South Africa's first black president. Mandela was a controversial figure for much of his life. Denounced as a communist terrorist by critics, he nevertheless gained international acclaim for his activism, having received more than 250 honors, including the 1993 Nobel Peace Prize, the US Presidential Medal of Freedom, and the Soviet Order of Lenin. He is well respected within South Africa, regarded as the "Father of the Nation".

Nobusuke Kishi (11-13-1896 to 8-7-1987) was adopted by his paternal uncle bearing the name Kishi; his original name was Sato Nobusuke related to a younger brother, Sato Eisaku. Prime Minister of Japan (11-9-1964 to 2-17-1967 and 1-14-1970 to 7-7-1972) an opponent to the Kissinger-Nixon's normalizing relation with China. Nobusuke Kishi graduated from the Tokyo Imperial law department (1920) and began a successful civil service career. In 1936 he became a vice minister of the Manchukuo government's industrial department and helped to promote the industrialization of Japanese-occupied Manchuria and China (Japan's continued war against China lasted till 1945). On his return to Japan (1940) he served as vice minister of commerce and industry, later in 1941 he served as commerce and industry minister in the Cabinet of Tōjō Hideki (known as the Japanese WW II Cabinet). In April 1942 he won a seat in the House of Representatives. Subsequently he served as Tōjō's vice minister of munitions.

Although Kishi was imprisoned in 1945 by the Allied Occupation authorities for his war services but Kishi was released (1948) without trial (Note: To this day, many current Japanese politicians have a historical background with the WW II). After reestablishing himself as a businessman, Kishi resumed his political activities, helped to organize the Japan Democratic Party, and was instrumental in merging with other conservative factions to form the Liberal-Democratic Party in 1955. He was first elected to the House of Representatives in 1953 and became the foreign minister in the Cabinet of Ishibashi Tanzan in 1954. When Ishibashi fell ill, Kishi succeeded him as prime minister in February 1957, but his term (1957–60) was marked by a turbulent opposition campaign against a new U.S.–Japan security treaty agreed to by his administration.

Kishi used his conservative parliamentary majority to ratify the revised treaty while the opposition parties were boycotting the Diet session. This was viewed as high-handed and undemocratic and provoked large-scale public demonstrations against Kishi; the protests led to the cancellation of a scheduled visit to Japan by U.S. President Dwight D. Eisenhower which cost his resignation.

Kishi advocates close relationship with the U.S. but seeking an equal basis for diplomatic relation. He initiated an official study of the controversial postwar constitution, which outlawed war, and he encouraged Japanese self-reliance in national defense. Although the section of the Japanese constitution outlawing the "potential to make war" was not altered, Kishi initiated a policy of interpreting this clause liberally, allowing the Self-Defense forces more armaments.

The history seems to repeat itself; as Abe Shinzo, a grandson-in-law of Nobusuke Kishi, now serving as the Japanese Prime Minister, appears to be continuing Kishi's wishes to 'Normalize Japan' and take a step further to bring Japan back to her WW II glory. This scenario is scary for not only the Japanese people but also for all Asians and the world population.

Chapter 15 Why Is Abe Shinzo Following Junichiro Koizumi's Footsteps on the Yasukuni Issue?

Yasukuni Shrine was originally Shokonsha established at Kudan in Tokyo in the second year of the Meiji era (1869) by the will of the Emperor Meiji. In 1879, it was renamed Yasukuni Shrine. Meiji Emperor was known for "Meiji Restoration" (1868-1912) which forced Japan to industrialize and adopt the Western values including the colonialism.

Yasukuni Shrine was established to commemorate and honor the achievement of those who dedicated their precious lives for their country. The name "Yasukuni," given by the Emperor Meiji represents wishes for preserving peace of the nation.

Currently, more than 2,466,000 divinities are enshrined here at Yasukuni Shrine. From the Japanese perspective, these are souls of men who made ultimate sacrifice for their nation since 1853 during national crisis such as the Boshin War, the Seinan War, the Sino-Japanese and Russo-Japanese wars, World War I, the Manchurian War, the China Wars and the World War II. These people, regardless of their rank or social standing, are considered to be completely equal and worshipped as national heroes at Yasukuni.

The dispute with Asian countries over the Yasukuni worship occurs because of that Japan enshrined the WW II war criminals in Yasukuni. Rubbing the salt into the wound is when the Japanese Government officially goes to the Shrine and worships the war criminals. This act plus the fact that (1) the Japanese imperial emperor never received any condemnation for the Japanese Imperial Army's war atrocities and (2) the Japanese government constantly denies the war history, be it massacres, comfort women, biological experiments, etc despite of ample physical evidence. In contrast to the German government and German people's remorse regarding the Nazi war crime, Japan has not shown any sincere remorse about the war atrocities the Japanese Imperial Army committed.

The UN has made effort to reconcile the sad part of WW II history; unfortunately, the Japanese government considers the UN recommendations as non-binding.

Junichiro Koizumi (born January 8, 1942) is a Japanese politician who was the 87th Prime Minister of Japan from 2001 to 2006. He retired from politics when his term in parliament ended in 2009. He was the fifth longest serving prime minister in the history of Japan. He is openly affiliated to the active revisionist lobby Nippon Kaigi which advocates the return to militarism, the denial of Japanese war crimes, and visits to Yasukuni Shrine. Koizumi also attracted international attention through his deployment of the Japan Self-Defense Forces to Iraq, and through his visits to the controversial shrine that fueled diplomatic tensions with neighboring China and South Korea. Abe Shinzo and Junichiro Koizumi appear to share a lot in common.

Hideki Tojo (12-30-1884 to 12-23-1948) was sentenced to death as a WW II war criminal by the International Military Tribunal for the Far East. Tojo was a general of the Imperial Japanese Army and the Prime Minister of Japan from October 1941 to July 22, 1944. He was directly responsible for Pearl Harbor attack and warfare in China and South Asia.

Chapter 16 The Difference of Germans and Japanese In Handling the Truth of WW II History

The **French Massacre** is referring to the 1944 massacre at the village and surrounding commune, burned out cars and buildings still litter the remains of the original village. The village of Oradour-sur-Glane in Haute-Vienne in Nazi occupied France was destroyed on 10 June 1944, when 642 of its inhabitants, including women and children, were massacred by a German Waffen-SS company. A new village was built after the war on a nearby site, but on the orders of the then French president, Charles de Gaulle, the original has been maintained as a permanent memorial and museum.

Nanking Massacre - In late 1937, over a period of six weeks, Imperial Japanese Army forces brutally murdered hundreds of thousands of people–including both soldiers and civilians–in the Chinese city of Nanking (or Nanjing). The horrific events are known as the Nanking Massacre or the Rape of Nanking, as between 20,000 and 80,000 women were sexually assaulted. Nanking, then the capital of

Nationalist China, was left in ruins, and it would take decades for the city and its citizens to recover from the savage attacks. The Chinese governments due to internal struggles received an unfair settlement of the Japanese surrender. The episode of the Nanking Massacre remains a painful memory in hundreds of millions people's minds. Due to the Japan's denial of this massacre, the wound would not heal. Recently, China at the urge of her people began to build memorials for the victims of the massacre and held memorial services each year.

Emperor Hirohito (4-29-1901 to 1-7-1989) was the ultimate commander of the Japanese Imperial Army which committed the WW II war crimes including the Nanking Massacre. Hirohito known as Emperor Showa was the 124th Emperor of Japan according to the traditional order, reigning from December 25, 1926, until his death on January 7, 1989. He was never brought to trial for the WW II crimes. However, the Japanese people may have to honestly revisit the WW II history in order to find justice and peace for themselves and for future generations to come. After all, Justice is far more important than blind loyalty.

Chapter 17 Tom Clancy and US-China Relationship

Tom Clancy (4-12-1947 to 10-1-2013) was born in Maryland in 1947. He was an American author best known for his espionage, military science and technological thrillers. Clancy worked as an insurance broker before writing his first novel, *The Hunt for Red October,* in 1984. Ten of Clancy's books earned No. 1 rankings on *The New York Times'* best-seller list. More than 50 million copies of his books have been printed, and four have been made into movies. Clancy died at age 66. Tom Clancy was a New York Times best-selling American author with 10 of his books earning No. 1 rankings on the NY Times best-seller list during his life time.

Chapter 18 Debate on the Logic in Great Power Diplomacy - Diaoyu Islands Case in Point

Paul D. Miller (BA and PhD Georgetown University and MA Harvard University) is a political scientist in the National Security Research Division at the RAND Corporation. He served as Director for Afghanistan and Pakistan on the National Security Council staff from 2007 through September 2009. Prior to joining RAND, Miller was an assistant professor at the National Defense University in

Washington, D.C., at which he developed and directed the College of International Security Affairs' South and Central Asia Program. He also worked as an analyst in the Central Intelligence Agency's Office of South Asian Analysis, and served in Afghanistan as a military intelligence officer with the U.S. Army.

Reference: Foreign Policy 12-26-2013.

Chapter 19 From 'Comfort Woman' Issue To US-China-Japan Relations

Comfort Woman were women and girls forced into sexual slavery by the Imperial Japanese Army before and during World War II. The name "comfort women" is a translation of the Japanese euphemism 'ianfu and the similar Korean term 'wianbu'. Ianfu is a euphemism for shofu, "prostitute(s)" in Japanese. Estimates vary as to how many women were involved, with numbers ranging from as low as 20,000 to as high as 360,000 to 410,000, in Chinese sources; the exact numbers are still being researched and debated. Many of the women were from occupied countries, including Korea, China, and the Philippines, although women from Burma, Thailand, Vietnam, Malaysia, Taiwan (then entirely occupied by Japan), Indonesia (then the Dutch East Indies), East Timor (then Portuguese Timor), and other Japanese-occupied territories. Comfort women were used for military "comfort stations" which were located in Japan and every war zone. According to testimony, young women from countries in Imperial Japanese custody were abducted from their homes. In many cases, women were also lured with promises of work in factories or restaurants; once recruited, the women were incarcerated in comfort stations in foreign lands.

Michael Makoto "Mike" Honda (born June 27, 1941) serves as the U.S. Representative for California's 17th congressional district, known as Silicon Valley, which is the only Asian American-majority district in the continental United States. The district encompasses all or part of the cities of Cupertino, Fremont, Milpitas, Newark, Santa Clara, San Jose, and Sunnyvale. He is a member of the Democratic Party and has been serving in Congress since 2001. Honda introduced House Resolution 121 (H. Res. 121), a resolution about comfort women in 2007. It asks that the Japanese government apologize to former comfort women and include curriculum about them in Japanese schools, citing 1921 International Convention for the Suppression of the Traffic in Women and Children that Japan has ratified and United Nations Security Council Resolution 1325.

Gay J. McDougall (born August 13, 1947 in Atlanta, Georgia, USA) was Executive Director of Global Rights, Partners for Justice (from September 1994 to 2006). In August 2005, she was named the first United Nations Independent Expert on Minority Issues, serving until 2011.

The Kono Statement refers to a statement released by Chief Cabinet Secretary Yohei Kono in 1993 after the conclusion of the government study that found that the Japanese Imperial Army had forced women, known as comfort women, to work in military-run brothels during World War II. The Japanese government had denied that the women had been coerced until this point.

In the Kono statement, Kono acknowledged that the Japanese Imperial Army had been involved, either directly or indirectly, in the establishment of comfort facilities. On top of that, the comfort women were recruited against their own will, through coaxing, coercion, etc., at times, administrative or military personnel directly taking part in the recruitments and lived in misery at comfort stations under a coercive atmosphere as the Kono statement articulates. However it is still debated whether the statement had acknowledged that coercion had been used in the recruitment and retention of the women by the Japanese Imperial Army directly, as the recruitment was believed to be mainly conducted by private recruiting agents (both Korean and Japanese). The statement was welcomed in South Korea. It also led to the creation of the Asian Women's Fund, which provided aid and support to women who had been forced into prostitution during the war.

The Kono statement has been the target of criticism by some conservatives in Japan. Current Prime Minister Shinzo Abe, during his first term as Prime Minister in 2007, stated that he did not believe women were coerced into working at military brothels. Members of the ruling Liberal Democratic Party had been discussing the possibility of the government, led by Abe, looking into revising the statement. After further reviews confirming reported facts and some foreign protests, Prime Minister Shinzo Abe has re-stated that he does not plan to revise the Kono Statement.

Reference: Website of the UN Office of the High Commissioner for Human Rights, http://www2.ohchr.org/english/issues/minorities/expert/index.htm, accessed 16 November 2009

Reference: "National Human Rights Depend on International Action, Says U.N. Expert", http://www.law.virginia.edu/html/news/2008_spr/mcdougall.htm, accessed 16 November 2009

Reference: "National Human Rights Depend on International Action, Says U.N. Expert", http://www.law.virginia.edu/html/news/2008_spr/mcdougall.htm, accessed 16 November 2009

Chapter 20 Nation Development of The U.S. and China in Past 250 Years and Forward

Opium War I - The First Opium War (1839–42), also known as the Opium War and as the Anglo-Chinese War, was fought between Britain and China over Britain's forced trade of opium into China. In defeat, China yielded to Britain with the Treaty of Nanking—the first of many unequal treaties imposed by the Western Power - granted an indemnity and extraterritoriality to Britain, the opening of five treaty ports, and the cession of Hong Kong Island.

Opium War II - The failure of the Nanking treaty to satisfy British goals of improved trade and diplomatic relations led to the Second Opium War (1856–60). The Second Opium War was a war pitting the British Empire and the Second French Empire against the Qing Dynasty of China, lasting four years. Again, Qing lost and signed the Treaty of Tianjin, another unequal treaty ceding part of Kowloon, opening Tianjin port, paying 8 million taels of silver and legalizing opium trade.

John V. Walsh is a scientist who lives in Cambridge, Mass. He is a frequent contributor to CounterPunch.org and Antiwar.com, discusses Paul Krugman's "economic chauvinism" regarding China's currency valuation, provocative US military postures in Central and East Asia, China's eons-long history of open trade and self defense and why the US should abandon the policy of "containing" China.

Reference: Unz Review 1-21-2014

Chapter 21 Interplay of US-China-Japan National Strategies - As Revealed By The Diaoyu Island Dispute

Maguan Treaty (April 17, 1895, Chinese (Pinyin) Maguan Tiaoyue, also known as Treaty of Shimonoseki) was an agreement that concluded the first Sino-Japanese War (1894–95) with China in defeat. By the terms of the treaty, China was obliged to recognize the independence of Korea, over which it had traditionally held suzerainty; to cede Taiwan, the Pescadores Islands, and the Liaodong (south Manchurian) Peninsula to Japan; to pay an indemnity of 200,000,000 taels to Japan; and to open the ports of Shashi, Chongqing, Suzhou, and Hangzhou to Japanese trade. The Triple Intervention (1895), secured by Russia, France, and Germany, subsequently required Japan to retrocede the Liaodong Peninsula to China in return for an additional indemnity of 30,000,000 taels.

Okinawa (Ryukyu, Liujiu) has long been a tributary state relationship with China under her protection against invaders from the feudal forces from Japan. The invasion from the Japanese was on and off from the 17th century to the 18th century. After Japan had won the Sino-Japanese war in 1895 and obtained Taiwan, she then captured the Ryukyu royal family and annexed Ryukyu in 1897 as Okinawa Prefecture. Post-WW II, Japan had to give up all captured territories such as Taiwan and Okinawa. The United States became the trustee of Okinawa Islands.

Chapter 22 Can Jade Rabbit (Yutu) Help Win The Space Exploration For Mankind?

Chang'e and Yutu – Chinese fairy tale said that a lady Chang'e ascended to the moon and became a fairy living on the moon with a bunny (Yutu, a jade bunny) whose job was making medicines for curing diseases. China's space program chose to name her space transport rockets Chang'e and the robot for conducting experiments on the moon as Yutu.

Alexei Leonov (Russian; born 30 May 1934 in Listvyanka, West Siberian Krai, Soviet Union) is a retired Soviet/Russian cosmonaut and Air Force Major General. On 18 March 1965, he became the first human to conduct extra-vehicular activity (EVA), exiting the capsule during the Voskhod 2 mission for a 12-minute spacewalk.

Neil Aiden Armstrong (August 5, 1930 – August 25, 2012) was an American astronaut and the first person to walk on the Moon. Before becoming an astronaut, Armstrong was a naval officer served in the Korean War. After the war, he earned his bachelor's degree at Purdue University and served as a test pilot at the National Advisory Committee for Aeronautics High-Speed Flight Station, now known as the Dryden Flight Research Center. There were three crew members on the Apollo 11 Moon Mission, Neil Aiden Armstrong, Edwin Buzz Aldrin and Michael Collins.

Chapter 23 From Russia's Annexation of Crimea to International Diplomatic Play

The **Crimean Peninsula**, also known simply as **Crimea**, is a major land mass on the northern coast of the Black Sea that is almost completely surrounded by water, hence possessing a strategic value for maritime and naval operation. The peninsula is located south of the Ukrainian region of Kherson and west of the Russian region of Kuban. It is surrounded by two seas: the Black Sea and the smaller Sea of Azov to the east. It is connected to Kherson by the Isthmus of Perekop and is separated from Kuban by the Strait of Kerch.

Chapter 24 Should The United States Believe Or Not To Believe China's Message in Körber Foundation?

Körber Foundation is founded by Kurt A. Körber. He as a German and world citizen believes that Social development calls for critical reflection. The foundation established by him takes on this social challenge at a national and an international level. Körber Foundation is the owner of the Körber AG (public limited technology company with 11,000 employees), has been developing its own profile for almost five decades guided by its committees. It brings together people from different political, social and cultural backgrounds. Acting as an operating foundation, it develops and promotes programs for which it retains full responsibility, while still remaining open to suggestions and cooperation. The aim of its work is to try out new ideas and methods and to transfer them to society. The Körber Foundation seeks to encourage others to take initiative into their own hands. As China is going through a tremendous social change in her as well as influencing other nations, it is extremely important to engage the leader of China to speak in an open forum.

China Threat is a term now frequently appearing in political analysts' writings, but no one is sure who has first coined the term and what has been its precise definition. The right-wing conservatives in Japan beat the 'China Threat' drums in terms of political and military perspective and the left-wing liberals in the United States seem to label 'China Threat' as an economic issue. There is a strange website using China-Threat as its domain name, www.china-threat.com. Two former Professors (Bill Smith and Doug Kaufman) from The University of Michigan (UM) created the site to take a stand against the corruption and short selling of America's future by the US Government and by UM. The site has a very long confusing mission statement and link to an interview posted on the YouTube somehow blaming China's rise to Chinese students and faculties 'stealing technologies from America' and UM's leaders and the Michigan Governor Rick Snider letting that happen. Based on incorrect historical facts and their personal assessments, they concluded that the China Threat is a commerce and military threat. Here is the link to Xi Jinping's speech at the Korber Foundation on 3-28-2014 for you to judge whether or not there is a China Threat. (https://www.youtube.com/watch?v=ZEXer7JUC7I)

Chapter 25 Is Japan's Democracy Really Working for the Japanese People?

Axial Powers in WW II: Germany, Italy and Japan

Allied Powers in WW II: Great Britain, France, Soviet Union, The United States and China

Supreme Command of the Allied Powers (SCAP): The title held by General Douglas MacArthur during the Allied occupation of Japan following World War II.

Chapter 26 State Visit of First Lady Michelle Obama to China – 'First' Comment

Michelle LaVaughn Robinson (born January 17, 1964) is an American lawyer and writer. She is the wife of the 44th and current President of the United States, Barack Obama, and the first African-American First Lady of the United States. Raised on the South Side of Chicago, she is a graduate of Princeton University and Harvard Law School, and spent the early part of her legal career working at the law firm Sidley Austin, where Barack worked as an intern with her. She helped campaign for her husband's presidential bid. She delivered a keynote address at the 2008 Democratic National Convention and also spoke at the 2012 Democratic National Convention.

Peng Liyuan (born November 20, 1962) is a renowned Chinese contemporary folk singer and performing artist. She is the wife of current Chinese leader Xi Jinping, and as such referred to as the "Chinese First Lady" by the media. Peng is the Dean of the People's Liberation Army Art Academy. She gained popularity as a soprano singer from her regular appearances on the annual CCTV New Year's Gala, a widely viewed Chinese television program during the Chinese New Year. She has won many honors in singing competitions nationwide. Peng is a civilian member of China's People's Liberation Army and holds the civilian rank equivalent to major general. She was the first in China to obtain a Master's degree in traditional ethnic music when the degree was established in the 1980s

Chapter 27 Condemn Pity Or Exonerate Japanese Kamikaze Pilots?

Kamikaze Pilots ("Divine" or "spirit wind"), were officially called Tokubetsu Kōgekitai ("Special Attack Unit"). These military aviators made suicide attacks from the Empire of Japan against Allied naval vessels in the closing stages of the Pacific campaign of World War II, designed to destroy warships with human precision diving into the target to destroy the enemy more effectively than was possible with conventional attacks. During World War II, about 3,860 kamikaze pilots were killed, and about 19% of kamikaze attacks managed to hit a ship. Kamikaze aircrafts were essentially pilot-guided explosive missiles, purpose-built or converted from conventional aircraft. Pilots would attempt to crash their aircraft into enemy ships in what was called a "Body Attack" in planes laden with some combination of explosives, bombs, torpedoes and full fuel tanks; hence, the payload and explosion larger. A kamikaze could cause damage even when the plane was hit. The goal of crippling or destroying large numbers of Allied ships, particularly aircraft carriers, was considered to be a just reason for sacrificing pilots and aircraft. The Japanese Imperial Army methodically recruited and trained young cadets for this special airforce. Chiran Airfield at Minami was where Kamikaze pilots took off for their death mission.

Chapter 28 Don't Let Japan Highjack The US 'Pivot' Policy To A Japanese '3FN' Strategy

FFFN or 3FN means friend near foe far as a diplomatic and/or military strategy. **NFNR** means neither friend nor foe maintaining an ambiguous relationship.

Purnomo Yasugiantoro is the Indonesian Defense Minister

Patrick Cronin is a Senior Advisor and Senior Director of the Asia-Pacific Security Program at the Center for a New American Security (CNAS). Previously, he was the Senior Director of the Institute for National Strategic Studies (INSS) at the National Defense University, where he simultaneously oversaw the Center for the Study of Chinese Military Affairs. Dr. Cronin has a rich and diverse background in both Asian-Pacific security and U.S. defense, foreign and development policy.

Reference: The Emerging Asia Power Web, New American Security, 6-2014

Chapter 29 Japan Can't Win the Diaoyu Islands Dispute by Increasing MOFA Budget

MOFA – Ministry of Foreign Affairs of Japan

Diaoyu Islands (See notes in Chapter 1)

Dokdo Islands are disputed islands between Korea and Japan; they are also known as The Liancourt Rocks, pronounced as Tokto in Korean (literally *solitary island* in Korean, and Takeshima (literally *bamboo island*) in Japanese, a group of small islets in the Sea of Japan. While South Korea has *de facto* control over the islets, its sovereignty over them is contested by Japan. South Korea classifies the islets as Dokdo-ri, Ulleung-eup, Ulleung County, North Gyeongsang Province. Japan classifies them as part of Okinoshima, Oki District, Shimane Prefecture.

Chapter 30 The Illusion of Cyber Security and Privacy Protection for Citizens

PRISM is a clandestine mass electronic surveillance data mining program launched in 2007 by the National Security Agency (NSA), with participation of the British equivalent agency, GCHQ. The Prism program collects stored Internet communications based on demands made to Internet companies such as Google, Yahoo, etc. under Section 702 of the FISA Amendments Act of 2008 requiring the internet companies to turn over any data that match court-approved search terms. The NSA can use these Prism requests to target communications that were encrypted when they traveled across the Internet backbone, to focus on stored data that telecommunication filtering systems discarded earlier, and to get data that is easier to handle, among other things. PRISM began in 2007 in the wake of the passage of the Protect America Act under the Bush Administration. The program is operated under the supervision of the U.S. Foreign Intelligence Surveillance Court (FISC) pursuant to the Foreign Intelligence Surveillance Act (FISA). NSA contractor Edward Snowden leaked its existence and warned that the extent of mass data collection was far greater than the public knew, including "dangerous" and "criminal" activities. The disclosures were published by *The Guardian* and *The Washington Post* on June 6, 2013. Later reports have shown a financial arrangement between NSA's Special Source Operations division (SSO) and PRISM partners in the millions of dollars. PRISM is claimed to be "the number one source of raw intelligence used for NSA analytic reports", and it accounts for 91% of the NSA's Internet traffic acquired under FISA section 702 authority. The FISA Court had ordered a subsidiary of telecommunications company (Verizon Communications) to turn over to the NSA logs tracking all of its customers' phone calls.

Reference: House Bill HR 4291, The bipartisan FISA Transparency and Modernization Act of 2014, introduced by House Representatives Mike Rogers and C. A. Dutch Ruppersberger http://intelligence.house.gov/sites/intelligence.house.gov/files/documents/FISAmar2514asintroduced.pdf

Charlie Savage is a Washington correspondent for The New York Times. He is known for his work on presidential power and national security legal policy matters.

Reference: Obama to Call for End to NSA's Bulk Data Collection, NY Times 3-24-2014

Chapter 31 A Warm Bilateral Relationship Is Always Better Than A Hate Or Love Triangle
– Vietnam and China Relationship –

The **Paracel Islands**, also known as **Xisha** in Chinese and Hoàng Sa in Vietnamese, is a group of islands, reefs, banks and other maritime features in the

South China Sea. It is controlled (and occupied) by the People's Republic of China, and also claimed by Taiwan (Republic of China) and Vietnam.

The Spratly Islands (Chinese: *Nansha islands*, Filipino: *Kapuluan ng Kalayaan*, Malay: *Kepulauan Spratly* and Vietnamese: *Quần đảo Trường Sa*) are a disputed group of more than 750 reefs, islets, atolls, cays and islands in the South China Sea. The archipelago lies off the coasts of the Philippines, Malaysia (Sabah), and southern Vietnam. Spratly is named after the 19th-century British explorer Richard Spratly who sighted them in 1843. However, these islands have been on ancient Chinese maps recorded as the "Thousand Li Stretch of Sands"; *Qianli Changsha* and the "Ten-Thousand Li of Stone Pools"; *Wanli Shitang*, which China today claims refers to the Spratly Islands. The Wanli Shitang have been explored by the Chinese since the Yuan Dynasty and they may have been considered within their national boundaries. They are also referenced in the 13th century, followed by the Ming Dynasty. When the Ming Dynasty and the Qing Dynasty. These islands have been continued to be included in territorial maps compiled in 1724, 1755, 1767, 1810, and 1817. The islands contain approximately 4 km^2 (1.5 mi^2) of actual land area spread over a vast area of more than 425,000 km^2 (164,000 mi^2).

References:
1. *Qing dynasty provincial map from tianxia world map*, 1724
2. *Qing dynasty circuit and province map from Tianxia world map*, 1755
3. *Great Qing of 10,000-years Tianxia map*, 1767
4. *Great Qing of 10,000-years general map of all territory*, 1810
5. *Great Qing tianxia overview map*, 1817

Chapter 32 Cold War I to Cold War II with A Changing Triangle

David F. Gordon is Head of Research at Eurasia Group, the political risk consultancy. He was previously the U.S. State Department's Director of Policy Planning, where he held a rank equivalent to a United States Assistant Secretary of State.

Jordan Schneider is a researcher at Eurasia Group.

Reference Foreign Affairs 5-22-2014.

Chapter 33 Democracy Is Not An Ideology But A Method for Achieving the Goals of Ideology

Communist Party of China (CPC or CCP) is the founding and ruling political party of the People's Republic of China (PRC). The CPC is the sole governing party of China, although it coexists alongside 8 other legal parties that make up the United Front. It was founded in 1921, chiefly by Chen Duxiu and Li Dazhao. The party grew quickly, and by 1949 the CPC had defeated the Kuomintang (KMT) in a 10-year civil war, thus leading to the establishment of the People's Republic of China. The CPC is the world's largest political party with a membership of 86.7 million as of 2014.

Reference: http://english.cpc.people.com.cn/

Chapter 34 Will Hillary Clinton Win the 2016 United States Presidency
-Views of Americans and Chinese and Bomb Shell Stories-

Benghazi Event – Is the Benghazi (Libya) attack killed J. Christopher Stevens on 9-11-2013 a spontaneous attack or a planned terrorists attack? Members of the House Select Committee tasked with investigating the 2012 terrorist attack on the U.S. Consulate in Benghazi, Libya, has met recently behind closed doors with the State and Justice departments but still plans to hold public hearings, said the committee's chairman. Saying there are still "far too many questions" unanswered, House Speaker John A. Boehner reappointed Rep. Trey Gowdy to lead his chamber's inquiry into the Benghazi terrorist attack just a few days after a House committee cleared the CIA of most wrongdoing, which signaled the GOP was not satisfied with those conclusions. The Obama administration's just-released criminal complaint against the alleged mastermind of the Benghazi terrorist attacks provides a final contradiction to its own evolving explanations for what happened that day.

References:
Walter Russell Mead, Washington Post Opinion, 5-10-2014
Jonathan Tkachuk, Politics 2-1-2013

Benghazi Attack under Microscope, http://www.washingtontimes.com/specials/benghazi-attack-and-scandal/#ixzz3PFxzRzVc

Chapter 35 Why Americans Need To Understand The Real China Issue?
Watch the Historical Visit of Zhang Zhijun to Meet Wang Yoichi in Taiwan

Christopher J. Marut, Director of AIT, was born in Connecticut and was educated at the University of Notre Dame, where he received his BBA in Finance and Business Economics, and at the University of California, Berkeley, where he received an MBA. He also studied at the College of Naval Warfare in Newport, Rhode Island, where he received a Master degree in National Security and Strategic Studies. Over the 29 years of his career in the Foreign Service, Marut has developed a deep understanding of Asian affairs, including U.S.-Taiwan relations. Marut's most recent assignment at the Department of State was Director of the Office of Australia, New Zealand and Pacific Island Affairs in the Bureau of East Asian and Pacific Affairs (EAP), where he served as one of the key advisers on U.S. policy in the Asia-Pacific region. Prior to that, he served as Deputy Consul General at the U.S. Consulate General in Hong Kong, one of two U.S. consulates general worldwide that function as independent missions similar to embassies, and as Director of the EAP Office of Regional and Security Policy in Washington. As a seasoned diplomat, Marut has the capacity to contribute to the peaceful unification of China with eventual benefits to China, the United States and the world.

Chapter 36 Japan Fast Copying President Obama in Circumventing Democracy

The **Article 9** of the Japanese Constitutionis a clause in the National Constitution of Japan outlawing war as a means to settle international disputes involving the state. The Constitution came into effect on May 3, 1947, following World War II. In its text, the state formally renounces the sovereign right of belligerency and aims at an international peace based on justice and order. The article also states that, to accomplish these aims, armed forces with war potential will not be maintained, although Japan maintains *de facto* armed forces, referred to as the Japan Self-Defense Forces which may have originally been thought of as something akin to what Mahatma Gandhi called the soldiers of peace or a collective security police (peace keeping) force operating under the United Nations. In July 2014, the Japanese government, under PM Abe Shinzo's engineered plan, approved a reinterpretation which gave more powers to its Self-Defense forces, allowing them to defend other allies in case of war being declared upon them, despite of concerns and disapproval from China and South Korea. The United States supported the move by interpreting herself as the ally gaining a military support when needed. However, the interpretation in the minds of Japanese right-wing is not so simple. Japan essentially view this a license to strike as a third party interfering in any conflict. Abe Shinzo has been busy signing up military alliances with Asia countries to make this 'license' far reaching. This change is considered illegitimate by some Japanese parties and Japanese citizens since the prime minister circumvented Japan's constitutional amendment procedure.

Chapter 37 A Stable World Under The Three-Legged Ding Structure

Ding (Chinese: *dǐng*) appeared as ancient Chinese cauldrons, standing upon legs with a lid and two facing handles. The object is one of the most important shapes used in Chinese ritual bronzes. There were two shapes: round vessels with three legs and rectangular ones with four, the latter was called fan ding (square ding). Dings were used for cooking, storage, and ritual offerings to the gods or to ancestors. The earliest recovered examples were pre-Shang ceramic ding at the Erlitou site but better known ones were from the Bronze Age, particularly after the Zhou King deemphasized the ritual use of wine practiced by the Shang kings. Under the Zhou King, the type of ding and the privilege to use it to perform rituals became symbols of authority.

The three legged ding was used by historians as a metaphor to describe a political situation that China is being ruled by three 'kings'. Hence it is appropriate to use ding as the metaphor today to describe the world situation where three great powers are maintaining the world peace. Metaphorically speaking A three legged ding is only stable when the three legs are of approximately the same strength.

Chapter 38 Bipolar (Hegemony) and Multi-Polar (Post-Hegemony) World View and Foreign Policy

Hegemony is the political, economic, or military predominance or control of one state over others. In Ancient Greece (8th century BCE – 6th century CE), hegemony denoted the politico–military dominance of a city-state over other city-states. The dominant state is known as the hegemon. In the 19th century, hegemony came to denote the "Social or cultural predominance or ascendancy; predominance by one group within a society or milieu". Later, it could be used to mean "a group or regime which exerts undue influence within a society." Also, it could be used for the geopolitical and the cultural predominance of one country over others; from which was derived hegemonism, as in the colonial era that the Great Powers meant to establish hegemony over Asia and Africa. The word or concept has been used in The Marxist theory depicting a cultural hegemony, where the ruling class can manipulates and impose their view and value system as the world view. In cultural imperialism, the leader state that can dictate the internal politics and the societal character of the subordinate states is essentially establishing her hegemonic sphere of influence which may be capable of changing the regime of the subordinate state is deemed necessary.

BRIC or BRICS – Brazil, Russia, India and China are grouped together as they are all deemed to be at a similar stage of newly advanced economic development. A related acronym is BRICS which includes South Africa.

Chapter 39 Does Leader's Dream Match People's Dream? Comparing Abe, Putin and Xi's Dreams

Chinese Dream is simply defined by the Chinese leader as to double the per capita income for the Chinese citizens.

Chapter 40 Bad Attitudes Impacting the US-China Relationship

ASEAN, the Association of Southeast Asian Nations, was established on 8 August 1967 in Bangkok, Thailand, with the signing of the ASEAN Declaration (Bangkok Declaration) by the Founding Members of ASEAN, namely Indonesia,

Malaysia, Philippines, Singapore and Thailand. Brunei Darussalam then joined on 7 January 1984, Viet Nam on 28 July 1995, Lao PDR and Myanmar on 23 July 1997, and Cambodia on 30 April 1999, making up what is today the ten Member States of ASEAN.

Chapter 41 Worldwide Turmoil Viewed By Brzezinski and Wordman

Zbigniew Kazimierz Brzezinski (born March 28, 1928) is a Polish American political scientist, geostrategist, and statesman who served as a counselor to Lyndon B. Johnson from 1966–1968 and held the position of United States National Security Advisor to President Jimmy Carter from 1977 to 1981. Brzezinski belongs to the realist school of international relations, geopolitically standing in the tradition of geographer and geostategist, Halford Mackinder and Nicholas J. Spykman. Brzezinski is currently Robert E. Osgood Professor of American Foreign Policy at Johns Hopkins University's School of Advanced International Studies, a scholar at the Center for Strategic and International Studies, and a member of various boards and councils. He appears frequently as an expert on the PBS program *The NewsHour with Jim Lehrer*, ABC News' *This Week with Christiane Amanpour*, and on MSNBC's *Morning Joe*, where his daughter, Mika Brzezinski, is co-anchor. In recent years, he has been a supporter of the Prague Process. His son, Mark Brzezinski, is an American diplomat and the current United States Ambassador to Sweden since 2011. Brzezinski still writes frequently on world affairs.

Chapter 42 Why Does Japan Keep Denying Her War Atrocities? - The Nanking Massacre, Comfort Women and Unit 731 Biological Experiments –

Nanking Massacre (See notes in Chapter 16)
Unit 731 was a covert biological and chemical warfare research and development unit of the Imperial Japanese Army that undertook lethal human experimentation during the Second Sino-Japanese War (1937–1945) and World War II. It was responsible for some of the most notorious war crimes carried out by Japanese personnel. Unit 731 was based at the Pingfang district of Harbin, the largest city in the Japanese puppet state of Manchukuo at that time (Northeast China).

It was officially known as the Epidemic Prevention and Water Purification Department of the Kwantung Army. Originally set up under the Kempeitai military police of the Empire of Japan, Unit 731 was taken over and commanded until the end of the war by General Shiro Ishii, an officer in the Kwantung Army. The facility itself was built between 1934 and 1939 and officially adopted the name "Unit 731" in 1941.

Between 3,000 and 12,000 men, women, and children—from which around 600 every year were provided by the Kempeitai—died during the human experimentation conducted by Unit 731 at the camp based in Pingfang alone, which does not include victims from other medical experimentation sites. Almost 70% of the victims who died in the Pingfang camp were Chinese, including both civilian and military. Close to 30% of the victims were Russian. Some others were South East Asians and Pacific Islanders and a small number of Allied prisoners of war. The unit received generous support from the Japanese government up to the end of the war in 1945.

Chapter 43 "In the Interest of the U.S." – We War!

Sun Tzu (also rendered as **Sun Zi or Sun Tzi**) was a Chinese military general, strategist and philosopher who lived in the Spring and Autumn Period of ancient China. Sun Zi is actually an honorific which means "Master Sun": His birth name was **Sun Wu** and he was known outside of his family by his courtesy name **Changqing**. He is traditionally credited as the author of *The Art of War*, an extremely influential ancient Chinese book on military strategy. Sun Zi has had a significant impact on Chinese and Asian history and culture, both as the author of *The Art of War* and as a legendary historical figure.

Sun Tzu's biography was sketchy. Sima Qian and other traditional historians placed him as a minister to King Helü of Wu and dated his lifetime to 544–496 BC. Modern scholars accepting his historicity nonetheless place the existing text of *The Art of War* in the later Warring States period based upon its style of composition and its descriptions of warfare. Traditional accounts state that the general's descendant Sun Bin also wrote a treatise on military tactics, also titled *The Art of War*. Since both Sun Wu and Sun Bin were referred to as Sun Tzu in classical Chinese texts, some historians believed them identical prior to the rediscovery of Sun Bin's treatise in 1972.

Sun Tzu's work has been praised and employed throughout East Asia since its composition. During the twentieth century, *The Art of War* grew in popularity and its philosophy and tactics were seen to be applicable outside of military theory. The book eventually saw practical use in Western society and it was translated and annotated for professionals of different disciplines such as marketing, trade, finance, enterprise, psychology even for marriages. It became one of the Chinese books that have had great impact in Asia, Europe, and America influencing culture, politics, business, and sports, as well as modern warfare.

Chapter 44 Robin Williams, Drug Problems and Opium Wars

Opium War I and Opium War II (See notes in Chapter 20)

Chapter 45 The US Leadership Transition at 2016-17 - Most Critical for US-China Relation

ISIS Started as an al Qaeda splinter group. The aim of ISIS is to create an Islamic state across Sunni areas of Iraq and in Syria. ISIS is known for killing dozens of people at a time and carrying out public executions, crucifixions and other acts. It has taken over large swaths of northern and western Iraq. The group currently controls hundreds of square miles. It ignores international borders and has a presence from Syria's Mediterranean coast to south of Baghdad. It rules by Sharia law. ISIS gets revenue from extortion and robbery, recently, shifted to generating resources through large-scale attacks aimed at capturing and holding territory.

Chapter 46 Chinese Americans Should Vote on Issues, not Party Line

The **Number of Voters** (in %) identified as Republican, Democrat versus Independent in 2012 Presidential election are 28, 31 and 40 and the independents are increasing in number. It certainly supports the thinking, the Chinese Americans should vote on issues not by party affiliation.

Chapter 47 Conclusion From The U.S.-China Commission (USCC) Military Assessment

USCC – U.S. – China Economic and Security Review Commission (Chaired by Senator James M. Talent and Dr. Katherine C. Tobin)

Senator **Jim Talent** is a national security leader who specializes in issues related to the Department of Defense. He has been active in Missouri and national public policy for over 25 years.

Reference: http://www.uscc.gov/Commission_Members/sen-james-talent#sthash.X0OYB3bj.dpuf

Dr. **Katherine Tobin** was appointed to the U.S.-China Economic and Security Review Commission by Senate Majority Leader Harry Reid in December 2012 for a two-year term expiring December 31, 2016. Dr. Tobin has fifteen years of experience as a business manager, market researcher and consultant in corporate America at institutions including Hewlett-Packard Corporation, IBM and Catalyst. She also has worked for fifteen years as a university faculty member and administrator.

Reference: http://www.uscc.gov/Commission_Members/hon-katherine-c-tobin-phd#sthash.48FsyAhH.dpuf

Chapter 48 From Nixon-Kissinger to Obama-Rice on US China Policy

The **Joint Communiqué of the United States of America and the People's Republic of China**, also known as the **Shanghai Communiqué** (1972), was an important diplomatic document issued by the United States of America and the People's Republic of China on February 28, 1972 during President Richard Nixon's historical visit to China. The document pledged that it was in the interest of all nations for the United States and China to work towards the normalization of their relations. Normalization did occur with the Joint Communiqué on the Establishment of Diplomatic Relations seven years later. The US and China also agreed that neither they nor any other power should "*seek hegemony in the Asia-Pacific region*". This was of particular importance to China, who shared a militarized border with the Soviet Union. (See notes in Chapter 38) Regarding the political status of Taiwan, in the communiqué the United States acknowledged the One-China policy (but did not endorse the PRC's version of the policy) and agreed to cut back military installations on Taiwan. This "constructive ambiguity" (in the phrase of US Secretary of State Henry Kissinger, who oversaw the American side of the negotiations) may be a legacy hindering efforts for complete normalization in a shorter schedule.

Reference: <u>Joint Communique of the United States of America and the People's Republic of China"</u>. <u>Taiwan Documents Project</u>. February 28, 1972

Chapter 49 Is War Between The United States and China Inevitable?

Robert Farley, The National Interest
Reference: http://nationalinterest.org/feature/should-america-fear-chinas-nuclear-weapons-11046

Aaron Friedberg, the International Security
Reference: *http://www.mitpressjournals.org/doi/abs/10.1162/016228805775124589#.VL2IfYtOyOO*

John Mearsheimer and Zachary Keck, The Diplomat
Reference: http://thediplomat.com/2014/01/us-china-rivalry-more-dangerous-than-cold-war/

Joseph S. Nye, World Affairs
Reference: http://www.project-syndicate.org/commentary/joseph-s--nye-wants-to-deter-russia-without-isolating-it

Paul Craig Roberts and Jeff Steinberg, Press TV
Reference: http://www.paulcraigroberts.org/?s=china+war

ASB and War:
Comment on 'Preparing To Go To War With China' by Prof. Amitai Etzioni at GWU
Ifay Chang, Ph.D. 9-30-2013

After reading the article written by Prof. Amitai Etzioni of George Washington University, I cannot help but share the concerns his article alluded to. Here are my comments:

Planning for war whether it is offensive or defensive, must be done on the basis of sound strategy. Prof. Etzioni rightly hinted that the U.S.' ASB plan seems to have been launched before a thorough debate and a sound strategy were well established, hence, giving rise to the concern that adversaries will counter their own military build-up eventually leading to a devastating nuclear war.

Famous Chinese military strategist Sun Tze said clearly in his world-known book, The Art of War, that war should be the last resort in settling differences. If war is inevitable, then the planning must be thorough and grounded in absolutely sound strategic thinking. I am not a military strategist, but based on my understanding of Sun Tze and common wisdom, I feel that any military plan such as ASB must pass some basic strategic thinking before it is implemented. This strategic thinking can be placed in three categories, Psychological, theoretical (or Ideological) and Practical (or Economic) considerations.

From a psychological point of view, is ASB a deterrent or provocative plan? The answer to this question is quite obvious; it does not take a military genius to know that it is a provocative plan. The U.S. pursued full-proof preemptive strike capability because she felt provoked, and in turn, ASB will provoke targeted country to think about an anti-ASB build up to retaliate against an ASB attack. Unless ASB is guaranteed to succeed in terms of wiping out the opponent totally, the consequence is unthinkable and unacceptable in the strategic sense. If the military strength of the target is wiped out, the people left would bear the devastating consequences and would develop a deep hatred which will dwarf the Islamic terrorists' hatred for generations. Can American people bear the psychological strain after the U.S. launches an ASB attack? I am not sure the U.S. citizens have been given a chance to think about this strategic question. The concept of ASB going beyond containment may have worked against a small and weak target, but would not have worked against the Soviet Union, for instance. With weapon so far technologies advanced (sophisticated electronics, communication and control involving satellite and global networks) a full-proof strike is hardly guaranteed, hence unthinkable. Cyber technology shrinks the timeline for war-time decision making (compared to WW II era warfare) and makes the military intelligence so vulnerable that there is no full proof solution. Even given NSA's ability to monitor and capture the entire world's communications and information, there is no way to guarantee that data did not contain planned information to lead to a false decision. Therefore, the current ASB plan does not pass the simple psychological test as a plan based on a sound strategy.

From Ideological or a theoretical point of view, is ASB the only solution to counter any rising nation seeking to challenge the U.S.' supreme power? The U.S. and China have cultural, historical and philosophical differences, but the most significant difference lies between their political systems. The U.S. has been the sole bearer of democracy that advocates people's voting power. However, this difference does not warrant adopting a plan of annihilation plan such as ASB. Any political scientist will tell you there is no and has never been a perfect political system in the modern world or in history. The U.S. democracy has not worked perfectly as evidenced by our grid-locked Congress and deteriorating economy, education, manufacturing and quality of life. No doubt, the U.S. system is attractive for many immigrants who want to enter this country including many Chinese citizens. If this trend continues, there is no need for the U.S. to worry that a rising China is threatening the US political system, is there? If that trend stops, then it has to be the result of political reform in China; then it would perhaps be time for the U.S. to examine and accelerate her political reform. Ideologically, China has never fully endorsed the Soviet style communism, and the legacies of its past leaders like Mao, Deng etc have been reevaluation. Thus there does not seem to be any ideological grounds for the U.S. to adopt ASB.

From practical or economic point of view, is ASB a feasible plan? First in the above discussion, the author believes there is no full-proof winning plan possible in the modern cyber-enabled war. Take the GPS system alone: It took many years and a lot of investments to build a satellite system (separately for military) but now China has developed her own system (provoked by the psychological reasons discussed above) to feel secure. The U.S. may still enjoy a technological lead but China is no longer a WW-II China; psychologically she has transformed from a weak victim psychology to a grown-up self-respect seeking psychology. The more pressure is applied to her the more resistance she will show. In its rise, China has definitely prioritized in growing economic strength not aggressive military power (she has only a carrier refurbished from a used Russian carrier hulk while the U.S.

is re-balancing her navy in the Pacific, namely encircling China's seas.) How would you feel and what would you do? By exercising the 'tolerant' policy as the weak Qing Dynasty reacted to the western power or leap frog the technologies to stand up to threats? China chose the latter because she has earned her economic power. She has the means to pay and expand militarily to ensure there will never be another Japanese invasion or eight western powers to divide the Chinese sea shore line. On the contrary, the U.S. is suffering economically partially due to her war diplomacy and partially due to a decline in world competitiveness in production because of a faltering political system. The U.S. maintained her military superpower status by outspending the world top ten countries combined, but this is not sustainable nor necessary from a strategic point of view, as we discussed above. Therefore, from a practical standpoint, we need to debate the viability of an ASB plan. If we have to finance the ASB alone and provide supports to all our partners, the cost is prohibitive. If we count on partners, like Japan, Korea, Taiwan, and the Philippines, to chip in money for the ASB, it gets more complicated than NATO. Japan has her own agenda which may not be beneficial to the U.S. Korea has her own national issues with Japan. Taiwan, which has been manipulated all these years by external powers, may finally have a wake-up call. Seriously, can US manage these partners in an ASB plan with an ill-defined objective? I seriously doubt it.

ASB is still not well explained by the Pentagon to the public. We may be overly worried, but in today's world, it is safer and wiser to be concerned about world affairs than not. I applaud GWU for hosting a debate on ASB to shed some light on the possible wrong assumptions made under ASB which may lead to an unnecessary all-out war with China, a war likely to include Russia and other nations in the world.

Preparing Go To War With China by **Amitai Etzioni**
http://icps.gwu.edu/2013/07/03/preparing-to-go-to-war-with-china/

Chapter 50 Common Interest, Objective and Understanding (IOU) Policies Make the U.S. and China Win-Win

Sun Zi and Sun Zi Bin Fa (The Art of War) (See notes in Chapter 43)

ISIS (See note in Chapter 45)

Chapter 51 Use Space Cooperation to Unite the Earth

Chang'e and Yutu (see notes in Chapter 22)

Neil Armstrong et al (See notes in Chapter 22)

The International Space Station (ISS) is a space station, satellite like, staying in low Earth orbit. ISS is a modular structure whose first component was launched in 1998. ISS is still the largest artificial body in orbit; it can often be seen with the naked eye from Earth. ISS consists of pressurized modules, external trusses, solar arrays and other components. The components in ISS have been launched by American Space Shuttles as well as Russian Proton and Soyuz rockets. In 1984, the ESA was invited to participate in Space Station *Freedom*. After the USSR dissolved, the United States and Russia merged Mir-2 and *Freedom* together in 1993. China is currently excluded from ISS participation for the same reason that the Soviet Union was excluded.

Chapter 52 Who Is More Stupid to Engage in Arm Race and Repeat the Cold War? The U.S. or China?

Jeremy Page, Deep Threat: China's Growing Submarine Capability Throws Others Off-Kilter Reference: The Wall Street Journal, http://blogs.wsj.com/china-realtime/2014/10/27/deep-threat-chinas-growing-submarine-capability-throws-others-off-kilter/

Chapter 53 APEC Past, Present and Future
Sprouting of the Two Great Nations Relationship

G-2 (See notes in Chapter 2)

Robert James Lee "Bob" Hawke (born 9 December 1929) is an Australian politician who was the 23rd Prime Minister of Australia and the Leader of the Labor Party from 1983 to 1991. After a decade as President of the Australian Council of Trade Unions, he was elected to the House of Representatives as the Labor MP for Wills in 1980. In 1983, he led Labor to a landslide election victory and was sworn in as Prime Minister. He led Labor to victory at three more elections in 1984, 1987 and 1990, thus making him the most successful Labor Leader in history. Bob

Hawke is the oldest living former Prime Minister in Australia. His idea of forming the APEC will earn him a bright spot in world history.

Chapter 54 Significance of APEC-Beijing and Post-APEC Agreements between the U.S. and China

APEC History (See Chapter 53)

Chapter 55 Is China So Difficult to Understand by the West? Why? Why Not?

Classical Chinese (*gŭwén*, "ancient text") is the language of the classic literature from the end of the Spring and Autumn period through to the end of the Han Dynasty, a written form of Old Chinese. The term is also used for **Literary Chinese** (*wényán wén*, "written text"), a traditional style of formal written Chinese used principally by educated people modeling the classical language, distinctly different from any modern spoken form of Chinese. Literary Chinese was used for almost all formal writing in China until the early 20th century, and also, during various periods, in Japan, Korea and Vietnam. While common Chinese folks and foreign Chinese learners have adopted plain written Chinese similar to modern spoken Mandarin, the vast amount of classic Chinese literature cannot be appreciated without acquiring the skills in reading Chinese classic literatures.

Chapter 56 Why Apologizing to Japan?

Paul Robin Krugman (born February 28, 1953), won the Nobel Memorial Prize in Economic Sciences in 2008 for his contributions to New Trade Theory and New Economic Geography. Krugman is known in academia for his work on international economics (including trade theory, economic geography, and international finance), liquidity traps, and currency crises. Krugman is ranked among the most influential economic thinkers in the US. Krugman has written over 20 books, published over 200 scholarly articles in professional journals and edited volumes as well as written more than 750 columns on economic and political issues. As a commentator, Krugman has written on a wide range of economic issues including income distribution, taxation, macroeconomics and international economics.

Krugman considers himself a liberal and his popular commentary draw plenty of comments.

Chapter 57 American TV Should Provide Lifelong Learning In An Entertaining Manner-Somers Record

David Michael Letterman (born April 12, 1947) is an American television host, comedian, writer, producer, and actor. He hosts the late night television talk show *Late Show with David Letterman*, broadcast on CBS. Letterman has been a fixture on late night television since the 1982 debut of *Late Night with David Letterman* on NBC. Letterman even surpassed his friend and mentor Johnny Carson as the longest-serving late night talk show host in TV history. On April 3, 2014, Letterman announced he would retire in 2015 with his last show on May 20, 2015 completing a 33 years career. Letterman is also a television and film producer. His company, Worldwide Pants, produces his show and *The Late Late Show with Craig Ferguson*. Worldwide Pants has also produced several prime-time comedies, the most successful of which was *Everybody Loves Raymond*.

Chapter 58 Why Do Putin and Xi Cling To The Theme of Patriotism But Not Obama?

The **Lewinsky scandal** was a political 'not-sex' scandal emerging in 1998, from a sexual relationship between 49-year-old United States President Bill Clinton and a 22-year-old White House intern, Monica Lewinsky. The news of this extra-marital affair and the resulting investigation eventually led to the impeachment of President Clinton in 1998 by the U.S. House of Representatives and his subsequent acquittal on all impeachment charges of perjury and obstruction of justice in a 21-day Senate trial. During the grand jury testimony Clinton's responses were carefully worded, and he argued, "It depends on what the meaning of the word 'is' is", in regards to the truthfulness of his statement that "there is not a sexual relationship, an improper sexual relationship or any other kind of improper relationship." The wide reporting of the scandal led to criticism of the press for over-coverage.

Dominique Gaston André Strauss-Kahn (born 25 April 1949, a.k.a. DSK) is a French economist, lawyer, politician, and member of the French Socialist Party

(PS). Strauss-Kahn became the Managing Director of the International Monetary Fund (IMF) on 28 September 2007, with the backing of his country's president, Nicolas Sarkozy. His promising career, in both the IMF and French politics was abruptly undermined in New York, on May 14th, 2011 when he was arrested and charged with sexual assault and attempted rape of Guinean-born Sofitel Hotel chambermaid Nafissatou Diallo. Shortly afterwards –(on May 18th, 2011)–, DSK tendered his resignation from the IMF. He was swiftly replaced by French Finance Minister Christine Madeleine Odette Lagarde. DSK pleaded not guilty and, eventually, all charges were dismissed (Los Angeles Times, 2011) after even public prosecutors became unable to believe the accuser's words (BBC, 2011).

Chapter 59 Significance of Okinawa, Taipei and Hong Kong Elections

Occupy Central is a civil disobedience campaign initiated by Benny Tai Yiuting, Associate Professor of Law at the University of Hong Kong, and advocated by Occupy Central with Love and Peace (OCLP). In the course of the 2014 Hong Kong electoral reform, OCLP intends to pressure the PRC Government into granting an electoral system which "satisfies the international standards in relation to universal suffrage" in Hong Kong Chief Executive election in 2017 as promised according to the Hong Kong Basic Law Article 45. Should such an electoral system not be achieved, OCLP sought to continue the occupation of Central, which OCLP vowed to be a non-violent event. As time went on, OCLP began to lose citizens support as it interrupted normal life.

Chapter 60 The Near-Term Future of The U.S. and China

The Asian Infrastructure Investment Bank (AIIB) is an international financial institution proposed by China. A new multilateral bank was created in October 2014 with the formal launch of the Asian Infrastructure Investment Bank (AIIB) located in Shanghai, China. The AIIB is backed by at least 21 countries in the region. The purpose of this new multilateral institution is to provide finance to infrastructure projects in the Asia Pacific region. The AIIB is backed by an initial guaranteed capital of $50 billion and with additional authorized capital of $100 billion. AIIB is regarded by some as a rival for the IMF, the World Bank and the

Asian Development Bank (ADB), which are dominated by developed countries like the United States and Japan.

Reference: Robert Bestani, Will China's AIIB succeed?, 12-8-2014 http://www.businessspectator.com.au/article/2014/12/8/china/will-chinas-aiib-succeed

APPENDICES

—m—

(Articles in Mandarin)

US – China Relations
Mainstream and Organic Views

Chinese Characters, Terms and Idioms
Removed from the Chapters

張一飛 Ifay Chang Chapter 2
小三 Xiaosan Chapter 3
安倍晋三 Abe Shinzo Chapter 25
東條 英機 Hideki Tojo Chapter 25
知覽特攻平和会館 Chiran Peace Museum for Kamikaze Pilots Chapter 27
百田尚書 Author of 'Forever Zero' Chapter 27
遠交近攻" 'Be Friend with the Far and Be Foe with the Near' Chapter 28
"戰國時代" Zhou Dynasty Chapter 28
孫子兵法 Sun Zi Bing Fa Chpter 28 and Chapter 43
于山島/亏山島 Usan-Do Yusan Island Chapter 29
韜光養晦 Laying Low to Focus on Priority Chapter 32
鼎 Ding An Ancient Chinese Utensil Chapter 37
王道 Wang Dao Rule by Kindness and Persuasion Chapter 40
霸道 Bah Dao Rule by Hegemony Behavior Chapter 40
師出有名 (any military action must be launched under a 'proper name'
a cause with sound justification) Chapter 43
知彼知己, 百戰不殆, originated from Sun Zi Bin Fa
(The Art of War by Sun Zi)
If you understand your opponent and yourself thoroughly,
you will win all the time. Chapter 50
錢莊 Money Bank Chapter 55
當舖 Pawn Shop Chapter 55
文言文 Classic Chinese Chapter 55
招安 'suzerainty' or 'tributary relation' Chapter 55
金 Jin Dynasty Chapter 55
元 Yuan Dynasty Chapter 55
清 Qing Dynasty Chapter 55
共贏 Win-Win Mutual Economic Prosperity Chapter 60

中美論壇週年感言 - 張一飛

美國有一句話, 大家都聽過, 那就是"You only live once", 這句話可有不同的意義, 它可以解釋說, 人來到世界上只活一輩子, 人要珍惜時間和生命, 一輩子要活得有意思。 可這個"有意思"就不能簡單的來定義了, 每個人都可能有不同的定義。我們姑且舉兩個不同的定義, 一個是努力工作, 以求立功,立名或立德。 另一個是盡情享受, 以吃,喝,玩, 樂,來不虛度此生。我想大多數人都可能在這兩個定義間徘徊過, 也大有可能在兩個人生定義裡多多少少都有些成就或滿足。那一個人到了退休年齡, 他或她的人生定義該是什麼呢?

中國也有一句話, 大家也都聽過, 那就是"人生七十方開始", 這句話也有不同的意義, 可是這句話在一個退休年齡的人來說, 倒只有一個定義, 那就是珍惜人生的寶貴經驗, 找新的目標開始新的生活。不管你是立了功, 立了名或立了德, 或者是在吃喝完樂上達到了很高的段數,人到了七十就該有個新目標和新開始。今在中美論壇一週年之時, 我就談一下我的新生活和新目標吧!

在我過了七十生日之后,我就在找一個新目標和新生活。如何能把我七十年的人生經驗用在新目標上。真是好的運氣, 就在我打算用寫作和製作電視節目作為我的新目標的時候, US-China Forum 在范湘濤,陳憲中, 馬在莊,傅建烈, 劉冰,佟秉宇, 張文基,周友道, 李慰華, 和江啟光幾位籌劃下誕生了。 我有幸被邀為中美論壇寫一個英語專欄 - Mainstream and Organic by Dr. Wordman。中美論壇就佔據了我新生活的大部分時間了。

時間過的很快, 中美論壇就已經一週年了, 我就以個人的經驗和想法來向大家報告一下為什麼我認為中美論壇是一個值得做的新目標,為什麼會充實一個新的生活。 讓我簡短的歸納一下:
1. 古人說天下事,匹夫有責, 為中美論壇服務是盡一己之責, 盡責任就能達到自己所定的新目標。
2. 分工合作,眾志成城,中美論壇在大家合作下,很有成績, 也會更有成績,有成績就能充實新生活。
3. 美國愚民多, 知識份子較客觀并接受意見,美國政客大多數沒有多年政治,外交,和戰略經驗。以我們七十年人生經驗和學術背景, 用我們的充份學識和不斷研討精神來教育, 辯駁,和引導美國民眾和政治人物對中美關係有正確的了解和建立良好的關係。這樣我們會有充實的新生活。
4. 華人媒體內向,影響力小,中美論壇替華人媒體打出和超出"各人自掃門前雪, 休管他人瓦上霜"的境界。我們要為論壇爭取更多篇幅, 出刊次數,多家報紙和網路媒體, 以更能發揮我們的力量。這樣我們可以不斷提高新的目標。
5. 中美論壇不只是退休人的新目標, 它也有年輕人參加我們的工作,我們要吸收更多年輕人,要使美裔華人能減小代溝,為兩岸和中美未來前途作出有效貢獻。讓美籍華裔后代及全球華人以有華人血統為驕傲。

以上就是為什麼中美論壇值得我們共同努力, 有錢出錢和有力出力。 希望大家都來為中美未來打造美好的前景!!!

Mandarin Article 1, Remarks on the 1st Anniversary of US-China Forum]

世界上引用最多的社会名词"小三"和美中关系
作者 张一飞　　译者 王胜炜
2014 年 1 月 1 日

我和我儿子杰瑞上个月的中国之旅十分愉快，令他兴奋，令我惊讶。杰瑞拍了 800 张照片，我希望他会在某个地方展示它们，而我想在这里谈论的是一个社会名词，"小三"。这是我此次在中国和中国以外的旅行中频繁听到和读到的字眼，特别是在互联网博客、报纸、电视、甚至电影中。如果你答应我从头到尾读完这整篇文章所影射的一个严肃的问题，我就不会让你悬留在这个名词的词意上。

"小三"就是普通话里"第三者"的意思。它是今天世界各地媒体最常用的字眼，因为它是一个邪恶的、强大的、可怕的、破坏婚姻、带来腐败、破坏政府和危及外交关系如美中关系的一个名词。最近，报纸上说，中国的离婚率正在迅速上升，其主要元凶是"小三"，即第三者进入婚姻，并拆散婚姻。小三往往也是引诱人背叛和腐败的原因，譬如，以侵吞的资金来支付小三占用的城堡别墅或秘密公寓。那个臭名昭著的薄熙来和中国许多其他腐败高官的审判表明小三现象如此猖獗，因此，开始谈论"小三"以及如何对付小三的文章、书籍和电影，都十分畅销。频繁刺探和测试您合作伙伴（企业员工）的手机和电子邮件，也成为被推荐的最低安全对策。美国的热门消息则有纽约市长候选人安东尼·韦纳的性短信和邓文迪和默多克高调离婚的故事，都属于小三八卦。文迪本人是不是破坏默多克婚姻的小三，也在互联网上引发了一个巨大的辩论。

现在您会奇怪，"小三"怎麽会扯上美中关系？请继续阅读下去。

马克·伦纳德是作家和记者，也是畅销书《欧洲如何打造 21 世纪》（2005 年出版，被翻译成 19 种语言）和《中国怎么想？》（2008 年出版，被翻译成 14 种语言）的作者。他写了一篇长文发表于 2013 年 9 月 6 日的《外交事务》杂志，文章的标题为"为什麽美中越来越多相似性却导致两国渐行渐远"（http://www.foreignaffairs.com/articles/139650/mark-leonard/why-convergence-breeds-conflict）。文中提出许多很好的意见和分析，但其标题所导致的结论在我看来却完全不合逻辑。与其相信这两个国家越来越类似是推动她们渐行渐远的原因，我宁愿设想，这两个国家都没有用足够的勤奋，通过历史事实和目前的发展，来审视她们的相似之处，以发现和培育一个温暖的关系。我进一步设想，这两个国家都正走在一条由错误的外交政策所引导(希拉里·克林顿制定，现在由约翰·克里执行)的危险道路上；这个政策是在一个缺乏诚实历史角度的错误假设下，对最坏的情况所作的分析。

人们似乎可以用婚姻来比喻美国与中国的关系。过去 150 年来，婚姻的形式和风格在许多方面经历了众多变化，美国与中国的关系也是如此。从两个在世界舞台上没有关联的双方到两国集团(G2) 关系（尚未被视为一个可行的方案），可以简单地看成是两个结婚的合作伙伴，正在经历成长和适应的阵痛；随着时间的推移，越来越多的相似之处逐渐形成，而一些固有的分歧也依然存在。这样的关系会成功或决裂，简单地看来，取决于两个合作伙伴如何审视她们的异同，并且为她们的关系和世界利益而认识彼此的分歧。

从历史上看来，美国对中国或中国人，在中国衰弱和遭受西方列强与日本帝国主义迫害之时，并没有进行任何有意义的关系。关系的形成，开始于当中国醒来面对现实，并以革命寻求形成一个共和制国家之时，美国对此表示同情，并且美国的历史和治理充当了中国的一个榜样。但是美国和中国的关系，直到第二次世界大战发生而成为媒介以前，从来不够接近和温暖。中国和美国通过二战，成为在任何意义上的真正盟友，彼此拯救许多战场上的生命，并对抗一个共同的敌人，日本（和德国）。这种关系给那个时代的所有中国人留下了深刻的记忆；不论苏联和中国早期共产主义政权如何种努力，至今都无法将之消除。然而，美国犯了一个战略性的错误，并不接受中国作为一个整体，以迫使其成立一个联合政府；这个联合政府可能已经演变成一个或多或少介于民主和社会主义国家之间的中国共和国。这两个中国派系不幸地也犯了战略性的错误，未视争议为一个内部问题，反而各自依附外部的两个对立、长期冷战的對手，苏联和美国。

之后，这两个中国派系外部的合作伙伴做出了一个武断，也可能是自私的协议，对待中国仿佛她是一个战败国，将她一分为二。这个协议并没有获得中国任一派的同意，这种待遇甚至还远不如真正被打败的侵略者，日本，至少日本还设法让她的國土主权保持了完整。这个协议不仅造成了中国的分裂，甚至更糟糕地造成亿万中国人民经历几十年的痛苦生活。美国的慷慨援助，帮助了日本和台湾在二战后快速恢复，但是美国与绝大多数中国人的关系，经历了几十年的黑暗时代。这一段历史，在美国和中国的关系往前行进时，应该得到承认与和解。

马克所描述的"中美共同体"关系，其存在之时，中国已经脱离了苏联式的共产主义，在政治稳定下追求经济增长。他描述这两个国家的不同有如锁和钥匙，在"中美共同体"时期，共生而互补。依我看来，这个关系的可行性，在于美国对世界有一个安全的"锁"和中国实践邓小平的"低调"（low "key"）理念。随着时间的推移，美国的锁不再那麼安全，因为9/11袭击和中东战争改变了美国的形象。美国作为一个崇尚民主的超级大国，却失去了联合国的支持（马克指出，美国发现许多世界组织并不可行），以依靠军事力量解决问题，中国则在世界上结交了更多朋友，并获得了联合国的支持。因此，"钥匙"已经变成比"锁"大了。同样地以婚姻或两国集团(G2)作比喻，这就像家庭中有两个负担家计的人，当他们的赚钱能力和外部情况改变时，他们就必须作出调整。如果他们希望继续保持温馨的关系，就必须做出互惠互利的调整。马克谈到"换位"和"两个搭桥"，但真正需要的是他们必须深入研究他们的相似与内在差异，以找到更多共生和互补的机会。这不是马克的文章中所提到的一盘西洋棋，也不是围棋，而是桥牌比赛。他们需要制定一个沟通的公约，以提升他们的相互了解。两国集团伙伴是桥牌的合作伙伴，当世界看到有一个两国集团的语言和所有牌友都明白的一个约定，他们在比赛中将不会有恐惧或争执。美国和中国应该开始练习一个有两个玩家的桥牌（真正的纸牌游戏中有一个蜜月桥牌），建立惯例、语言、规则和双方的玩风。我相信通过这種对话，我们会发现從历史、地理和政治方面的觀點看来，有很多理由能够让这两个国家共享技术和诀窍，其利益更超过彼此帮助对方国内生产总值的增长，而世界也会因此获益。

马克正确地指出，美国和中国相争的不是思想理念，而是地位尊嚴。那麼，两国应该做些什么来创建一个新的"中美共同体"时代，尊重彼此的地位？在我看来，认识历史和当前的事实是第一步。每个国家都必须诚实地审视过去的历史，以重振美国人和中国人追寻至二战时的温暖关系。如同任何关系，承认和尊重历史，是建立一个未来温暖关系的基础，不应该以臆想和错误的假设而人为地创造口号，或依据最坏的情况而作出分析。一个具有良好意图和适当行为的两国集团关系，就像一个好的婚姻，会彼此互利和造福世界。

现在我们可以点明小三为什么与美中关系有关连了。正如在婚姻中，与第三者调情以挑激伴侣既不明智，又极其伤害彼此的关系。目前美国与日本右翼领导人安倍晋三的暧昧，正是中美关系的禁忌。日本这个第三者，拒绝承认历史及其对中国、韩国、菲律宾和美国等地的战争罪行，永远不能获得信任；这个视中国为她的供应地、市场和禁脔，并野蛮地对中国人及中美戰俘使用化学和细菌戰劑的第三者，也永远不能成为一个公平的局中人。中国被"小三"这个字眼吓坏了，然而，你会发现媒体描绘日本为"小三"，是破坏美中关系的"小三"。那么，为何美国一面与安倍晋三调情，同时还试图让一个G2两国集团行之有效呢？安倍晋三，受到克林顿甚至麦凯恩的鼓励，希望修改日本的和平宪法，建立她攻击性的军事力量。任何人都不应该为奥巴马的G2两国集团想法得到冷淡的反应而感到惊讶；中国还没有准备好接受它，或者她认为应该建立的是一种新的超级大国关系。一个可行的G2两国集团，就像一桩婚姻，必须耐心地建立互信和诚意，从来不能以眼还眼。马克对"美中越来越多相似性却导致两国渐行渐远"的描述，引用了弗洛伊德对"微小差异的自我陶醉"。我想说，如果将上述小三的情况告知弗洛伊德，他可能会称之为调情疯狂，因为它会导致决裂、毁坏和一个可能的世界战争。现在我能理解为什么"小三"这个可怕的名词会被用在美中关系中，你不能理解吗？希望美国人和中国人都具有足够的智慧，找到一个治疗方子，停止这种与小三调情或被小三调情的疯狂。

Mandarin Article 2 Page 2, Most Used Social Term 'Xiaosan' in US-China Relations

回憶 2013 之中國
張畢鳴 (張一飛筆名)

2013 年我在中國住了一個月頗增見聞，也對中國事物特別注意，再加上在中美論壇上開始寫些中美關係的問題，我的 2013 真有身在美國心在中國的現象．在此年假時期回憶去年瞻望未來，不免提筆寫下一些感想，想與美國華人及全球所有對中國關心的人分享．

去年中國最大的一件事當然是中央權力順利交替，習近平和李克強分別當選國家主席及國務總理．交替之前前中央政治局委員兼任重慶市書記薄熙來貪污瀆職收賄一案，由王立軍投奔成都美國領事館引發薄熙來妻子谷開來殺人案，進而牽扯出薄熙來一大籮筐罪行．薄案關係大到習李上位，非同小可，在定案之前，傳說謠言南北各地紛起，最有幻想力的是說整個事件是因為美國人怕薄熙來的重慶模式會變成全中國的模式，所以設計扳倒薄熙來．如果美國真有此遠見和深算，那中東的伊拉克，伊朗，舒立亞就不會搞的如今的情況了，是不？

其次該是中共的十八大三中全會，中共公佈大會公告全文．此公告誠可供全球參考，尤其是其他國家要想效法中國如何改革建造自己模式的現代化國家．中國有她特別的問題像人口問題，戶口制度，城鄉區別，國有企業，市場開放，金融系統，科技創新，國防更新，政府體制，憲法維修，國家統一等等，中國問題很多也複雜，但是由此公告也看出中共的決心和信心．

中國的經濟在去年裡還是令人羨慕的．雖然中國的房地產有泡沫現象，政府似乎已經在用戶口政策促使人口向中小城市轉移．當然工作機會也需要轉移，人口大量由鄉入城，造成城市人口膨脹，房價飛揚，交通擁塞，空氣污染，生活品質下降，要解決這些問題可不是一件輕鬆和短期的事．這就難怪三中全會把城鄉問題定為重要議題來提出解決辦法．大家拭目以待吧！

網絡商業在全球高速成長，中國的淘寶在台灣已經成為第二大的線上商業做了超過三億美元的生意．如何利用網絡商企業幫助調整城鄉人口就業居住等問題倒是很值得研討．淘寶前年的調查中說中國每人平均購買是大城$740 小城$900，整個網絡商業$260 億．這個數字定是在增長，城鄉人口調整與網絡商業是因果還是果因關係也是值得研究的問題．

2013 年月亮上從中國來了一個玉兔訪客當然是一件大喜事．雖然美日沒有多加報導，但是這個玉兔表現了中國在航太技術上的進步和實力．讓中國可以與美俄在航太研發上增加合作．大國能把精力和競爭從武器上換在航太上是件好事．除了有野心和嫉妒的國家，大家都願意看到人類向太空發展．

在國際事務和外交上，中國的成績單可說是相當不錯．習近平的訪美與奧巴馬唔談及其他中美的接觸，尤其是軍事方面的，對兩國關係有良好的幫助．中國的維穩中求進步發展是好的政策，但還要與美國保持友好關係起碼不是敵對關係．在釣魚島爭議上，中國的表現以強硬和有計劃的作法來對付日本的無理舉動是可嘉的，中華人民的表現也很好．最近提出的 ADIZ，航空識別區，也是好的招數，不過如果與美國事先打個招呼，給個面子，效果更好控制．幸好日本安培急於復古增軍讓美國猶疑不定，ADIZ 上中國算是贏了一仗．外交上中美關係保持友好還是上策．中國在亞太以大國身份辦事原則上美國不會過份干預．只要中國與美保持友好關係，島鏈戰略是把中國當作假想敵的，如果中國是友好國，甚至日本是假想敵，那美國的戰略思維就完全不同了．

三中全會強調說明中國走自己的路是對的，但還要加強對外的說服工作．中美遠距，華人在美表現良好，也漸能參與政治發表意見，是促進中美友好合作的一大資源．2013 年可以看見不少世界華人參與保釣，反日，及溝通中美文化交流及友好活動，中美論壇就是一個例子．想今后這些活動更會提升，如今網絡發達以成強國必需的基礎設備，控制網絡不如善用網絡．中國政府在這方面得下點工夫．司若登事件把美國弄的啞口無言，也幫了中國應付美國的控訴．中國應當借鏡深思．

由 2013 往前看，中國的未來是看好的！

Mandarin Article 3, China in 2013

回憶 2013 之中國
張華鳴 (張一飛筆名)

2013 年我在中國住了一個月頗增見聞，也對中國事物特別注意，再加上在中美論壇上開始寫些中美關係的問題，我的 2013 真有身在美國心在中國的現象．在此年假時期回憶去年瞻望未來，不免提筆寫下一些感想，想與美國華人及全球所有對中國關心的人分享．

去年中國最大的一件事當然是中央權力順利交替，習近平和李克強分別當選國家主席及國務總理．交替之前前中央政治局委員兼任重慶市書記薄熙來貪污瀆職收賄一案，由王立軍投奔成都美國領事館引發薄熙來妻子谷開來殺人案，進而牽扯出薄熙來一大籮筐罪行．薄案關係大到習李上位，非同小可，在定案之前，傳說謠言南北各地紛起，最有幻想力的是說整個事件是因為美國人怕薄熙來的重慶模式會變成全中國的模式，所以設計扳倒薄熙來．如果美國真有此遠見和深算，那中東的伊拉克，伊朗，舒立亞就不會搞的如今的情況了，是不？

其次該是中共的十八大三中全會，中共公佈大會公告全文．此公告誠可供全球參考，尤其是其他國家要想效法中國如何改革建造自己模式的現代化國家．中國有她特別的問題像人口問題，戶口制度，城鄉區別，國有企業，市場開放，金融系統，科技創新，國防更新，政府體制，憲法維修，國家統一等等．中國問題很多也複雜，但是由此公告也看出中共的決心和信心．

中國的經濟在去年裡還是令人羨慕的．雖然中國的房地產有泡沫現象，政府似乎已經在用戶口政策促使人口向中小城市轉移．當然工作機會也需要轉移，人口大量由鄉入城，造成城市人口膨脹，房價飛揚，交通擁塞，空氣污染，生活品質下降，要解決這些問題可不是一件輕鬆和短期的事．這就難怪三中全會把城鄉問題定為重要議題來提出解決辦法．大家拭目以待吧！

網絡商業在全球高速成長，中國的淘寶在台灣已經成為第二大的線上商業做了超過三億美元的生意．如何利用網絡商企業幫助調整城鄉人口就業居住等問題倒是很值得研討．淘寶前年的調查中說中國每人平均購買是大城$740 小城$900，整個網絡商業$260 億．這個數字定是在增長，城鄉人口調整與網絡商業是因果還是果因關係也是值得研究的問題．

2013 年月亮上從中國來了一個玉兔訪客當然是一件大喜事．雖然美日沒有多加報導，但是這個玉兔表現了中國在航太技術上的進步和實力．讓中國可以與美俄在航太研發上增加合作．大國能把精力和競爭從武器上換在航太上是件好事．除了有野心和嫉妒的國家，大家都願意看到人類向太空發展．

在國際事務和外交上，中國的成績單可說是相當不錯．習近平的訪美與奧巴馬唔談及其他中美的接觸，尤其是軍事方面的，對兩國關係有良好的幫助．中國的維穩中求進步發展是好的政策，但需要與美國保持友好關係起碼不是敵對關係．在釣魚島爭議上，中國的表現以強硬和有計劃的作法來對付日本的無理舉動是可嘉的，中華人民的表現也很好．最近提出的 ADIZ，航空識別區，也是好的招數，不過如果與美國事先打個招呼，給個面子，效果更好控制．幸好日本安培急於復古增軍讓美國猶疑不定，ADIZ 上中國算是贏了一仗．外交上中美關係保持友好還是上策．中國在亞太以大國身份辦事原則上美國不會過份干預．只要中國與美保持友好關係，島鏈戰略是把中國當作假想敵的，如果中國是友好國，甚至日本是假想敵，那美國的戰略思維就完全不同了．

三中全會強調說明中國走自己的路是對的，但還要加強對外的說服工作．中美遠距，華人在美表現良好，也漸能參與政治發表意見，是促進中美友好合作的一大資源．2013 年可以看見不少世界華人參與保釣，反日，及溝通中美文化交流及友好活動，中美論壇就是一個例子．想今后這些活動更會提升，如今網絡發達以成強國必需的基礎設備，控制網絡不如善用網絡．中國政府在這方面得下點工夫．司若登事件把美國弄的啞口無言，也幫了中國應付美國的控訴．中國應當借鏡深思．

由 2013 往前看，中國的未來是看好的！

Mandarin Article 4, Op Ed in United Newspaper on Taiwan's Defense

讀彭文逸東亞博弈趨熱，凸顯台灣獨特角色感言
張語人 (Dr. Wordman 中文筆名)

彭文道理清晰，主要闡述自 1949 美國發表白皮書-台灣地位未定論-至今超過一甲子，台灣從 "風雨飄搖" 到 "勿忘在莒"，到 "反攻復國"，到後來的無數篇 "台灣往何處去？" 的論述，如今仍在原地地位未定。彭先生認為一國兩制走向乃比地位未定為較光明之路，在此釣魚島爭端炒熱的時機，台灣與香港是最早為了釣魚島抗爭的，所以最是有權發言。以釣魚島在美國島鏈戰略中的重要性，台灣以香港為例走向一國兩制并與大陸合作奪回釣魚島最能出言有聲且能發揮力量。

讀彭文后不但起共鳴而且認為此想法必須詳加解說推廣論述以能得到更多兩岸人民認同并取得國際尤其華僑一致贊助。因此筆者冒大不諱寫此文以求有學有志人士共襄盛舉幫助台灣從不定位走向有國有名自治自強繁榮發達的道路。為此目標，筆者認為應當以下兩個問題論述說服。第一是台灣應不應該走這一國兩制的路？第二是台灣要如何走好這條一國兩制的路？

對於第一個問題，其實在書刊雜誌上已經有不少的論述，大多數的反應是正面的，要不是台灣陰錯陽差讓李登輝做了兩任總統，他以日裔心態陰謀親日挫統，台灣或許早已走上一國兩制之路，台灣已然成為四小龍之首，而中國也早一步達到全球第一大經濟國。台灣受民主之利也受民主之弊，飽受外在壓力內部紛爭弄得政治混亂，把不定位弄得日況愈下無所適從。其實台灣有了民主經驗多年當知少數服從多數的原則，民主方可行。同時也應當了解民主之名方能與美國以民主掛帥的國家打交道，走向一國兩制保存民主，而美國無理由反對。中國也樂見其成。說民主，它是草根性的概念，民主從下而上，多少存在，只是看上面壓多少，上面壓的少，民主就比較多，上面壓的多，民主就比較弱。在一國兩制下，只要訂的國法保護了沒有從上面來的壓力，那下面的民主作業就是真民主要比現在不定位下的民主要強的多，因為它沒有了外在來的各方壓力。所以，台灣是應當走一國兩制的路，重要的是要定下沒有上方壓力的制度。這個要求不但合理而且會得大陸民心，因為大陸各省區也有此需，大陸的改革也必然往這方面漸進。台灣的大陸委員會應當提出這樣的構想，用全民表決方式來表態，以訂成一國兩制的架構。台灣就可以從不定位日況愈下走上自治繁榮的路了。

至於第二個問題，前面已經點到了，那就是要在台灣民主的範疇下來真心誠意的推動。當然這得要有遠見和擔當的政治家來領導，用公民投票來導致全民共識，以此方法來表態和定下底線。台灣每個政黨都可以提出構想計劃交由公民投票表態，在每次全台灣選舉的時候，讓各政黨自由提出各黨對一國兩制的看法和推行的辦法。最初提出的想法和辦法都可能得不到大多數人民的認同，但是各黨可由選舉投票結果來修訂改進再次提出，直到那一個計劃和辦法得到全民大多數的支持。在這公投的步驟中，大陸自然也在觀望學習。如今網絡通訊極為發達之下，這種由下而上的民主自會有其影響，大陸公民也可能表態，在這種情形下，時間會促成互相了解，在沒有時間表的原則下，最終一定達到共識。在這種民主的運作過程中，外在的影響和壓力也比較無法發生作用。這種漸進穩妥的作法是真正為人民著想，也是全球華人所願意看到的。

穩紮穩打，時間是對兩岸有益的，最終中國將會統一成為世界第一強國！讓兩岸同胞和全球華人一同來努力吧！

Mandarin Article 5, Comment on East Asia 'Chess Match' by Peng Yi-Wen

讀王師凱外交不休兵難道還修兵有感
張畢鳴（張一飛筆名）

王師凱在中國時報（7-10-2013）發表"外交不修兵難道還修兵"一文， 主題是講中華民國（台灣）的外交及李登輝與南非曼德拉打交道的醜事。曼德拉讀毛書信共產主義，在獄中時受中華人民共和國（中共）幫助， 南非則與台灣（中華民國）有邦交。曼德拉出獄后當選南非總統沒有立即和台灣斷交原因是李登輝送了曼德拉一千萬美元， 再送一千萬買了李登輝訪南非之行，但兩年后南非仍然與台灣斷交。這就是台灣用錢買朋友的外交政策，行不通，但是給喪心病狂的人趁作不法勾當時貪污。王先生以一個公務員寫此文章可以想像他是一個有正義和愛國家的人， 非常令人佩服。

讀王文之后除起敬意外也感到此文言有未盡， 標題提到修兵但文內未加闡述。這使我想起台灣向美國購買軍火的策略。一心一意想買軍火以防共， 看著美國臉色要賣不賣， 最後出高價買個后進美國要淘汰的軍備。老百姓的錢化的真冤枉。 其實如果台灣不要買軍火， 美國還急的要把軍火送上門， 原因很簡單， 沒有台灣這一環， 美國的亞太軍事佈局就漏氣了。 日，韓，菲都看的出來， 可是台灣有賣台的李登輝， 挖台的陳水扁和忘祖棄宗的媚日份子及只求私利的政客做愚味的台獨的夢。台灣在美，日壓力之下能真正獨立嗎？那個夢只是往附屬地的附屬地的路上走。美國壓著日本， 日本壓著台灣， 不是嗎？如果真的兩強拼起命來， 台灣是作馬前足呢還是充炮灰？中國大約不會用核武對付台灣，千秋歷史交代不過去， 喊台灣同胞雖合統戰邏輯， 也還是本著中華歷史的根源。但是弄急了， 中國對日本用核武可是天經地義的， 日本在二戰殺的中國人（包括台灣人）還不夠多馬？日本不懺悔還要再打中國， 那還能夠不拼嗎？如果這個仗打了， 台灣想不受池魚之殃是不太可能的了。

可惜啊！台灣學到了民主的皮毛動作但沒有造就有遠大目光和真正愛民大公無私的政治家，小鄉小鎮小市的選舉只選出了勾心鬥角唱作欺騙和短視愚民的政客，所謂國會只不過是爭權奪利的地盤。沒有大政治家也就不會有對世界大局和政治走向的深刻認識。美國是世界上最強的國家， 以她的立場， 她是不會希望有另外一個強國與她爭霸。 冷戰美國贏了，俄國被逼退了，如今中國站起來了，美國就不想讓中國強大。但是美國的獨霸會能永久持續嗎？應該永久持續嗎？ 連許多美國人都不認為她能或一定要持續， 所以就有 G2 的說法， 但也有許多鷹派要想維持美國的獨霸地位。將來如何走向沒有人能預知， 但是每個國家都是為自己的利益和未來作打算的。日本人想利用美國站起來（夢想 Japan is back）， 俄國人就永遠甘休了嗎？ 中國能不繼續成長嗎？在這種情況下， 台灣要跟著日本屁股后冒作池魚之殃的險還是站出來促成一個穩定的 G2 中美關係和局面？ 後者是有可為和有長遠利益的路， 而前者是死路一條最好不過是三敗俱傷。美國應當不會不顧自身利益為救死而傷了自己的。

王先生的文章在中國時報發表的， 它對我海外華僑啟發了感想，但希望台灣人也多想想，切勿短視而自滅。曼德拉死了， 連 Obama 都去參加他的喪禮， 他到底是個政治人物為南非的百姓作了供獻。

Mandarin Article 6, Comment on Taiwan Diplomacy by Wang Shi-Kai

評辭理泰：釣魚島或將由契子變為棄子
張畢鳴 (張一飛筆名)

辭文確是一篇好的分析論文，顯示作者為史丹福國際安全合作研究所成員背景。其六條推測皆有邏輯。但國際大事之推測比對股票市場或經濟動盪推測更難， 更吃力不討好。即使測對也不能像股市上有立即名利雙收之可能。不過以天下事匹夫有責的觀念來看，辭文之類還是應當多鼓勵，多傳閱和多分析的。本文就以推理來分析一下辭文之推測，也盡一點匹夫之責。

首先我們把辭文的六條推論規納一下以便分析， 其重點如下：
一，美國戰略規劃老辣，不會犯下低級錯誤， 為幾塊大石與有核中國對抗。
二，釣魚島為作平衡用的契子， 一旦有了軍事衝突就無契子作用變為棄子， 原因有三，i，不涉及核心利益，ii，美接受中國'G2'條件 及 iii，中國處理有方。
三，美未准，日不敢擊落中無人機， 揚言擊落只為測量中方，未必實行。
四，日可能冒險，但中方反應后， 日不得美同意不敢繼續， 美使中日坐談，對民意可有交代。
五，中日皆無準備包括心理，最後歸于平息可能性大。
六，美未制定以'抗'代'防'之策略，排除立即介入之可能。

本文作者對辭文仔細考量之後認為他的以上六點推論實際上是繞著一個基本想法， 那就是美，日，中 三方都沒有準備， 所以都不敢也不會莽動。但是以我個人觀察， 美國在此問題上還沒準備好或許正確。 美國仍然在揣摩如何與中國建立什麼樣的關係。美國用日本作棋子來試探而不願日本莽撞是可能的。但是説日本不敢莽動， 這依據就很薄弱了。日本現任首相，安培，祖傳遺訓畢生立志恢復日本軍國舊日榮耀，時不我與， 機不可失，第二次得來首相不易，似乎在作孤注一擲之打算。日本現在全力製造民氣，極力媚美及造訪中美之鄰國， 居心甚為明顯， 目的在修憲擴軍，所以我不敢苟同辭氏的看法。

辭文認為中日未準備交鋒。但是就如他文中所説像 NHK 這樣非右派的媒體都已轉向，不能説日本不在作心理和交鋒的準備。以中方來説， 自習近平任中國國家主席以來，他對外的演講雖然一再表明中國要在和平中求經濟發展， 其目的是達到中國夢 - 提高中國人民生活水平。可是以他的軍中關係及與軍方講話內容也可看出中國在無奈中，也不得不作有備之舉。面對美國之不明態度與日本的積極希望修憲和擴軍，中國也似乎在作最壞的打算，與日本作一次一百年的清算。

所以個人認為辭文以及前星加坡總理李光耀等之關於中日美的論文雖皆有邏輯， 但總是有悲天憫人怕天下大亂的心理。作者本人也不免有此心理。可是觀察美中日近年來的行為，繼續演變下去，后果實難像辭氏所推測。在美國不即早表明立場採取行動情況下，中日遲早會擦槍走火發生軍事沖突。除非美國民意發聲，美政府策略透明化，釣魚島的情勢不會成為棄子。

其實要美國人民發聲促使美政府明朗化她的亞洲外交政策， 讓日本民心停止向右轉， 和使中國人民不再 擔憂日美聯手打擊中國，不是不可能的。這要靠所有關心美中日的有識之士，一起把美中日近百年的歷史公正坦白的告知給各國人民。一旦各國人民都了解了這共同的歷史， 民意就可以發聲了， 美政府依民意則非得把外交政策明朗化， 日本極右派也必會被民意軟化下來， 而中國也當能就民意走向大國應走的路與美日建立互利的關係。作者這段話是發自內心匹夫之言以盡匹夫之責。

Mandarin Article 7, Comment on Diaoyu Island by Xue Li-Tai

評馬立誠鳳凰台談話'用民族主義的武器時要認識到雙刃性'
張一飛 9-26-2013

中國人崇尚仁愛受佛教影響都認為有菩薩心腸是好事。可是人是要有理智的，尤其在國家
大事和國際政治上，尊重歷史辨明事實是最基本的原則。馬立誠和李楊在鳳凰台的對話
談中日情結，聲稱戰后日本政府已道歉 25 次仇恨沒有未來，實在令人吃驚，不但談話
中引述不實，分析不深，甚至不合邏輯，完全沒有說服力，其立場實令人髮指。 本
文就其網上摘要分項作一評論：
一，日本真愛中國文化，是唯一推揚中國文化的國家？
絕對不是。日本輕視中國及中國人，把中國文化辯為己出，不像新加坡真正的尊崇中華
文化和尊敬中國人。問問日本人，什麼是圍棋，一個源自中國的棋藝，他們怎麼說，
不知道還是沒聽過？
二，日本政府道歉了 25 次嗎？
一次真誠的道歉就足夠了。但是我們可以查一下日本人作了多少次道歉和否認，有多少
次在道歉后立馬有人否認，特別是官方人士。 在靖國神社拜祭日本二戰戰犯絕不是一個
真誠道歉的表現，與德國來比較，日本人殘忍有甚但懺悔全無。原因請看第六項。
三，二戰罪行真正解決了嗎？2200 次審判 900 人判死刑？及日本人釣魚島行為正確嗎？
戰爭罪行是要由戰勝國制定的公約裁定的。中國和中國人至今仍然承受著不公平的戰后處
理結果。日本人保有了國土完整，而中國一分為二沒經任一方中國人認可。釣魚島雖小但
為中國固有領土，日本不知懺悔侵略罪行反倒要想恢復日本軍國主義擴張領土領海。日
本最近行為完全暴露了它的野心真面目。至於審判死刑 900 人完全胡說沒有證據，指的
是中國的審判和處決嗎？不是！
四，日本人在中國大投資供給了大量就業機會
投資做生意應當是互利的，但是投資的目的是控制那就有陰謀了。為什麼日本人要霸佔
中國的飲水市場？甚至啤酒。為什麼砍伐中國的森林不砍自己的木材？為什麼把關鍵的
生產技術總是扣在手中不放？當然中國人不能抱怨別人技術高超和經營策略高明，天下
沒有白食。中國人要用智慧在商場上戰勝日本人，不管別人說什麼民族主義，中國人必須
團結抵制日本的經濟和軍事侵略，才有永久和平的希望。
五，老大，老二 和小三的關係
為什麼中國在世界上願意屈居末位？ 日本一個小國都不願意，做了老二還想做老大，
只是美國太大太強。現在妒忌中國趕上來了，想做小三媚美打中。馬先生太天真了，說
什麼聯日抗美，其實中國長遠的安寧是聯美和走向第一。日本人知道遠交近攻，中國人
不懂嗎？記住歷史的教訓，日本人太殘忍，用菩薩心腸對日本就有吃武士刀的一天。
六，教科書的禍害
馬先生又錯了！ 中國教科書正確多了也仁愛多了。日本教科書隱瞞歷史真相，欺騙兒童。
難怪馬先生要被罵為漢奸國賊。

馬先生任職人民日報，想不致於賣國，怕是菩薩心腸想法太幼稚了！

Mandarin Article 8, Comment on Nationalism May Be Double-Edge Sword by Ma Li-Chen

Made in the USA
Middletown, DE
20 July 2015